December 1, 2002

Dear Toby,

I hope that some of these
stories will inspire you in your
religious journey.

May God continue to bless you
now and always.

Much love
Ruth Mayfatola

Jewish Tales

of
Holy Women

Jewish Tales
of
Holy Women

Yitzhak Buxbaum

JOSSEY-BASS
A Wiley Company
www.josseybass.com

Published by

 **JOSSEY-BASS**
A Wiley Company
989 Market Street
San Francisco, CA 94103-1741

www.josseybass.com

Jossey-Bass books and products are available through most bookstores. To
contact Jossey-Bass directly, call (888) 378–2537, fax to (800) 605–2665, or
visit our website at www.josseybass.com.

Substantial discounts on bulk quantities of Jossey-Bass books are available to
corporations, professional associations, and other organizations. For details
and discount information, contact the special sales department at Jossey-Bass.

We at Jossey-Bass strive to use the most environmentally sensitive paper stocks available to us. Our publications are printed on acid-free recycled stock whenever possible,
and our paper always meets or exceeds minimum GPO and EPA requirements.

Jossey-Bass also publishes its books in a variety of electronic formats. Some content
that appears in print may not be available in electronic books.

Design by Paula Goldstein.

Library of Congress Cataloging-in-Publication Data

Buxbaum, Yitzhak.
    Jewish tales of holy women / Yitzhak Buxbaum.— 1st ed.
        p. cm.
    Includes bibliographical references.
    ISBN 0-7879-6271-6
    1. Zaddikot—Legends. 2. Legends, Jewish. I. Title.
BM532 .B84 2002
296.1'9—dc21   2002006596

FIRST EDITION
HB Printing 10 9 8 7 6 5 4 3 2 1

Contents

S'micha
as a Maggid

*W*hen my spiritual master, the holy and pure Rabbi Shlomo Carlebach, gave me *s'micha* (ordination) as a *maggid,* a teller of sacred Jewish tales, he put his holy hands on my head and said:

B'ezrat HaShem
Maggid devarav l'Yaakov.
Aileh hadevarim asher tidabeir el bnai Yisrael.
Bizeh anu somchim v'tomchim u'm'chazkim yidei
Reb Yitzhak ben Meir Buxbaum
sh'yichyeh lihiyot machzir al hap'tachim, pitchaihem miku-
vanim
petach habayit sha'arei halev liban shel Yisrael
l'hachzir otam avaida mida'at da'at Elyon
b'divrei aggada sh'moshchim liban shel Yisrael
b'divrei hitorerut.
Kumi ori ki va oraich.
Yagid yagid
Y'orair y'orair
Yachzir yachzir
am Yisrael b'tshuvah shleima mitoch ahavah.
Koh t'varchu v'yizkeh lirot b'haramat keren Yisrael mitoch
simcha.

With the help of God,

Be a *maggid,* a teller of tales, and speak sacred words to the
seed of Jacob.

These are the words you shall speak to the Children of Israel.

With this, we support, strengthen, and uphold the hands of

Reb Yitzhak son of Meir Buxbaum

To live a life of the spirit, making the rounds, knocking on all
doors, the doors facing each other, the door of the Temple, the gates of the heart, the Heart of Israel

To return those who are lost, lost to mind,

the Mind of the Most High,

With stories that draw the heart of Israel and cause them to
awaken.

Arise, shine, for your light has come!

Tell, tell

Awaken, awaken

Return, return the People of Israel in complete repentance,
from love.

So shall you bless, and merit to see the raising of the honor
of Israel, in joy.

Acknowledgments

I would like to gratefully acknowledge the help of Carole Forman and my editor, Alan Rinzler, who read the manuscript of this work and offered valuable suggestions to improve its clarity. I would also like to thank Rabbi Gershon Winkler, who provided me with source materials on holy women that he had gathered in doing research for his book, *They Called Her Rebbe* (New York: Judaica Press, 1991), about the Maiden of Ludomir. I am grateful also to Rabbi Meir Fund of Brooklyn, who was always ready to provide information or advice when needed about any Jewish topic.

ABOUT GOD LANGUAGE

Although the language in this book sometimes refers to God as "King," "Father," "He," and "Him," God is not corporeal and has no gender. Men and women are made in God's image (Genesis 1:27), and God has both masculine and feminine traits.

ABOUT HONORIFIC TITLES AND MISSING NAMES

Many of the women about whom stories in this book are told were *rebbetzins,* rabbis' wives, which is undoubtedly a main reason why stories about them were known and preserved. But a holy woman's worth does not depend on a title derived from her husband's status. There are a few women in this book who were not wives of rabbis, and much as I would have wanted to bestow on them titles of honor, there is a problem in doing so. The traditional female equivalent to the male honorific *Reb* (Mr.) is *Marat*—a title not used outside traditional circles and one that would strike most ears as unfamiliar and strange. So I have decided to leave these holy women without honorific titles, knowing that we honor them all the same.

Because many of the stories collected lack the names of the holy women, who are identified only as this rabbi's wife or that rabbi's mother or daughter, I had to do special research to try to find the names and respect the dignity of the women involved. I often succeeded but sometimes did not. In order to honor the remaining handful of unnamed women, I gave them fictitious names. These are identified in the Notes so that no one will be misled to think that these are the actual names.

Jewish Tales
of
Holy Women

Proverbs 1:8 says:
"Listen, my son, to the musar *[instruction]*
of your father and do not forsake the torah
[teaching] of your mother." This book is
dedicated to those Jewish holy women who
have been forgotten through our neglect.
May we always remember the sacred
teachings of our Torah mothers.

Preface

Stories, particularly Hasidic tales, have provided me with spiritual nourishment for all of my Jewish religious life. But I have long been troubled by the lack of tales about holy women. I have read scores and scores of Hebrew books of Hasidic and other traditional Jewish tales, and the number of stories about holy women is minuscule, almost negligible. And to add to the embarrassment, when a book contains an anecdote or a story about a holy woman, her name is often left out; she is identified only as this or that rabbi's mother, wife, or daughter. Because of my distress at this unfortunate lack of stories of holy women, for about ten years I have made it a point to collect stories or anecdotes of holy women as I came across them— one here, one there, a few here, a few there. Happily, in recent years, things have been changing. A few collections of stories about women have finally appeared, and I've selected tales from these sources too. And at long last, with God's help, I've collected enough material for this book.

Most of the tales I have included are newly translated from the Hebrew. Some were heard orally and are appearing in print for the first time. Others have been retold.

I am aware that as a man, my perspective as expressed in my comments on these tales may have certain limitations. I ask my Jewish sisters to forgive me if I have made a misstep. My only desire is to enhance the glory of God, our people, and our holy Jewish women.

Introduction

What is a "holy woman"—or a "holy man" for that matter? According to Jewish mystic teaching, all people should strive to be holy. Everyone is granted a pure soul and has the potential for holiness. Someone once asked Rebbe Yisrael of Rizhin what was meant by saying that a person had the holy spirit. He answered, "When a person has spirit and keeps it from becoming impure, it is the holy spirit." In Hebrew, a Jewish holy woman is called a *tzaddeket* (plural, *tzaddikot*), and a holy man is called a *tzaddik* (plural, *tzaddikim*). The male term is also used inclusively for both genders. Some people are tzaddikim—holy and good—in almost every aspect of their life. Others are tzaddikim in only certain aspects. There are people who are tzaddikim just with their immediate family. Others are tzaddikim in their relation to everyone they meet. Whereas some stories in this book are about women who were perfect *tzaddikot* with God and with people, other stories are about women who rose to holiness in particular instances.

God said to the prophet Isaiah about the Jews, "Your people are all tzaddikim."[1] Everyone is a tzaddik, but some are smaller tzaddikim; others are bigger tzaddikim who can extend their love farther afield.

There is a ladder of holiness, from the little to the great. Most of us do some good in this world, do something that is pure and holy. When we hear tales of women who reached awesome levels of piety and holiness, we might think, "Oh, I can't attain that! What does that have to do with me?" Or we can be inspired by their holy deeds to think, "I may not reach the level she attained, but with the example of her holiness before my eyes, may I reach a little higher!" The ancient Rabbis taught, "Every Jew should say, 'Oh, when will my deeds reach the level of the deeds of Abraham, Isaac, and Jacob!'" The Hasidic rebbes (leaders) understood this to mean that each of us should say, "When will my deeds have the merest connection with the deeds of my ancestors!" and we can add, "with the deeds of our holy female ancestors—Sarah, Rebecca, Rachel, Leah, and all the other holy women who followed them!" Every Sabbath night, pious parents bless their daughters: "May God make you like Sarah, Rebecca, Rachel, and Leah!"

One of the benefits of reading these tales of Jewish holy women is that we become aware of a pattern of spirituality different from that prevalent among Jewish men. Judaism rests on three pillars: Torah study, prayer, and kind deeds. With almost all male tzaddikim, the central pillar is either Torah study or prayer, although of course they participate in all three areas to some degree. But for *tzaddikot,* the central pillar is usually kindness and occasionally prayer. Traditional holy women study Torah, but their study is less central to their spiritual lives, and their devotion to Torah is often expressed through supporting and encouraging the men to study. This produces a different pattern of holiness, which is useful even for men to know about because not all men are scholars. And it is valuable for everyone to have a model of a devout lifestyle in which the essence of life is compassion—doing good, helping others, doing favors—constantly and at every minute. According to Jewish mystic teaching, continuous spiritual practice leads to continuous God-awareness. Although such mystic attainment is rarely spoken about explicitly in the stories about women in this book, more than a few of the women mentioned undoubtedly reached high levels of the holy spirit and of divine wisdom.

In most collections of Jewish or Hasidic religious tales, many of the heroes are famous individuals. If a story tells about a famous rabbi or rebbe, there are many other stories about him that serve as a background and context. In this collection, however, the heroines are, with a few exceptions, relatively unknown. Frequently, we have only a story or two about a particular holy woman. This unfortunately lessens our ability to appreciate a certain woman in the context of her whole life.

There is another problem in collecting stories about holy women. In the past, women were traditionally relegated to supportive roles. A wife was praised, for example, for aiding her husband's spiritual elevation in Torah study and prayer. Her own spirituality was generally given less attention. That is one reason why there are so few traditional stories about holy women. This attitude fails to satisfy most Jews today. But I hope people will see that just because a pious woman of former times expressed her devotion in a supportive way does not mean that we cannot appreciate and be inspired by her piety. The difference between a woman who served God by sacrificing herself to spiritually and materially support her husband and a husband who served God by sacrificing himself for the sake of Torah study may be less than people might suppose. Both wife and husband were devoted, and each was holy. One expressed his spirituality by Torah study and prayer, the other expressed her spirituality by devoted service to her husband. The archetypal aspiring tzaddik sits and studies Torah and *davvens* (prays) confined in the *beit midrash,* the house of Torah study; his wife is confined to their home, caring for the children and him. But they each act out of pure spiritual motives to serve God. By their devotion, they are released from the restricted confines of their egoism to fly freely in the exalted heavens of holiness and bliss.

Most of us today expect women to have a broad and equal scope for their spiritual lives. But we can still be inspired by the devotion of the holy women of former times or of today who choose to follow a supportive lifestyle. One can appreciate and be inspired by another person's devotion and holiness, even if one pursues a different path. Some very pious Jewish women cut off all their hair and wear a kerchief. I sometimes tell modern Jewish women, "If you heard of a Buddhist nun who cut off all her hair, you might say, 'Wow!' Why not give the same credit to your Jewish sisters, to say, 'They're trying to attain something spiritually. They're going all the way!' It is a mistake to impute the highest motives to women of another religion but to impugn the motives of one's traditionally pious Jewish sisters. You don't have to tread the same path or want to cut your hair to appreciate and be inspired by their sincerity and spirituality."

There are few traditional tales about holy women. If we reduce their number still further by excluding those that show women in a supportive role, we are left with nothing in our hand. Some tales showing women in supportive roles are unworthy and demeaning, but many are inspiring, if one has an open heart and the eyes to see. Why should we look down on our pious grandmothers and great-grandmothers? Why should we disparage their holiness and piety? I have included some tales in this collection that may challenge the reader's values. I hope those tales will be appreciated in the spirit they are offered and will be pondered. I favor the full development, appropriate for our time, of women's religiosity and spirituality, as they choose. But I want to revere the ways of our forebears, of our holy women of former times.

Much of the unfortunate animosity and disrespect among religious people of different persuasions would be dissipated if people understood that they can pursue one path and yet appreciate another. The ancient Rabbis gave us concepts to apply to sincere people of contrary views, such as "These and those are the words of the living God" and "Leave him alone, for everything he does is for the sake of heaven"—meaning that someone may seem to be acting contrary to what you consider the correct path, but you should not trouble him because of that because in truth, everything he is doing is for the sake of God.

I hope this book inspires people to holiness and piety. Let it be seen as part of a movement toward a fuller appreciation of tales of Jewish women's holiness. Let me make two practical suggestions toward that goal. First, Jewish tales of holy women are still unfolding today; let us begin to notice and record the pious deeds of women we know—our family, friends, and teachers. Second, how wonderful it would be if many of us who observe the Sabbath and Jewish holidays made it a custom, at our festive table, to always tell or even to read aloud a tale of a holy woman—perhaps from this book. Others can find different contexts for the telling of these tales. But the ultimate purpose of sacred tales is to elevate our religious life. In fact, many of the tales in this book describe spiritual practices that can be imitated.

A traditional Jewish text states, "There are angels—divine messengers and servants—above and angels below. There are also 'female' as well as 'male' angels."[2]

May we be more aware of the female angels here on earth below and learn to tell their tales and imitate their ways.

The Tales

Sabbath Candle-Lighting Prayers

The Sabbath is the focus of much of Jewish religious life. It is inaugurated by the woman of the household lighting candles as dusk descends on Friday. The Hebrew for Sabbath is *Shabbat;* in Yiddish, the word is pronounced *Shabbos.* Friday during the day is called *erev* Shabbat, and the time right after the Sabbath ends at sundown Saturday is called *motza'ei* Shabbat.

The *tzaddeket* Rebbetzin Hayyeleh Aharonowitz, wife of Rabbi Avrum Aharonowitz, the Israeli tzaddik, was totally devoted to the holiness of Shabbat. On *motza'ei* Shabbat, she prepared wicks for her candles for the coming Shabbat, already expectantly looking forward to the next week's holy day of rest. And every day of the week, she did something to prepare for the next Shabbat, so as to remember the Sabbath constantly.[1] Her preparations reached a zenith on *erev* Shabbat, when she exerted herself so that everything would be fully ready and prepared in the best way, without any tension or pressure.

When the setting sun had reached the tops of the trees, the rebbetzin stood beside her candles, her white Shabbat *tichel* [head covering] on her head, gripped with the holiness of the entering Sabbath. With great love and reverence, she lit the candles and then did not move from her place. She stood standing in front of the precious light of the flickering flames, her hands covering her eyes, her whole body swaying in heartfelt prayer. She prayed, pleaded, and entreated, laying out her supplications before the One Who Sits on High. Thus she spent the time after lighting Shabbat candles, which is known as a time of special grace, when prayers are answered. For two hours, she kept her hands over her eyes, pouring out her heart's desires to God. As she stood there, her face shone in the supernal light of the Shabbat candles, and her tears glistened like pearls as they exited from the corners of her eyes.

Only when the last congregants had returned from the synagogue did the rebbetzin move away from her candles and softly bless, with great feeling, her daughters—"Good *Shabbos!* Good *Shabbos!* Good *Shabbos!*"[2] ✑

Tears Before Candle Lighting

✑ The *tzaddeket* Rebbetzin Rivka Miriam of Belz, the wife of Rabbi Yehoshua, the second Belzer Rebbe, excelled in acts of kindness and gave away large amounts of money for *tzedaka* [charity]. Rebbe Yehoshua said that his wife's *tzedaka* could be compared to that of the holy Rebbe Hayim of Tzanz. The Tzanzer was so devoted to *tzedaka* that he even borrowed money and went into debt to give to the poor!

One *erev* Shabbat, the Belzer Rebbe heard the sound of weeping coming from the rebbetzin's room. He immediately sent someone to ask her why she was crying. She replied that the whole week, she had not had money to give to the poor, as she usually did. Every day of the week, she could hope that she would still get some money the next day. "But now," she said, her voice choking, "in a few hours, it will be candle-lighting time. I have no more hope. I can't bear it anymore." So she broke down and cried.

Rebbe Yehoshua sent back a message, saying, "I don't have any money to give you. But if you'll give me something of value, I can loan you money to give to the poor." [The rebbe was undoubtedly holding other people's money for charitable purposes, which he could not freely give but could loan if a valuable item was left pawned with him.] The rebbetzin gave him her ornamented Sabbath *tichel*. He loaned her the money, and she rushed out and gave it to the poor people, in just enough time for them to buy their Sabbath needs right before the day of rest began. Then she went home and later, with elevated spirits, joyfully lit her Sabbath candles.[1] ⊰◈⊱

This tale and the preceding one about Sabbath candle lighting each provide a glimpse into a world of holiness. When one hears a tale about a holy person, one should realize that it is just a glimpse, a peek, into a different realm. How holy does a person have to be to stand, like Rebbetzin Hayyeleh, for two hours in front of the candles with her hands over her eyes! And how holy must a person be to cry, like Rebbetzin Rivka Miriam, because she has no money to give to poor people! Each anecdote is just a detail that intimates much greater things. We should understand many of the tales in this book that way. Sometimes what seems to be only a small act can reveal spiritual greatness.

In the Merit of the Sabbath Candles

⮞ When Rabbi Yaakov Yitzhak (later known as the Seer of Lublin) and his wife, Shprintza, were young, they were very poor. One *erev* Shabbat, Shprintza had no money for Sabbath candles. Candles cost only a few kopecks, but she had no money at all. An hour before candle lighting, not knowing what to do, she went out of her house and was standing in the street, confused and distraught. Overcome at not being able to light Sabbath candles for the first time in her life, she began to cry and pray to God, "Master of the world, it's not for my honor that I want to light candles but only for Your honor and for the honor of the holy *Shabbos!* I want to bring Your light into the world!"

God heard Shprintza's prayer, and suddenly, a fancy carriage with a wealthy man inside came rumbling down the street. When the rich man, who was Jewish, saw a Jewish woman standing in the street crying, he told his driver to stop. He got out and said to her, "Why are you crying?"

She said, "I don't have money for *Shabbos* candles, although it's only a few kopecks."

"Here are a few kopecks," he said. "Please get yourself candles."

Although outwardly he seemed to be just an irreligious rich man interested only in externals, Shprintza saw that inwardly he was much more. He gave her merely a few coins—nothing for such a wealthy man—but she could see his soul shining in this act of compassion.

She said, "May God bless you with the light from the *Shabbos* candles that you've bought for me."

He got back into his carriage and continued on his trip. He would be traveling on Shabbat, but he was not religious and did not care. Shprintza ran to the last store in town that was open and bought candles to light in honor of the holy Sabbath.

Soon afterward, when Shprintza was lighting her Sabbath candles, she prayed with all her heart that her blessing be fulfilled and that the light of her candles reach the soul of that wealthy man and that he be brought back to the Source of light and life, in the merit of his kind deed. And the holy Rebbetzin Shprintza was on a spiritual level that, as the Rabbis teach, a tzaddik—or *tzaddeket*—decrees and God fulfills. So a miracle occurred.

The rich man was traveling in his carriage when he suddenly felt an expansiveness, an openness within himself that made him wonder why he was alive and what his purpose on earth was. Then he remembered how he had felt when he had done his kind deed. He immediately told his driver to turn the carriage around. He went back to Lublin; found the house of the rebbetzin; met her husband, the Seer; and stayed with them that Shabbat. He became the Seer's disciple and eventually became a tzaddik and a holy man himself.[1] ⊲⧖⊳

A truly pious person who loves doing God's will is pained at not being able to perform a *mitzvah*, a divine commandment. In answer to Shprintza's heartfelt prayer, God sent her a benefactor to provide her with money for Sabbath candles. But divine providence worked

for the rich man as well, because spiritually, she became his benefactor. Why did God make the rebbetzin needy? To save a lost soul
who would be rewarded for helping her. Rebbetzin Shprintza was
so radiantly holy that she could bring even an irreligious man, who
casually came into contact with her, back to God.

A Prayer over the Challahs

≈◎≈ A prayer has come down to us from Perl, the wife
of Rebbe Levi Yitzhak of Berditchev. Whenever she
kneaded and baked challahs for Shabbat, she would
pray, "Master of the world, I beg You that when my husband Levi Yitzhak says the blessing over the challahs,
he has the same holy intentions I have now when I'm
kneading and baking them!"[1] ≈◎≈

Husband and wife are partners in the Jewish spiritual mission of becoming holy. Traditionally, the woman bakes the challahs for Shabbat, and the man makes the blessing over them at the table. If both
have holy intentions, in the baking and the blessing, the bread flies
up to heaven as it is eaten.

The Taste of the Garden of Eden

≈◎≈ The tzaddik Rabbi David of Lelov was good friends
with another tzaddik named Rabbi David, who lived in
the nearby village of Zellin. They were both Hasidim
and disciples of the Seer of Lublin and always traveled
to Lublin together. Sometimes Rabbi David of Lelov

traveled first to Zellin, and sometimes Rabbi David
of Zellin traveled first to Lelov—and then they set out
together for Lublin.

Once, Rabbi David of Lelov went to Zellin to begin
their trip, and his friend, Rabbi David of Zellin, told his
wife, Miriam Shulamis, "My dear, please prepare something to eat quickly, because we have a very special
holy guest!"

Now, Rebbetzin Miriam Shulamis and her husband were desperately poor. They had nothing in
the house, not even coals for the oven! All she had in the
way of food was a little bit of flour. How could she prepare a meal for this tzaddik who was visiting them? So
she went out into the field to gather some wood chips
for the oven and brought them home. She then mixed
the flour with some water, without any fat or spices,
and served this meager meal to her husband and their
guest. After the meal, the two traveled to Lublin.

When Rabbi David of Lelov returned home from
their trip to the Seer of Lublin, he told his wife, Rebbetzin Hanna, "I want to tell you, my dear wife, that I was
in the home of my friend Rabbi David of Zellin, and his
wife made us the most delicious dish I ever ate. It actually had the taste of the Garden of Eden."

When Rebbetzin Hanna, who knew how far her
holy husband was from relishing simple earthly pleasures, heard that, she hurried to Zellin to learn the secret of the other rebbetzin's cooking. When she arrived
there, she asked her, "With what did you season the

food you served my husband? He said that it was the
most delicious food he had ever eaten, that it had a
taste like the Garden of Eden!"

Rebbetzin Miriam Shulamis told Rebbetzin Hanna
that she really had nothing to serve or anything with
which to season the food. But while she was preparing
her meager meal, she was begging God, "Master of the
world, You know that if I had something to serve,
I wouldn't spare a thing to give to this holy tzaddik!
But what can I do? We don't have anything in the house!
So I'm begging You to put the taste of the Garden of
Eden in this dish I'm making so that this tzaddik will
enjoy my food." And she continued to pray this way
until the food was prepared. "So it seems that God answered my prayer," she said. "And your husband tasted
the flavor of the Garden of Eden in my food."[1] ⁓

What gives food its taste is not its physicality alone but its spiritual
aspect. Rebbe Simha Bunim of Pshis'cha laughed at Hasidim who
praised their rebbes by saying that they were so holy, so ascetic,
they did not even taste their food. He said that true tzaddikim are
the only ones who really taste the food they eat! Why? Because they
don't just taste the food itself; they taste God in the food, or as this
tale puts it, they taste the Garden of Eden. Food served and offered
with love tastes of love. Rebbetzin Miriam Shulamis put her devotion to God and God's servants into the dish she prepared, and the
rebbe was on a spiritual level to taste it.

Some pious women, while preparing food for Shabbat, continually repeat, like a mantra, the words *l'kavod Shabbos,* "for the honor
of the Sabbath." Jewish religious tales often recount acts of piety that
seem to be unique but are actually practices recommended by the
rebbes and rabbis. We can learn from them for our own spirituality,

from this tale, for example, to use a mantra while preparing food and to pray while cooking that those who eat our food taste God in it.

Healing Food

In earlier generations, there were great Hasidic rebbes who could heal the sick. For example, when sick people went to the Tzanzer Rebbe paralyzed, the rebbe would bless them and say, "Get up and walk," and they would walk out.

At the turn of the twentieth century, before the First World War, there were still great rebbes who could heal, but not all of them healed by the laying on of hands or by words, with spoken decrees like the Tzanzer Rebbe.

For example, there was the Kerestirer Rebbe, Reb' Yeshaya. He did not lay on hands or speak—but if you ate food in his house, you went away healed.

When his wife, Sarah, died, the rebbe wept terribly and would not be consoled. He told the Hasidim, "You might have thought that people who ate in my house were healed because of me. That's not true. It was because of my holy wife, Sarah. Now that she is gone, I can tell you. Listen to this story of what happened.

"In our earlier days, we were desperately poor. If we ate one meal a week, we would have food to eat on the Sabbath, but we wouldn't be able to have any guests. So we fasted from Sabbath to Sabbath. Then we had enough food for ourselves and for some guests. One week, my holy wife was cooking on Friday for the Sabbath when a drunkard knocked on the door and was invited in. He was reeking of alcohol, but he said to my wife, 'I'm starving. Do you have anything to eat?' We hadn't eaten that whole week, but who knows how long *he* had been without food? And when someone says he's starving, how can you not feed him? So my wife gave him from the food she'd prepared for the Sabbath. But after finishing what she gave him, he asked, 'Is there more?' Each time, he ate whatever was put before him and asked for more, until she said, 'There's not a crumb left.' She gave him everything she had prepared for our Sabbath meals. And she gave him everything gently and respectfully, because she was doing a great *mitzvah* and a good deed. She didn't judge him by how he looked or for his crude behavior, for who knows what troubles he had had?

"Then this drunkard did something unusual. He asked, 'Can I speak with your husband?' My wife came to my room and told me about his request, and when I agreed, she sent him to me. When he came in, he no longer smelled, and he didn't appear drunk. In fact, his face was glowing, and I realized at once that this was Elijah the Prophet.

"He said to me, 'I only came here to bless your wife. Her kindness has made a great impression in heaven. But we wanted to give her a final test to see if she was worthy of the great blessing we have in store for her. She passed the test.'

"What was the great blessing? It was the blessing of healing. And that," said the rebbe, "was why the food my holy wife served healed whoever ate it."[2]

Food that is prepared and served with love can heal the sick and revive the weary. Rebbetzin Sarah's food, offered with such self-sacrifice, contained a heavenly blessing. This quality is not unique to this *tzaddeket*. There are other stories in which the healing powers of a holy woman come through the food she serves.[3] And many women who prepare and serve food to their family put in their healing love as a main ingredient.

Women's holiness is too often hidden. That is sad, because as a result, holy women are not given the honor and respect they deserve. But it is also true that the traditional ideal of Jewish piety is *kol k'voda bat melech p'nima,* "all the glory of a princess is [modestly hidden] within."[4] It is a regular theme in Jewish tales that a rebbe or a holy man tries to hide his piety and his miracles. That would be even more true of a holy woman, for traditionally women have held themselves to stricter standards of modesty and concealment. This story suggests that out of humility and modesty, Rebbetzin Sarah of Kerestir told her holy husband to keep her miraculous powers secret, and only after her passing did he feel entitled to reveal them.

Watching at the Market

⁌ A certain *tzaddeket* in Jerusalem used to go out to the market on Thursday, when all the women did their shopping, to see which of her neighbors did not come to the market. "Whoever doesn't come," she thought, "certainly doesn't have any money to buy for her needs on Shabbat."

Then she would hurry to the home of any woman who had not appeared and give her some money, saying, "Please take this from me, just as a loan," since she knew that her pious neighbor would not want to take charity. Later she would tell her to forget about the loan.

The neighbor would say with embarrassment, "You've saved me, my sister. I didn't want to accept a gift of charity from flesh and blood. Thank you so much."

The *tzaddeket* would then quickly leave and seek other favors and other *mitzvot* to do.[1] ≈≈

Sometimes we might think that what God wants from us is to perform great deeds and to save lives. More often what is required of us is to do small deeds that save lives. People sometimes have a difficult time responding openly and charitably to needy individuals who approach them. But perhaps even more often, needy persons do not approach others at all, out of embarrassment. When we strive for holiness and goodness, we will be sensitive to hear the silent cry of a friend or a neighbor or someone who cannot bring himself to ask for help. That was the holiness of this *tzaddeket*. She was what the Jewish tradition calls *maskil el dal,* aware and alert to the needs of the poor.

Two Pious Peddlers

≈≈ In the Jerusalem market were two small stands next to one another where two pious Jewish women each sold tasty and fragrant cakes and cookies that they themselves had baked. Different from most peddlers, who loudly announce their wares, these two women sat modestly and patiently at their stands, waiting for the customers to come on their own. "*Parnossah* [a livelihood] is from heaven," they often said. "What a person deserves in this world, he'll receive—even if he doesn't call out about his merchandise." So the two women sat at their stands, occasionally conversing. They were good friends and companions to each other.

Neither one was jealous of the other's business. When there were few customers, each of them would become absorbed in reciting psalms from the book that was always resting on her stand. If one of them had many customers, she would say, "Why have you come just to me? My friend's cakes and cookies are at least as good as mine! Go over there and see how fine her baked goods are. And I can tell you that they're delicious. I know!" The customers would smile at hearing this, and some would go over to the other stand. Her friend and neighbor would do the same favor for her when the situation was reversed. "You're looking for honey cake, my dear sir? Honey cakes are not my specialty. Go over to my neighbor's stand. Her honey cakes are the best—they taste just like manna!" The customer would rush over to the other stand, somewhat amazed and confused by this strange behavior, thinking, "Maybe they're sisters, and she's worried about her sister's livelihood." Each one would send customers to the other so that one of them would not profit more and the other be heartbroken.

Once, when one of them became aware that her neighbor had debts, having recently married off her daughter, she said to her husband, "My neighbor who sells cookies and cakes in the market stand next to mine is burdened with many debts. I was thinking that I won't go to sell in the market this week. Let me take a little vacation from baking and selling cakes. She needs the money more than me. Let the customers go to her this week." Her pious husband nodded in agreement, saying, "That's a very good idea, my dear." He understood very well the ways of his pious wife.

The other woman stood in the market that week, selling her cakes. Every once in a while, she looked over at her friend's stand, wondering where she was and what might have happened to her. It was already four days that she had not seen her. "Maybe she's sick," she worried. "I'll go visit her today." After she closed her stand, she went to her friend's house. "*Shalom*," she said as she entered her house. "I expected to find you in bed. *Baruch HaShem* [Thank God], you're healthy! I was worried that you were sick and came to help you out. What's the matter?"

Surprised and not knowing what to reply, her friend said, "I felt tired and fatigued this week and thought I'd take the week off and rest."

"Come," said her friend, "I know you're not rich and need *parnossah*. Let's go into the kitchen. I'll help you bake some cakes and cookies to sell tomorrow. Come into the kitchen. Why am I bothering you with a lot of useless talk?"

She already had an apron on and began to vigorously sift flour for her friend. Then she energetically and diligently kneaded the dough in a trough, with the joy of doing a *mitzvah*.

These two women peddlers in the Jerusalem market loved each other without needing any special reason. Both of them had great faith and trust in God, blessed be He. They were truly *tzaddikot*.[1]

Most of us want to be good and do good. But self-interest and the supposed "demands" of the marketplace can interfere with our benevolent intentions. Not so for holy people like these two pious women peddlers. The Rabbis teach that a person should not be jealous of his fellow merchant, whom the secular world calls his "competitor," because God alone determines what each person deserves and receives. Everything that happens happens by divine providence. The Rabbis say that someone else cannot affect what is decreed for a person from heaven, not even by a thread. No human, no "competitor," can ultimately affect what happens to another individual. And the lesson of this tale applies not only to business but also to any area where people might seem to be competing. It is an idyllic description of a better world in which love overcomes obstacles and selflessness defeats selfishness. But holy people live in that better world now.

Are You Not Our Father?

Rabbi Yisrael—the Baal Shem Tov ("Master of the Good Name")—was the founder of Hasidism. He is also known as the Besht, an acronym for his title.

⊰⊱ When the Baal Shem Tov once saw that there was a serious accusation in heaven against the Jewish people, he and his disciples prayed and engaged in many fasts, but for all their efforts, they were unable to change the situation for good.

The Besht used his influence with the rabbi of Medzibuz to declare a fast for all the townspeople so that they would offer prayers and supplications on the fast day for the annulment of the heavenly decree. (The rabbi did not know the real reason, but by giving him some justifications as an excuse, the Besht was able to convince him to declare a fast.)

Both men and women came to the synagogue, where they wept, prayed, and recited psalms. But even the communal fast, the prayers, and the tears did not remove the evil decree.

Suddenly, the Besht's face, which had been clouded over with worry, began to shine joyfully. He turned to his disciple, Rabbi Nachman Horodenker, who stood beside him in the synagogue, and said, "Thank God, the decree has been annulled in heaven!"

Later, after the conclusion of the fast, when the Besht was sitting with his disciples, he told them in whose merit the decree was removed. "When a certain woman in the women's section of the synagogue heard the congregation sobbing, she spoke to the Holy One, blessed be He, saying, 'Master of the world, are You not our Father, and are we not Your children? I have five children, and when they all begin to sob and wail at once, my insides turn over within me. And You, our Heavenly Father, have so many children, and all of them are crying pitifully. Is Your heart made of stone that You don't hear their cries and pleas? Should You not answer them? Master of the world, answer us!'

"At that moment," said the Baal Shem Tov, "a heavenly voice proclaimed, 'The decree is annulled!'"[1] ◀◈▷

This compassionate mother knew God's ways as a parent from her own experience. It is a great secret of prayer to speak to God as to a parent, which evinces and evokes a feeling of intimacy with our Father in Heaven. Rabbi Shalom Noah, the late Slonimer Rebbe in

Jerusalem, wrote that when one prays, calling God "Father," there is no heavenly accusation, and mercy is aroused.[2]

God is also our Mother. The Rebbes of Komarna and Shpitevka saw visions of the *Shechinah*—the indwelling Divine Presence—in the form of a woman.[3] "During sleep, Rebbe David Biderman of Lelov-Jerusalem would burst out with longing for the holy *Shechinah* and cry out in a voice suffused with love and yearning, 'Mother! Mother!'"[4] Rabbi Eliezer Papo, in his famous book *Pele Yo'aitz,* speaks of a person's "Father and Mother, the Holy One, blessed be He, and His *Shechinah.*"[5]

Riveleh the Tzaddeket

≪◈≫ The Baal Shem Tov was traveling from his home-town of Medzibuz to Satinov in Podolia, and as he approached the city, he saw with his holy vision that a divine light was shining above one of the townspeople. Stopping briefly and standing in place to look more closely, he saw that the light was resting on a woman. When he entered the town and was greeted by its prominent men, he told them what he had seen and asked if they knew which woman might be the one over whom he had seen the light. They replied that undoubtedly it was Riveleh the Pious. Anxious to meet this holy woman, the Besht asked them to send for her, but they told him it was unnecessary, since she was very active in collecting *tzedaka* and in performing deeds of kindness and would certainly come on her own to ask him for a donation.

The next day, after prayers, the Baal Shem Tov saw with his holy spirit that she was on her way, and he said

to the people with him, "I see her coming here. And
she's made up her mind not to accept anything less
than a certain large sum of money from me. Pay attention to how I'll act with her and the way she responds,
and you'll see her holiness."

When Riveleh came, she said to the Baal Shem Tov,
"Holy Rabbi, there are several poor people in town who
are sick. Will you please make a generous donation for
them?" When the Besht offered her a small amount of
money, she said nothing but made a slight gesture with
her hand to indicate that she would not accept it. He
then offered her twice that amount, which was still a
small sum, but she would not accept that either. Feign-
ing anger, he rebuked her, saying, "Who made you the
charity collector, so that you could steal from the fund
whenever you pleased?" She did not answer a word or
show the slightest anger or annoyance at this insult; the
words made no impression on her whatsoever, because
she was as humble and lowly as the dust. But she refused to leave the Besht until he had given her the entire
amount she had decided she would take from him. For
although she was as soft and pliant as a reed in the face
of abuse to her own person, she was as hard and unyield-
ing as a cedar when it came to doing good and helping
the needy. The Besht, who had seen her great light, had
tested her resolve and patience by offering her small
donations and trying to provoke her so that the townspeople would see her pious humility as he saw it.

That evening, Riveleh came to the Baal Shem Tov
a second time and said, "A certain doctor in the city is

very sick. Please pray for him to live, because he's in
critical condition."

"Let there be one less adulterer in the world," said
the Besht.

"Who told you that he's an adulterer?" she protested.

The Besht turned to the men standing there and
said, "Is what I say true?"

"Yes, it's true!" they answered.

She responded firmly, "First, they haven't the least
evidence for this. And he's a complete innocent, sexu-
ally; he's the sort of person who's never even seen a
paintbrush in a tube. Even if he did what they say, it's
only because he's ignorant of the Torah and didn't know
the severity of the sin. If he had known how serious it
was, he would never have transgressed!" Kind and
compassionate as she was, she easily found reasons to
judge others favorably and to excuse their faults, just
as the Besht taught his disciples and followers to do.

The Baal Shem Tov, who had heard an accusation
about the doctor's adultery made against him in heaven,
repeated it to her intentionally so that she would defend
him and speak in his favor. When she did so, her arguments on his behalf were accepted above, and the doctor
immediately recovered from his illness.[1] ◈

According to the Baal Shem Tov and the Hasidic rebbes, the opinion
of certain very holy people—like Riveleh—is heeded in heaven. The
pious and humble Riveleh had come to the holy Baal Shem Tov to ask
him to pray for the doctor. But the Besht knew that she was so holy
that her prayers too would be answered—perhaps, in this case, even
more readily than his own. The Besht made his mock accusation in

order to elicit her defense of the doctor, knowing that her words would be heard and heeded in heaven; he had played the "devil's advocate" only to cast her in the role of a defending angel before the Throne of Glory.

The Besht was an expert at discerning holiness. He saw a person's hidden light when others did not. This was the case with men whose virtue was veiled by their humble exterior; how much more was his expert eye necessary with women, who are even more concealed because of their modesty and because of the common failure of men to appreciate their holiness. The men of Satinov knew that Riveleh was a pious *tzaddeket,* but they did not know to what extent. The Baal Shem Tov revealed it to them.

Holy Spirit

Rebbetzin Mirl was the wife of Rebbe Yitzhak Meir of Zhinakov. One day, when the rebbetzin went to the synagogue to pray, as she entered the women's section, she saw the women animatedly conversing. "Haven't you heard," they greeted her, "that Reb Yaakov the Wagon Driver passed away?"

"*Oy!*" sighed Rebbetzin Mirl. "My dear friend, the holy Reb Yaakov, is gone!" and she broke out in tears. Her friends were all surprised: Why was she so emotional? Was Reb Yaakov related to her? Or was she close to him because he had worked at some time for her husband, the rebbe?

"Listen, my friends," said the rebbetzin, when they asked her about it, "and I'll tell you why I'm so saddened by the death of that dear tzaddik Reb Yaakov."

All the women came closer to her to hear what she would say. "One day," said the rebbetzin, "I ran out of firewood. I didn't even have any wood chips to start a fire. My house was freezing cold. So I went to Reb Yaakov the Wagon Driver and asked, 'Reb Yaakov, could you please bring me a little wood?' Without delaying for a minute, he immediately hitched his horse to the wagon, drove off to the forest, and before long brought back a wagonful of wood. I used the wood to warm my house and also the *beit midrash* [Torah study hall]. In his merit, Jews sat and studied Torah in a warm and pleasant room!

"I remember another time when I had no water in my house on *erev* Shabbat. I couldn't cook for Shabbat without water. To whom did I go? To Reb Yaakov! When I asked him to please get me some water, he didn't wait or delay for a moment; he immediately hitched his horse to his wagon and quickly brought a barrelful of water to my house!"

After telling this to the women, the holy rebbetzin lifted her eyes to heaven and said, "Master of the world, may it be Your will that every little chip of that wagonful of wood be a defending angel for Reb Yaakov in heaven. And may every drop from that barrelful of water be a great merit for him, to plead for him and support him in the Upper World!"

The rebbetzin then prayed during the synagogue service with great *kavvanah* [devotional focus] and returned home.

Later, when Rebbe Yitzhak Meir, her husband, came to the synagogue, his Hasidim told him what the rebbetzin had said about Reb Yaakov. Rebbe Yitzhak Meir said, "Now you know that the rebbetzin too has *ruach ha-kodesh* [the holy spirit], because I tell you, when Reb Yaakov died, I heard them saying in the Heavenly Court exactly what she said just now."[1] ✑

A holy woman like Rebbetzin Mirl has compassionate eyes that can see the greatness of even a simple person. Reb Yaakov was not a Torah scholar, but he was ready to help a needy fellow human without delay. The holy rebbetzin, who appreciated the holiness and goodness of a humble wagon driver, called him a "tzaddik."

A pious person like Rebbetzin Mirl does not forget a favor. Judaism cultivates one's feelings of gratitude and deepens one's appreciation of goodness. The rebbetzin remembered Reb Yaakov's kind deeds and pleaded for him before the Heavenly Throne. She was on a spiritual level to be a defending angel for others in the Heavenly Court, fulfilling the task of the archangel Michael, who pleads on behalf of the Jewish people. Her holy husband, the rebbe, who could hear heavenly proclamations, stated that he had just heard in heaven what she had said; his wife was, so to speak, making the same argument as Michael and the other defending angels. Certainly, her pleas were heeded in heaven.

Deeds Great and Small

✑ When the *rosh yeshiva* [headmaster] of the Lomzeh Yeshiva, Rabbi Yehiel Mordechai Gordon, was visiting London during the Second World War, he received a letter from his daughter Batsheva. At that time, she was engaged to be married to Reb Yitzhak

Kastiokovsky, an outstanding young Torah scholar in Lomzeh. Her father had earlier written to her, promising to borrow five hundred dollars from relatives so that her wedding should not have to be postponed any longer for lack of money.

In her letter, Batsheva replied, "I recently met a friend, also a *kallah,* a bride-to-be, and asked about her wedding plans. She tearfully confided to me that because she was lacking five hundred dollars, her engagement was in danger of being broken off. Therefore, dear father, I'm asking you to please borrow money for her instead of for me. With God's help, Yitzhak and I will somehow manage without that money."

The letter touched her father's heart. He decided to show it to one of the most important rabbis in London, Rabbi Yehezkel Abramsky, who then took it upon himself to collect money for the needy *kallah.* When Rabbi Yehezkel had collected the entire amount, he himself went to mail the envelope containing the check. His students asked him why he went to the trouble of mailing the money personally, rather than sending his aide to do it. The rabbi replied with a story.

"Hanna, the wife of the Vilna Gaon,[1] made a pact with her best friend. They promised each other that whichever of them passed away first would appear to the other within thirty days and tell her what had happened in the World to Come. The friend died first and appeared to Hanna in a dream. This is what she told Hanna: 'Do you remember the day we went from door to door together, collecting money for charity? We spotted a wealthy woman some distance away, and I raised my hand, motioning for her to stop. We went over to her and received a nice donation. Well, this simple act of raising my hand was recorded in the divine Book of Remembrances, and I received an extra reward for that gesture. . . .' That is the reason," concluded Rabbi Abramsky, "that I chose to mail the envelope myself. One can never know the true value of even the smallest deed for the sake of heaven."[2] ⊸

The first part of this story is about loving your neighbor as yourself—or, for pious people like Batsheva, loving them more than yourself, for she passed on money she needed for her own wedding in favor of a friend who had a similar need. It seems that Batsheva had learned her generosity from her parents, and it is notable that her father, rather than resisting her suggestion and trying to divert her from her selfless deed, as some parents might, was so proud of her that he showed her letter to his friend, Rabbi Yehezkel Abramsky.

The second part of the story, the tale within the tale, about Hanna, the Vilna Gaon's wife, has a different lesson. It teaches that holy deeds are never lost. Even seemingly small deeds and even gestures are noted and "recorded" because they are precious to God and are, in truth, the meaning of life. The first part of the story is about a great deed—giving up five hundred dollars; the second part is about the great worth of every small deed. In both parts of this tale, it is inspiring to see holy rabbis appreciating and being inspired by the deeds of holy women.

How I Envy You!

The Torah teaches a person to be humble, even to the extent of receiving abuse with love of God, not from a lack of self-esteem but from such high self-esteem that it cannot be shaken by the lowly acts of anyone else.

⪦⪧ The holy Rebbetzin Rachel Leah was the second wife of Rabbi David Moshe, the Chortkover Rebbe. When she went to live at the rebbe's court in Chortkov, she was subjected to the abuse of one of the female servants, who had a terrible temper and regularly insulted and harassed Rachel Leah. But the holy rebbetzin received all of the abuse with love for God and never even mentioned it to her holy husband.

The situation became so bad that it reached a point where this woman servant threw a pot at the rebbetzin that hit her on the forehead and wounded her, causing a deep gash. The rebbetzin simply put a bandage on her forehead and continued with her business.

The rebbetzin's custom was that after the evening prayers, when night fell and her husband's single meal of the day was brought in to him, she would go to his room and sit opposite him while he ate. Some days, the rebbe was so immersed in his God-consciousness and divine service that he did not even lift up his holy eyes and did not speak with her at all; other days, he looked at her and asked her about this or that.

That evening, when the rebbetzin went in to her husband, the rebbe, with the bandage on her forehead, the rebbe looked up and noticed it and asked her what had happened. Since her holy husband had already asked about it, she decided to tell him that she was being abused by one of the women servants, who regularly insulted her and had even thrown a pot at her earlier in the day that hit her on the forehead.

Instead of reacting angrily, saying, "Who dared to do such a thing!" and so on, the rebbe quietly asked her, "What did you say when she cursed and insulted you?"

"I said nothing," the rebbetzin replied.

"What did you say when she threw the pot at you?" the rebbe asked.

"I didn't say anything when she hit me with the pot either," answered the rebbetzin quietly.

As if speaking to himself, the rebbe then continued, "So even though she cursed and actually injured you like that, you didn't say a word?"

"No," answered the rebbetzin.

"Then," said the rebbe with great emotion, "how I envy you!"[1] ◈

Some people might be inclined to think that a person should always defend himself from abuse. But the holy rebbetzin accepted the abuse not because of her low self-esteem but because of her high self-esteem, because she was a devoted servant of God and was above answering lowly abuse with lowliness. Rebbetzin Rachel Leah was humble because she was a holy woman. And in her great humility, she could not be humiliated.

The Rabbis say:

> "Those who are humiliated by others,
> and do not respond in kind;
> Who hear themselves abused,
> and do not answer with abuse;
> Who act from love of God and rejoice in affliction:
> Of them does scripture say:

'Those who love Him shall be as the sun
when it comes out in full strength.'"[2]

A Fence to Wisdom

Sarah Shneirer was the founder of the network of Beis Yaakov schools for girls.

Once, during the change between classes at her first Beis Yaakov school, she overheard a group of girls noisily arguing about some petty matter. She stopped what she was doing to listen and heard one girl say to another, "You insulted me, but I won't answer you back! The Rabbis say, 'Silence is a fence to wisdom.'"

Sarah smiled with amusement. She called that girl over and asked her, "Havveleh, if silence is a fence to wisdom, what is wisdom itself?"

The girl did not answer.

Sarah Shneirer continued, "The fence to wisdom is restraining oneself when insulted, without answering back. But wisdom itself is not to be insulted at all."[1]

How can you "not be insulted" when someone insults you? It is only possible by being above insult, by putting yourself totally in God's hands. A truly pious Jew, a holy Jew—like Sarah Shneirer—on a certain level cares only "what God thinks" and is beyond the praise or blame of flesh and blood. A mother might teach a child that "sticks and stones can break my bones, but names can never harm me." A holy woman like Sarah Shneirer taught a similar but awesomely higher lesson to her spiritual children: not to be insulted.

A Saving Prayer

According to Jewish law, if a woman's husband has disappeared and is missing, she cannot remarry; a woman with such an unfortunate status is called an *agunah*. When a wicked, unconscionable husband abandons his wife, making her an *agunah,* she may have no recourse unless her husband can be found and pressured to give her a writ of divorce, a *get.* Abandoned wives—a long-standing problem in traditional Judaism—suffer greatly; their situation is truly wretched.

The following tale about an *agunah* was told by Rabbi Hayim Shmuelevitz, a teacher in the Mir Yeshiva in Jerusalem.

During the Six-Day War [in 1967], Rabbi Hayim was in a bomb shelter together with his yeshiva students. "The rumble of the bombs was deafening," he said. "Everybody was withdrawn and concentrated within himself. Fear pervaded the cramped space. Suddenly, my ears heard the desperate plea of a poor woman whose husband had abandoned her ten years earlier, leaving her an *agunah.* Broken and crushed during those moments of fear and trepidation, when all our lives hung in the balance, this poor woman cried out from the bitterness of her heart, 'Master of the world, I forgive my husband for all the grief he has caused me, all the humiliations and pain he has inflicted on me by having left me alone and abandoned all these years. Please, I beg You, Master of the world, that You too forgive the sins of all these people sitting here, just as I completely and wholeheartedly forgive my husband!'"

Rabbi Hayim was deeply moved by these sincere words of a pious Jewish woman. Whenever he told this story, he would say, "If we stayed alive then and survived the bombs and bullets of death, it was not due to the prayers we prayed in our distress but due to the merit of this woman, this *agunah,* who forgave the sins of her husband. This was the pinnacle of overcoming one's evil inclination and lower nature. This stood by us in our time of need, and her prayer tipped the balance of the heavenly scales toward life."[1] ◈

Who could be more bitter than an *agunah* against her husband? Yet we know that to ask God to forgive us our sins and keep us in life, we must, so to speak, "show the way" by forgiving those who sin against us. Some readers, particularly women, may be justifiably angry against all men who submit their wives to the humiliation and suffering of being an *agunah*. It may also distress some women that the *agunah* in this tale forgives her husband. But unrestrained bitter feelings may poison our lives and destroy us spiritually. This story's heroine conquered her bitterness.

Some of us may also be disturbed by the notion that God determines life and death in crisis situations according to the sins of the potential victims. But whether you share that belief or not, is it not noble for a crushed and afflicted woman who held this belief to plead with her Creator on behalf of her fellow human beings by releasing her anger? Such a forgiving prayer moves God to forgive too.

Why did she pray this prayer? Because in a critical moment, when life and death hang in the balance, we intuitively know that our negativity, our seething anger, makes us less worthy of life. That is not why God put us into this world. Indeed, it could be a cause for Him to remove us from it. When we are humbled by a disastrous situation and our pride is broken, our anger may fade, and we are ready to forgive. Nor was this woman thinking of herself alone. She offered up her anger to God on behalf of all those in the shelter. What is the greatest sacrifice that pleases God? The sacrifice of our evil inclination, the sacrifice of our lower nature, of our anger and hatred. How could God not hear and accept this woman's cry of repentance and her plea for divine mercy for all those in the shelter?

What can we learn from her example? Perhaps we can be inspired to consider giving up our anger at this or that person as a sacrifice to God, as a way to reach our goal of true spiritual clarity and purity, of gentleness and love. Do we diminish our wish to do everything possible to help or alleviate the situation of *agunahs* by tempering our anger? Do we weaken our fight against wickedness by removing our own share in the world's lowliness? I think not and hope not. May God help us move forward on the path of love and truth.

Insulting Her Husband

Who is a good wife? The Rabbis taught that a good wife is "one who does her husband's will." Many modern women would object to this teaching, yet there are ways to understand it that change its meaning. For example, Rabbi Menachem Mendel Schneersohn, the Lubavitcher Rebbe, interpreted the Hebrew to mean that a good wife "makes" or forms ("does") her husband's will, directing him to spirituality. But I hope that this controversial saying will not prevent some readers from appreciating the following tale.

⬥ A great and pious woman, the wife of a great rabbi, told Rabbi Sholom Schwadron, the *Maggid* [preacher] of Jerusalem, that her husband once asked her to always insult him publicly. Of course, this was a very unusual request to make of a religious woman, who held her husband's honor in the highest regard! Nevertheless, he asked and urged her to do this for him. She did not know what to think or do and said to him, "My dearest husband, I understand that this is what you want. And the Rabbis say, 'Who is a good wife? One who does what

her husband wants.' But how can I humiliate myself
publicly by the very fact of humiliating you, my husband, whom I should respect? Everyone will say, 'What
a terrible wife!'"

Her husband said, "Let me tell you an amazing
story about Freida, the daughter of Rabbi Yehezekel
Landau, the Noda BeYehuda.¹ She was the wife of the
Rabbi of Posen in Poland, whom everyone called Rabbi
Yosef the Tzaddik because he was so righteous. His
famous father-in-law, the great Noda BeYehuda, spoke
of him with the highest praise, saying he was the greatest of his generation in Torah and *mitzvot.*

"But whenever people came to this Rabbi Yosef
the Tzaddik to ask a question in *halacha* [Jewish religious law], his wife would say to them, 'To whom are
you coming to ask a question? To a hypocrite and a
fraud, whom I know intimately. I tell you, he's worth-
less, less than zero. He hasn't a single good trait of a
tzaddik!' Rabbi Yosef the Tzaddik would hear her and
not answer a word. Of course, everyone in the city was
shocked by her behavior. Her own father, the famous
Noda BeYehuda, respected and revered her husband so
much, and she belittled and humiliated him publicly!
They were all very distressed that the wife of the Rabbi
of Posen did not appreciate his greatness.

"But when Rabbi Yosef the Tzaddik passed away,
the rebbetzin made it known that she wanted to eulo-
gize him! Everyone was astonished. She had lowered
him his whole life, and now, when he was dead, she
wanted to praise him? But she insisted, so they had to

agree. In her eulogy, she said, 'Rabbi Yosef the Tzaddik, Rabbi Yosef the Tzaddik! Rabbi Yosef, you certainly were a tzaddik! But you made a condition with me at our engagement that I agree to publicly insult you, so you would not become proud, since everyone knew of your genius in Torah and your righteousness. What I did was only because you asked and pleaded with me to do it, not because I was bad-hearted. I was only a good wife, as the Rabbis say, who did the will of her husband. Who more than I,' she said, 'knew your greatness and goodness?'

"When she had finished, everyone present saw with their own eyes that the head of the tzaddik lying there nodded in agreement, testifying to the truth of her words."

This was the story that the rabbi told his wife. Then he added, "I'm not Rabbi Yosef the Tzaddik; I can't nod my head after death to show everyone that you're a good wife. But I'll write a note for you that I'll sign—that you did everything only because I asked you, because a good wife does what her husband wants."

This rabbi's wife told this whole story to Rabbi Sholom Schwadron. She then said to him, "He always begged me to insult him publicly, and I did it only because of the note he gave me."

Rabbi Schwadron said, "I asked her to show me the note, but she absolutely refused. Only after I begged and urged her did she show it to me, with her husband's signature. But before she showed it to me, she warned me in every way never to tell this story to anyone while

she was alive. I asked her, why didn't she want to reveal
this story or the note? Didn't she want the note to prove
that she insulted her holy husband only because she
was a good wife and not because she was bad-hearted?

"She answered me, 'The daughter of the Noda
BeYehuda was a great woman. She merited that heaven
reveal the truth of her words to everyone by her husband's nodding his head. But I'm not so great. Let me
at least have the merit in the World to Come of having
done this one *mitzvah* perfectly—that I was a good wife
who did what my husband wanted.' I told her, 'I can
name many *mitzvot* you've done,' because in fact she
was famous as a great woman. But she insisted and did
not budge from her resolve, saying, 'No *mitzvah*
matches this one.'"[2] ◁◈▷

In this story and in the story within the story, each husband wanted
his wife to do him the great spiritual favor of insulting him publicly
so that he would not become proud. How holy a man must be to ask
this! But the wife in each case humiliated herself even more by humiliating her husband publicly! Why did she do it? To fulfill the Rabbis' dictum that a good wife does what her husband wants. But she
also did it because, *like her husband,* she knew that by lowering herself in this way and humiliating not only him but herself, she would
reap the great spiritual reward of humility.

We could ask why each husband would ask his wife to humiliate herself in this way. The only answer would be that he wanted for
her what he wanted for himself: to achieve humility through humiliation. The behavior of each couple expressed an unspoken agreement between them to strive for holiness and humility—and they
succeeded.

In each case, the husband's secret remained hidden until after
his death. In the second case, of the rebbetzin who told this whole

story to Rabbi Schwadron, she too wanted her secret to remain hidden until after her death; then she would have fulfilled the *mitzvah* of doing her husband's will perfectly, without seeking to repair her damaged reputation. How great was this woman's husband, to desire to be publicly humiliated in order to remain humble! But his wife was even greater: she allowed herself to be publicly abased even more by humiliating him.

How can a person bear this or desire this? The answer is that holy people are above praise or blame and care only what God thinks of them. And humility has great spiritual rewards.

Rebbetzin Devorah Cohen"

The following three tales are told by Sara Levinsky Rigler of Jerusalem about her encounters with a contemporary hidden *tzaddeket*—a holy woman who has gone virtually unrecognized—whom she calls Rebbetzin "Devorah Cohen." All the names and places in the stories were changed, as a condition set by the holy woman for allowing Sara Rigler to write about her.

A Hidden Tzaddeket

℮ I was in Israel, hot on the trail of a hidden holy woman. I had only an address and a name—Rebbetzin Devorah Cohen. Her husband, Rabbi Emanuel Cohen, was considered by Israel's greatest rabbis to be one of the thirty-six hidden tzaddikim by whose merit the whole world exists. "Rebbetzin Devorah is as great as he is," my source had told me. As the bus pulled out of Jerusalem's Central Bus Station, I settled in for a long ride, grateful for the time to think. I had been in Israel for barely two months, studying about my Jewish background. Having spent the last fifteen years living in an Indian ashram, I had many unresolved issues with Judaism. My major obstacle, which I called, "Issue Number One," was accepting the Jewish emphasis on having children. For fifteen years I had invested myself in a celibate path, having been taught by my guru that sexual relationships dissipated spiritual energy and that children were little noisemakers who made it impossible to meditate. I believed that children and spiritual practices were mutually exclusive and that if I pursued the path of Judaism, all my spirituality would end up in the diaper pail. My "Issue Number Two" was a sense of spiritual alienation from most of the other Jews I met in Israel. Although I was convinced that Torah was true, I felt that it applied to "them," but not to me. I was a unique exception.

When I finally alighted at Rebbetzin Devorah's ramshackle rural community, I made my way to the home of Nomi, who had arranged the meeting. She filled me in on Rebbetzin Devorah's life. Born in Hungary, she had been taken to Auschwitz at the age of twenty. Her parents and sisters were killed in the gas chambers the first night, but the young Devorah had been kept alive to be experimented upon by the notorious "angel of death," Dr. Mengele. Right after the war, she made her way to Palestine, where she married Emanuel Cohen, also a survivor. The couple never had any children, although they raised many unwanted children who were left on their doorstep, including one

Down Syndrome boy who, thirty years later, was still living with them. They lived in abject poverty, eking out a meager income from raising poultry. "Through it all," Nomi concluded, shaking her head in wonder, "Rebbetzin Devorah is always smiling. I see her almost every day, and she is never without a smile. I still can't figure out what she has to smile about."

On Shabbat morning, I attended the service at the community's simple synagogue. Suddenly the door swung open, and a woman walked toward me, smiling broadly, her arms outstretched. She greeted me with a bear hug, like a long-lost daughter. I knew immediately that this was Rebbetzin Devorah. As I stared at her, she took my new prayer book from my hand. She leafed through it until she found the "Ethics of the Fathers," aphorisms by the sages of two millennia ago. Handing the prayer book back to me, she pointed to a passage and asked, "Have you ever seen this one?" As I read the words she was pointing to, I broke out in goose bumps. Here was a rejoinder to my Issue Number One: "Rabbi Shimon ben Yehuda says . . . Beauty, strength, wealth, honor, wisdom . . . and children—these adorn the righteous and adorn the world. . . ." While I stood there dumbfounded, she took my prayer book again and turned a few pages. Handing it back to me, she pointed to another passage and asked, "And have you ever read this one?" Staring at me were the words: "Hillel said: Do not separate yourself from the community." Issue Number Two in stark rebuttal. I looked up in consternation. The holy woman laughed, then turned and left.

Later that afternoon, I followed Nomi's directions
to Rebbetzin Devorah's home, which looked like a shack
from some Hasidic story. I came upon Rebbetzin Devorah
as she was setting out a dish of food for the stray cats.
She greeted me with a beaming smile and invited me in.
Soon we were engrossed in conversation. We spoke
Hebrew, a language which I barely knew, but somehow
I understood everything she said. She asked me about
my background. I told her about the ashram. Then I
asked her about her experiences in the Holocaust, a
subject which had always absorbed me. She described
how, on that first night in Auschwitz, a veteran inmate
had pointed to the smoke issuing out of the chimney of
the crematoria and told her, "That's your parents."
Nevertheless, she asserted, "Auschwitz was not a bad
place." What? I must have misunderstood. I asked her
to repeat her statement. "Auschwitz was not a bad
place," she repeated clearly. "There was a group of religious Hungarian girls. We stuck together. And all the
mitzvot we could do, we did do. For example, one girl
kept track of the days, so we knew when it was *Shabbos,* and we avoided doing any forbidden work whenever possible. On Passover, we didn't have any matzah
or wine, of course. But one of the girls had memorized
the *Haggadah.*[1] She would recite a line, and then we
would all repeat after her. In this way, we were able to
fulfill the *mitzvah* of reciting the *Haggadah.*" The holy
woman fixed me with her pale blue eyes. "A bad place
is a place where Jews can do *mitzvot* but don't do them.
For you, the ashram was a bad place." She had just

turned my whole reality upside down—a bad place had
nothing to do with bad things happening you. No matter that the Nazis had murdered her whole family.
No matter that Dr. Mengele had experimented on her
and probably sterilized her. All that really matters is
what issues *from* you.

No wonder she was always smiling, despite her
barrenness, despite her poverty, despite the grueling
hardship of her daily life. She was performing *mitzvot.*
She was bonding with God. She was projecting her own
light even in the darkness of hell.

I had met many holy masters in India. I had sat
at the feet of great swamis and had bowed before
Anandamayi-ma, the woman considered by millions to
be the incarnation of the Divine Mother. But sitting in
that bare room with its tin roof, eating cucumbers and
farmer's cheese across a rickety table from Rebbetzin
Devorah, I felt like I had just emerged from a whole
lifetime spent through the looking glass. I had been
seeing everything in reverse. Now here I was at the top
of the rabbit hole, awakened from the dream, squinting
my eyes at the brightness of a world of total spiritual
clarity. I looked long and hard at Rebbetzin Devorah.
She gazed back at me, and laughed.[2] ◀▨▸

As mentioned previously, Sara Rigler was required to change names
and places to protect the holy woman's anonymity as a condition for
being allowed to write about her. Rebbetzin "Devorah"'s modesty
and hiddenness add to our appreciation of her holiness. This tale
speaks for itself, but it is noteworthy that Rebbetzin Devorah was always smiling and that at the end of each encounter with Sara, she

laughed. This signifies something important. The ways of tzaddikim sometimes appear comical to us because they act in a manner opposite to what we consider rational or normal. The reason is that most of us put ego at the center of our reality, whereas tzaddikim put God at the center. That makes some of their behavior seem topsy-turvy. But the reverse is also true: our ways may seem comical to them. A *tzaddeket* knows that everything that happens is good, and she experiences joy and bliss in her life. When the core value is changed and God replaces ego, everything else changes value: good and bad rotate and swing into different places. And when a great *tzaddeket* who sees the divine truth of life has a chance to lift the cloud of confusion hovering over someone yet unenlightened, she may sometimes even be aroused to joyous laughter, as in this tale.

The Hot Water Heater

◈ For some two decades, Rebbetzin Devorah Cohen took care of brain-damaged, multiply handicapped children and young adults, sometimes numbering as many as seven at one time. All this in her three-room shack, which initially lacked electricity, telephone, and running hot water.

When the children started coming, she and her husband, Rabbi Emanuel Cohen, decided that kerosene lamps were a fire hazard, so they installed electricity. They also decided that in case one of the children had an emergency, a telephone was a necessity. As for luxuries like paint on the walls or flooring on the concrete floor, they never indulged themselves. This is the story of the running hot water.

Rabbi Emanuel would rouse himself at two o'clock every morning to pray and study Torah. When he did, he would find Rebbetzin Devorah making the rounds of the children. In those years, long before disposable diapers, the incontinent children (including those in their early twenties) would wear cloth diapers, easily soaked by urine and feces. At night, not only the diapers got wet and dirty but also the pajamas and the sheets. Rebbetzin Devorah would check each child regularly during the night and change diapers, pajamas, and sheets when necessary. When someone suggested that she give herself an occasional full night's sleep, she replied that she was afraid that if she let these helpless human beings lie in their filth, there would be an accusation against her in heaven.

Of course, washing the children required heating water on the stove, which added many minutes to the nighttime changes. Finally, Rebbetzin Devorah decided that she would buy a boiler to provide running hot water. She and her husband were farmers; the potato fields that year had yielded a good crop. While her husband was away in England (he went away six months of every year, but that's another story), Rebbetzin Devorah decided to use the money from the sale of the potato harvest to buy a water heater.

The potatoes were duly harvested and sold. Rebbetzin Devorah put the money safely away in her closet. The next morning, she would take a bus into town and buy a hot water heater.

That night, her husband telephoned from England. He told her that a family somewhere in Israel desperately needed money. He asked her to take all the money from the sale of the potato harvest and send it to that family, whose name and address he gave her.

Rebbetzin Devorah did as he asked. The next morning, she went to the post office and sent a postal money order for the full amount of the cash she had to the name and address her husband had given her. The hot water heater would have to wait.

"How did you feel when you sent the money to the other family?" I asked Rebbetzin Devorah three decades later. Having heard the story from someone else, I had gone to her to verify the details. Knowing that I, in a million years, would never have given up the water heater, I wondered how she had felt making this incredible sacrifice for the sake of total strangers.

"What do you mean, how did I feel?" she asked with a quizzical expression. Whereas I take my emotional pulse every fifteen minutes, Rebbetzin Devorah goes for years without worrying about how she feels.

"You must have been disappointed," I prompted.

"No, I wasn't disappointed," she replied, surprised at the very idea. "Why should I have been disappointed?"

Yet again I felt like Rebbetzin Devorah and I come from different planets. The law of gravity on my planet pulls everything toward me. The law of gravity on her planet pulls everything upward.

"You wanted the hot water heater," I reminded her.

"Yes, I wanted the hot water heater," she remembered, her eyes with a faraway look, remembering those years, which she considered the best years of her life.

"So you must have been disappointed when your husband told you to send the money to other people, people you didn't even know."

Rebbetzin Devorah sat there puzzling over what this thick-headed American woman was having such a hard time understanding. Suddenly, she broke into a smile.

"You don't understand," she explained, as to a child. "The money wasn't wasted. They used it for something they needed."

"But you didn't have it for what you needed," I countered.

She looked at me uncomprehendingly. What was the difference?[3] ᢒᢒ

It Must Have Been Hard!

ᢒᢒ For forty-five years Rebbetzin Devorah Cohen lived in a house with only an earthen floor, without running hot water and without a bathtub or shower. During those years, she raised numerous handicapped and retarded children whose parents had abandoned them on her doorstep. "It must have been hard," I remarked, sitting across the table from her for another of the interviews I subjected her to for the sake of the book I'm writing about her.

"No, it wasn't hard," she replied simply.

"Of course it was hard," I insisted. "At one point you had seven handicapped children you were taking care of, all by yourself, when your husband was away half the year. It must have been very hard."

She shook her head. "It wasn't hard," she repeated. I was annoyed. The rebbetzin had this maddening habit of turning my reality upside down. I wasn't going to let her get away with it this time. "You had to cook for them, bathe them by heating up water on the stove, change their diapers before there were disposable diapers, even change the diapers of grown children, keep them from hurting themselves and each other . . ."

"And do the laundry," she chimed in.

"Yes! The laundry. How could it not have been hard?" I asked petulantly.

"For meals, I would just take a big pot, fill it with vegetables or chicken or noodles, and cook it up," she chuckled. "It wasn't hard."

Aha! I had done my research, and now I had her. "Isn't it true," I asked like a wily lawyer, "that Hindeleh, who lived with you for fourteen years, had to be spoon fed? It wasn't just a matter of cooking up the stew and calling, 'Come and get it!' You had to sit and spoon feed her."

"Yes, I spoon fed her," Rebbetzin Devorah admitted.

I continued my cross-examination. "Were there other children who had to be spoon fed?"

By now her face was shining and she was smiling broadly as she remembered those years. "Yes," she replied simply.

Checkmate! "You had to feed seven handicapped children, and spoon feed more than one of them. Then it must have been hard!" I proclaimed triumphantly.

"No," she shook her head, and repeated, not insistently, just matter-of-factly, "It wasn't hard."

I left her house in a state of total cognitive dissonance. "How could it not have been hard?" I asked Rebbetzin Tziporah Heller, my occasional companion for these interviews. She thought about it for a minute and explained that, for Rebbetzin Devorah, spoon feeding and changing the diapers of adult children was exhilarating, because it stretched her to her full capacity as a human being. "Didn't you see the light pouring out of her face as she remembered it all?" ⚘

Sara Rigler comments about this tale:

"When faced with an undertaking, my inner question is: How hard is it? Rebbetzin Devorah's inner question is: Does God want this of me? That's why I see her life as full of hardships, while she sees her life as full of opportunities. . . . And that's why, at the age of seventy-six, light shines from her face brighter than any gilded medieval picture of a saint with a halo."[4]

If It's Difficult, It Must Be Good

⚘ The holy Rebbetzin Hinda Adler, the daughter of Rebbe Hayim Meir of Vishnitz, left behind her a trail of great deeds of self-sacrifice that elicit astonishment. Her amazing acts of *tzedaka* are engraved in the hearts of many who learned from her about the love of kindness.

When she was a girl of only eight or nine, her great father sent her out to collect *tzedaka.* She rejoiced at the chance to fulfill this *mitzvah* as his emissary. Each time she went, she strode through the streets of Vishnitz stretching out a holy chain of good deeds—of *tzedaka* and kindness—as she went to visit the wealthy of the town. On these early missions for her father, she absorbed the holy fire of self-sacrifice for deeds of *tzedaka* and kindness. She knew no boundaries or obstacles, and nothing stood in her way when she was engaged in collecting *tzedaka.*

One example among many occurred about two years before her passing: This was in London, when she heard about a wedding celebration of a certain wealthy family who were the descendants of Hasidic rebbes. At that time, Rebbetzin Hinda was involved in collecting money for a needy family. She did not worry about her honor and made great efforts involving much difficulty to be present at the wedding in order to collect money for *tzedaka.*

[In traditional Jewish religious culture, it is not considered intrusive for beggars or charity collectors to show up uninvited to solicit money at celebrations and other events where people gather. But Rebbetzin Hinda was not a beggar, and although she collected for charity, she came from a famous family and was a distinguished elderly public figure.]

During the wedding, Rebbetzin Hinda went around collecting for charity. Afterward, when one of her grandchildren asked her if she had been invited to the wedding, she said, "No."

"It's not fitting," he said, "for a woman of your standing and lineage to just show up uninvited like this at a wedding."

She replied firmly, "In heaven, after a hundred and twenty years,[1] how will I be able to look my holy father in the face—when this other family is suffering from such terrible problems involving great expense—if because of a foolish sense of honor I didn't help?"

Rebbetzin Hinda had certain set times when she stood on the street collecting *tzedaka* from Jews. She utterly refused to accept—as applying to her—the talmudic characterization of such an act as being "beneath an elder's dignity."[2] She rejected the idea that collecting for charity could be "shameful" or "embarrassing." So she stood collecting money for *tzedaka* at the time of the *tashlich* prayers[3] during the Ten Days of Repentance [between Rosh HaShanah and Yom Kippur], on Hoshanna Rabba—the seventh and last day of Sukkot, and on other occasions when people gather. Sometimes, in the tradition of her holy mother, who was also a rebbetzin, she even refused to accept less than she demanded.

Moreover, Rebbetzin Hinda was not content to simply collect for charity and bring merit to people.[4] She encouraged others and spurred them on to support the needy, just as she did. She was so dedicated and devoted to collecting for charity and helping the poor that she could not truly understand why everyone did not act as she did.

Once, an important woman told her that she needed money for a poor family but had no idea how to get it. The rebbetzin said, "Do what I do: walk around collecting money for this great *mitzvah.*"

"I can't do that. It's too difficult for me," her friend replied.

"If it's difficult," said the rebbetzin, "that's a sign that it's good."[5] ❧

Rebbetzin Hinda was a heroine of *tzedaka* on behalf of the poor. She was burning with a holy fire of self-sacrifice for deeds of *tzedaka* and kindness. Her personal honor was of no concern to her. She ignored difficulties. How does one reach such an exalted spiritual level? The final incident in this story gives us a clue. The rebbetzin's attitude was that if it's difficult, it must be good. In her view, nothing worthwhile spiritually comes without effort. If we avoid discomfort, we will never overcome our limitations and reach our spiritual goal. If we do not stretch ourselves, we will never grow. Spiritual development is like physical exercise: the muscles expand and grow only when stretched and used. The Rabbis say, "According to the painstaking is the reward." The reward is spiritual growth.

Using Every Device

❧ Rebbetzin Rivka, the wife of Rebbe Shmuel of Lubavitch, was constantly occupied with good deeds and charity work—outfitting brides, supporting Torah sages, and so on. Her husband, Rebbe Shmuel, frequently traveled outside the country and would always ask his wife to accompany him. She would say she did not want to go and would ask him instead to give her the money he was

ready to spend on her travel and expenses. She would
then use the money for charitable purposes.

She was not satisfied with this. Whenever the
rebbe traveled, she would pawn her jewelry and receive
additional money for it, which she gave for charity. Her
husband already knew of her custom, and every time he
returned from a trip, he would ask her, "Where did you
pawn your jewelry?" She would tell him, he would give
her some more money to redeem it, and she would go to
the pawnbroker to get her jewelry back.[1] ◈

The holy Rebbetzin Rivka used every device to obtain money from her
holy husband, and he went along with her goodness and generosity.
If he had money for her to travel with him, she preferred using it for
charity. If he wanted his wife to have jewelry, he had to pay for it each
time. Certainly, Rebbe Shmuel appreciated that his holy wife's greatest ornament was her love for kindness and for the poor.

The Shofar

◈ Having fled before the invading Nazi army, the
Pesten family suddenly found themselves cast adrift in
some remote nowhere land in the Soviet Union, wandering through the mud of Uzbekistan, remembering all
the adventures they had met with since deciding to
pack their bags and flee. They felt a nagging yearning
for home and even envy of their friends who had decided to remain there (no one yet knew about the concentration camps and the gas chambers). But they did
not really have time for second thoughts, regrets, or
longings. They had to wake up early every morning and

search for food, even for a slice of moldy bread; in those days, that too was worth a fortune.

The woman of the family, Hanna Golda, was very worried. It was only a few days before Rosh HaShanah, and there was no food at all in their meager, temporary home. But that is not what concerned her. She was troubled that in this remote place, they would not hear the *shofar,* the ram's-horn blasts of *Tekiah! Shevarim! Tekiah!*—and so would miss the holy shudder they always experienced in those exalted moments of the *shofar* blowing on Rosh HaShanah.

But the situation was not yet hopeless. Hanna Golda walked the long distance to the nearby town until she came to a massive garbage heap. Not deterred by the foul stench, she began to sift through the garbage for hours, although it seemed like an eternity. Would she even find what she was looking for? Or would her long walk and great effort be for nothing?

The pounding of her heart increased by the minute until, with a broad smile on her face, she pulled out from the smelly heap the rotten head of a ram that had been slaughtered a few days earlier but, providentially, was still there.

The slender moon of the end of the month was slowly traversing the gloomy skies of Uzbekistan, above the wretched huts of the town's sleeping inhabitants. From heaven, the angels looked down in amazement at a tiny, frail woman, who was bent over sitting on a low stool, cleaning a curved ram's horn with a small metal wire as she quietly sang a melody of thanks to God. She scraped and scraped without cease and without fatigue, with tremendous effort, until she finally managed to thoroughly remove the inner bone from the *shofar.*

That year, the stirring sounds of the *shofar* blasts echoed through the narrow lanes of Uzbekistan. Because of Hanna Golda's devotion, the community of Jewish refugees merited that this beloved *mitzvah* was not missed.[1] ✣

A holy woman like Hanna Golda aches if she cannot perform a *mitzvah.* Her pain indicates how much she cherishes the *mitzvah,* how attached she is to it, how deeply it has entered her heart, and the difficulties she is willing to confront to fulfill it. This is the painstaking that brings a great spiritual reward.

An Angel for the Poor

✣ Hayya Ziv of Kelm was a great woman, famous as a Torah scholar and as a *tzaddeket.* She was expert enough in Jewish laws to make halachic rulings, particularly laws affecting women. Her son, Rabbi Simha Zissel Ziv, one of the great teachers of the early Musar movement,[1] testified that his mother never walked four steps without meditating on Torah. She was occupied all her life with charity organizations and groups that did kind deeds. Her main concern was caring for the sick. To that end, she frequented the inns where carriages passing through Kelm made stops and solicited donations from the travelers.

Once, a famous tzaddik named Rabbi Mendli of Tevrig stopped at an inn in Kelm. When he was told that

the famous Hayya—about whom he had heard much—
was present, he immediately sat across from her and,
as a sign of respect, dipped some cake in wine and
offered it to her as a refreshment.

When another of the visitors passing through
then saw the great respect and honor that everyone
was showing her, he gave her a large donation of three
rubles. She was so happy at receiving such a generous
donation for her poor people, but—being humble as the
dust—she was so upset at the honor shown her that
she burst into tears.

Another characteristic anecdote shows Hayya
Ziv's exalted spiritual level. In her position as a charity
collector, she used to frequent funeral processions to
solicit donations for the poor.[2] Once, she had the misfortune that her only daughter passed away. Yet she did
not change her custom, and so at her own daughter's
funeral procession, she went around asking for donations to benefit the poor! She said, "If I'm mourning
and in distress, why should the poor suffer?"[3] ✍

One of the great Musar teachers said that the spiritual goal is to learn
to hate honor as much as you once loved it. It is unknown if Hayya Ziv
ever loved honor, but it is clear that she attained the rare trait of hat-
ing it. Like some other great women devoted to God and the needy,
she put the poor first, before her own comforts or concerns.

A Generous Wife

✍ There was a rich, pious man, knowledgeable in the
Torah, who had a beautiful daughter named Dina. Like

her father, she was intelligent and wise, but above all else, she loved to help the poor. She welcomed every beggar who came to the door and sat him down to a fine table laden with good food, and as he left, she gave him a generous donation of money to help him on his way.

Among Dina's suitors was a certain wealthy man who owned many flocks and herds. Dina agreed to marry him, and the wedding celebrations lasted the customary seven days. What Dina did not know was that as kind, generous, and charitable as she was, her new husband was mean, miserly, and selfish. In his whole life, he had never once given even a dry crumb of bread to a poor man.

One day, a ragged beggar appeared at their door. He had not eaten in two days and was famished and fatigued. Dina received him warmly, as was her way. "Welcome to our home," she said. "Come sit at our table and eat with us!"

But the moment her husband saw the man, he shouted, "Don't you dare enter this room! Get out of my house this minute. No dirty beggar eats at the table with me!"

Dina was shocked. But now she knew what her husband was like. So she left him, went back to her father's house, and was divorced from him.

After that, other suitors came to ask for Dina's hand. But as soon as they heard about how charitable she was, they left. "She'll give away all my money!" they cried. And "Should I eat at the same table with beggars? Never!" So no one would marry her.

But one man said, "What could be better than a charitable woman with a good heart?" So the two of them were wed.

One evening, they were sitting at the table, dining, and there was a knock at the door. When Dina got up from the table and opened the door, she saw in front of her a beggar—weak, tired, and hungry from much walking. But looking more closely at his face, she gave out a cry and fainted. She had recognized him: It was her first husband, the miser, who had lost all his money and was now begging from door to door!

When she recovered, her new husband revealed to her why he loved her generous nature. He said, "I was the beggar whom your first husband threw out of the house." He had received a new start in life and had become wealthy.

Reflecting on what had happened, Dina replied, "Great are the deeds of God. God enriches and makes poor. God raises one up and lowers another to the dunghill. Great are God's deeds!"[1] ⋙

A husband who complains about a holy woman's excessive charity might not realize that he too may one day be in need.

A Blessing

⋙ Rebbe Zusya of Hanipol's mother and father were very wealthy, pious people. His mother, Mirl, traveled every Wednesday to a town near where they lived to give money to the poor people to buy what they needed for Shabbat.

Rebbe Zusya said about her that she did not know how to pray from a *siddur,* a prayer book. She just recited a blessing every day in the morning.

"And wherever she uttered that blessing," he said, "the holy *Shechinah* rested for the whole day."[1] ◈

The Rabbis say in the Talmud: "It is all the same whether a person does little or much, as long as his heart is directed to heaven." Zusya's mother, Mirl, did not study much Torah or pray much. But her heart was directed to heaven. The Jewish mystics say that an impression of a holy person remains at the spot where he or she studies or prays. Rebbe Zusya was explaining his pious mother's profound impression on him, despite her illiteracy. God does not count how many pages one recites from the prayer book; as the Rabbis say, "God wants the heart." Rebbe Zusya knew his mother's heart. He also knew her greatness, though others may not have recognized it.

Yenta the Prophetess

◈ It is told that Yenta, the daughter of Rebbe Yehiel Michal of Zlotchov, ceased intimacy with her husband and in many ways conducted herself like the most pious of male Hasidim: she immersed herself in the *mikveh,* the ritual bath, several times a day; she *davvened* with great outpouring of her soul while wearing a *tallis*–the prayer shawl usually worn by men; and she practiced self-mortification and fasts. We are also told that as she listened in the fields or forests to the birds singing, she would "jump *Kedusha,*" that is, rise on her toes three times while saying the "Holy, holy, holy" response, as during the *Kedusha* prayer recited in the synagogue, in which Israel below imitates the adoration of the angels above.

Once, her husband, Reb Yosef, happened upon Yenta as she was sweeping the house. Suddenly, she threw her broom away and "jumped *Kedusha.*" Reb Yosef thought that his wife had lost her mind due to the severe poverty that reigned in their home. When he asked her what she was doing, Yenta revealed to him that while sweeping, she had heard the angels singing hymns before God's Throne and saying "*Kadosh, kadosh, kadosh, Hashem Tz'va'ot*" ["Holy, holy, holy is the Lord of Hosts; the whole earth is full of His glory!"]. So she said *Kedusha* with them.

Hearing this, Reb Yosef ran to the Baal Shem Tov and told him about his wife Yenta's delusions.

The Baal Shem Tov comforted him. "Your Yenta has seeing eyes and hearing ears," the Besht said, and advised Reb Yosef not to trouble her or interfere with her. "She has *ruach ha-kodesh* [holy spirit]" he said, calling her "*Yenta di Neviah*"—Yenta the Prophetess.[1] ◈

Yenta the Prophetess, who "knew the language of the birds," the mystic language manifested in the sounds of all living beings, heard the birds singing their praise of God and joined her voice to theirs by reciting *Kedusha*. A person who focuses day and night on God may eventually hear the sounds of all creatures singing God's praise, not untypically in verses from the liturgy. Did Yenta perhaps use the *Kedusha* as a mantra until she finally heard it in all the sounds that reached her ears?

In the *Kedusha* prayer, Jews imitate the ministering angels in their praise of God. The angels are the heavenly hosts; Jews are the earthly hosts. Yenta also heard the angels singing *Kedusha* while she was sweeping. Most people do not hear the angels singing even when they are praying in the synagogue! Yenta heard them because her mind was always on God. Even when doing her housework, her heart was prayerfully directed to the One and Only One. Perhaps she was uttering "Holy, holy, holy!" with each sweep of her broom.

This anecdote contains a teaching about how to do housework. It also tells us that a woman engaged in doing housework may be the holy of holies. The heavenly choirs may be heard not only in the synagogue but also when communing with nature in the fields and forests and even when performing the humblest daily household tasks.

Loud Davvening

◄❧► Rebbetzin Devorah Sternbuch was a *tzaddeket* of recent times who lived in London. Among her many pious habits, was that she always *davvened* loudly with intense *kavvanah,* often with her hands outstretched in supplication. During the High Holidays–Rosh HaShanah and Yom Kippur–her *davvening* reached a pitch of fervent devotion.

Once, her loud voice and emotional outpourings on the High Holidays disturbed some women in the women's section in the balcony of the synagogue, and since she would not quiet down, they told her they were going to ask for a halachic ruling from the rabbi forbidding her to be so noisy. "I'll go with you," she said.

The rabbi replied definitively. "By no means should Rebbetzin Sternbuch quiet down," he said. "Her fervent *davvening* inspires the men below, and in her merit, all of our prayers will be heard above, in heaven."

When Devorah Sternbuch died, a man visiting London who made a condolence call during *shiva,* the seven-day period of mourning, told the family that although he had left London forty years earlier, Rebbetzin Sternbuch's *davvening* still inspired him.[1] ❧

Why were some people inspired by Rebbetzin Devorah Sternbuch's loud *davvening* and others disturbed? The answer may that when someone is *davvening* loudly and demonstratively with utter sincerity, others nearby who are less focused will be disturbed but those who are also *davvening* sincerely will be inspired. They are not annoyed by the outer cry because they hear the inner cry of a heart turned to God and they are gratified and aroused to even greater fervor of their own.

All Prayer

❧ Rebbetzin Mirl Gafner and her husband, Rabbi Mendel, were utterly devoted to the practice of prayer. Mirl's essence was crying out and making supplication to God. When she prayed after the Sabbath candle lighting—a time of divine favor—she extended her prayers, weeping mightily. She would sometimes sob beyond her own capacity until she fainted and fell and she had to be revived with water.

She was once in Meron in the Galilee, pouring out her heart in prayer at the tomb of the great kabbalist of ancient times, Rabbi Shimon bar Yohai, author of the *Zohar.* Suddenly, there was a commotion and clamor. Rebbe Hayim Meir, the Vishnitzer Rebbe, was coming up the hill. His Hasidim wanted to bring him into the

inner recesses of the cave and were asking all the
women praying there to make way for a few minutes so
that the rebbe could pray for the people of Israel in the
place at which he was accustomed to pray.

One side of the cave was almost cleared, but next
to the tomb marker itself was heard the sound of the
voice of the pious Mirl. She had not moved or budged
from her place. Immersed in prayer before the King of
Glory, supported by the merit of Shimon bar Yohai,
she did not even turn her head for a moment toward the
commotion that was occurring behind her. Her face
was buried in the Book of Psalms, with tears flowing
down her cheeks. She had left her children and infants
and her chicken store in Jerusalem and had come all
this distance to pray here. Should she spend her time
and turn her attention to matters other than her
prayers? So she continued to beseech her Heavenly
Father amid tears.

By then, the rebbe was standing at the cave's entrance, increasing the confusion. When Rebbe Hayim
Meir saw Hasidim here and there anxiously whispering
to each other and wondering what to do, he asked them
what was going on, what the problem was. They told
him that right next to the tomb, Rebbetzin Gafner was
praying, completely immersed in her prayers, without
an opportunity to ask her to move away. The rebbe
well knew the pious rebbetzin and her husband. "She's
all prayer," said the rebbe. "Let her pray. Perhaps her
prayers will accomplish what is needed for all of
Israel."[1] ⁂

The late Slonimer Rebbe, Rabbi Shalom Noah, said that it is not enough for a Jew to pray three times a day. The Jerusalem Talmud says, "Would that a person prayed continually!" The Slonimer Rebbe explained that a Jew's essence should be prayer. He should never do anything without inwardly turning to the One and Only One, because no act should be done unless it conforms to the will of God. And no act can succeed without the will of God. The tradition ordains prayer three times a day, said the rebbe, but the inner prayer should be constant. A person should always be standing before God and inwardly turning to God. That was the essence of Rebbetzin Mirl Gafner. The Vishnitzer Rebbe described her perfectly: "She's all prayer."

Edel, Daughter of the Baal Shem Tov

The Jewish mystics say that by prayer and meditation, a holy person can "select" the kind of soul he wants for his child from the heavenly treasury of unborn souls.

The Baal Shem Tov once said that he took the soul of his daughter Edel from the Torah verse *Esh Daat Lamo,* "A fiery law unto them"[1]— because she was a fiery personality, fervently devoted to God.[2]

The Sleeping Child

As a young girl, Edel would sometimes misbehave. But being clever and bold as well, she was also able to defend herself against charges of wrongdoing.

One Rosh HaShanah, the Baal Shem Tov refused to begin the sounding of the ram's horn, the *shofar,* because his little daughter Edel was not present, and he wanted her to hear the *shofar* blasts correctly, according to *halacha.* When the whole congregation attended the *shofar* service under his supervision, the blasts would be properly sounded, and everyone would hear them and fulfill the *mitzvah*.

After searching for Edel, they found her sleeping in her bed.

Now, to sleep during the day of Rosh HaShanah, when one is being judged in heaven, is considered perilous. Her father woke her and said, "You know that one is not supposed to sleep during the day on Rosh HaShanah, don't you?"

Edel replied, "Mother always says that when a child sleeps, they keep for him the best portion." [This saying encourages a child to sleep or nap by telling him that although he might be asleep when the meal begins, the best portion of food will be kept for him until he awakens.]

On hearing these words, the Baal Shem Tov immediately went, with Edel, to the synagogue and began the sounding of the *shofar*.[3] ⊰◈⊱

One purpose of the *shofar* is to awaken the "sleeping" Children of Israel and call them to repentance. Yet that they are asleep itself gives a pretext for heavenly judgment against them: Why are they asleep? Edel's clever reply gave her father, the Baal Shem Tov, an answer to the heavenly accusations against the Jewish people, and he went immediately to wake them up to receive the best portion that had been kept for them. When they will fully awaken, the final redemption will come.

The Gates of Divine Help

⊰◈⊱ When she was a grown woman, Edel once debated with the Besht's disciples about the recitation said at

the end of Shabbat: "May the Holy One, blessed be He,
open for us the gates of light, the gates of long life,
the gates of patience, the gates of blessing, the gates of
understanding, the gates of joy, the gates of greatness,
the gates of redemption, the gates of courage, the gates
of bliss, the gates of knowledge," and so on, a long list of
many different gates.[4] They argued about which of the
gates was the most important, each offering his opinion.
Edel said that the gates of divine help were the greatest
of all and that all the others were included in it.

When they went and asked the Besht, he said,
"She's right, because when a person attains any one of
these gates spiritually—the gates of Torah, wisdom, or
repentance—or materially—the gates of sustenance,
livelihood, and so on—he should understand that it was
all due to divine help and that that gate includes all the
others, for without God's help, it is impossible to accomplish anything or to make even the smallest movement.
Even the understanding that everything depends on
God and that you yourself do nothing—this *also* comes
from God, blessed be He, who has granted you this
understanding."[5] ✎

Trust in God!

✎ Rebbetzin Tzippora Hanna, the holy wife of the
Jerusalem tzaddik, Rabbi Arye Levin, had great trust in
God. Rabbi Arye once said about his deceased wife, "My
wife, peace be upon her, reached such an exalted spiritual level that if something was decreed against her

from heaven, she wouldn't even need to accept it with
love for God. She simply wouldn't feel or notice anything—no pain, no discomfort, no suffering. That's an
even higher level than someone who experiences suffering and accepts it with love."

Rabbi Arye also said that any good traits he had
came in the merit of her holiness, because she never
complained and never worried about the next day.
Her faith in God was unlimited. He added, "If not for her,
I would never have been able to hold on in the time of
starvation during the First World War, because when it
came to trust in the Holy One, blessed be He, she was
much greater than me." He then told the following story.

During the First World War, there were periods
of terrible starvation in the Land of Israel. Finally, the
situation became unbearable. Rabbi Arye did not know
from whence his help would come. His children were
crying—they had not eaten for two days.

Rabbi Arye had heard about a certain man in
Jerusalem who had been loaning money during the war
to people in need. Since he had once done this man a
favor, he gave in to his wife's urging, took a few valuable holy books he owned, and went to this man's home
to ask him for a loan, planning to leave the books as
security. The man refused to offer him a loan. "Why
are you refusing to give me a loan," asked Rabbi Arye,
"when you're loaning money to many other people?"

"I have to loan money to them," the man replied,
"because they know I'm wealthy, and if I don't loan
them, they'll be angry at me. But I know that you're a

tzaddik, and you won't hold a grudge against me and hate me if I don't loan any money to you."

Rabbi Arye returned home greatly disappointed and dejected. He secluded himself in his room and cried bitterly. "Is it right for him to refuse to loan me money because I won't hate him for it? Should my family and I starve?"

Rebbetzin Tzippora Hanna, who was a woman of valor and had great faith and trust in God, began to encourage and console him. "Rabbi Arye, Rabbi Arye," she said, "where is your Judaism? Where is your trust in the Holy One, blessed be He? Consider: Why did this wealthy man refuse to loan you money? Because he has none? He's wealthy! Because it's not his custom to loan money? He's been giving to everyone who's needy! Is he not loaning to you because he doesn't believe you'll return the money? Last month, you went to his house late at night to return one extra coin he'd given you when he exchanged some money for you that day! So he knows that you're honest! Why, then, won't he loan you any money?

"My dear husband, it's a *mitzvah* to judge everyone favorably," continued the rebbetzin. "But what should we do when there's simply no way at all to explain a person's behavior, when there's no way to justify or excuse it, as in this case? The only answer is that there's something supernatural going on here, something strange and out of the ordinary! You must conclude that heaven is preventing him from giving you a loan because your help and salvation are destined to come from elsewhere, from a different source! Rabbi

Arye," said his wife, "'cast your burden on God and He'll support you'!"

Rabbi Arye calmed down and stopped weeping after hearing his wife's encouraging words. He realized that she was right and that he should have more faith.

Just a short while later, the postman knocked on the door and delivered a letter from America. Rabbi Arye opened the envelope and found inside a twenty-dollar bill. The accompanying letter said that some years earlier, when Rabbi Arye was visiting in Petach Tikva, a certain man came over to him and said, "Are you the grandson of so-and-so?" Rabbi Arye said he was. The man said, "You look like your grandfather, whom I knew and revered." With that, they separated. That American Jew had passed away and he had left in his will that on the anniversary of his death, they should send a check to Rabbi Arye for that sum.

So Rebbetzin Tzippora Hanna was right: Heaven had intended that Rabbi Arye's help come from another source.[1] ≪◈≫

How common it is for a person to be depressed because what he had expected and hoped would be the source of his happiness and support failed him. The tradition teaches us to cast our burden on God and to realize that when one avenue of support disappears, another will soon appear, if such is God's will. King Solomon said in Ecclesiastes: "Two are better than one, because they have a good reward for their toil, for if one falls, the other will lift him up. But one person alone has no one to lift him up when he falls."[2] Happy is the person who has a spouse like Rebbetzin Tzippora Hanna to provide support when he falls and to help him up when his faith fails!

Elijah's Cup

According to tradition, Elijah the Prophet will appear at the end of days to herald the coming of the Messiah. But he also appears from time to time to save Jews in trouble and to teach Torah secrets to mystic adepts. At the Passover *seder,* a special cup is placed on the table for Elijah. It is believed that he mystically visits toward the end of the *seder* and drinks wine from his cup. He can sometimes be seen by those who are worthy.

≈≫ There was once a wealthy couple named Elkana and Penina. They were generous to the poor, and their large house was always open to strangers. Their most valued possession was a beautiful Elijah's cup that graced their *seder* table each year at Passover.

Then the wheel of fortune turned for Elkana and Penina, and they were forced to pawn all of their possessions to buy food. The only thing of value that they had left was their Elijah's cup, which they agreed never to sell, no matter how desperate their fortunes became.

As Passover approached, they discovered that they did not have enough money to buy matzahs, wine, or food for the *seder.*

"Dearest Penina," said Elkana with a heavy heart, "I'm afraid we have no choice but to sell Elijah's cup."

"Never!" replied Penina, and nothing Elkana could say would change her mind.

On the day before Passover, Elkana went off to study in the *beit midrash.* It pained him too much to stay at home and see the empty Elijah's cup sitting in the middle of a bare table. How sad their Passover would be this year! How could they celebrate Israel's liberation from slavery without matzah or wine?

While Elkana was gone, there was a knock on the door. Penina opened it to find an elderly, well-dressed man standing before her.

"I'm a stranger in this town," he said. "May I celebrate the *seder* with you?"

"We have no money to buy anything for a *seder* this year," said Penina sadly. "We have nothing at all in the house."

The man handed her a heavy purse and said, "Take this money and go buy what you need. I'll return tonight for the *seder.*"

With a joyful heart, Penina hurried to the market and bought everything that she needed for the *seders.* Then she ran home and prepared a great feast. When Elkana returned, Penina told him what had happened and asked him to bring their guest home with him from the synagogue that evening. But Elkana returned from the synagogue alone. "I looked everywhere," he explained, "but there was no well-dressed stranger there."

They decided not to begin the *seder* until their benefactor arrived. But it began to grow late, and still there was no sign of him. At eleven o'clock, they could wait no longer, for the *afikomen*—the matzah consumed toward the end of the *seder*—must be eaten before midnight. They recited the first part of the *Haggadah* and then began the feast. Right after they ate the *afikomen,* Elkana fell asleep. But Penina stayed awake, still hoping that the stranger would appear. And a short while later, when she opened the door for Elijah the Prophet, the elderly man walked in.

She ran to wake Elkana, but by the time she succeeded in arousing him from his heavy sleep, the stranger was gone. Elkana fell back to sleep, and Penina finished the *Haggadah* by herself.

Shortly after this, Elkana died. When he appeared before the Heavenly Court, they wished to admit him to paradise at once, but Elijah appeared and said, "If he wanted to sell my cup, he has to remain outside!" So for several years, Elkana waited outside the gates.

Then Penina died, and the gates of paradise opened before her. But as she moved forward to enter, she noticed someone in the way. It was her beloved Elkana.

"I won't enter without him!" she cried.

The Heavenly Court tried to persuade her to change her mind, but she stood firm. So they were forced to admit them both.[1] ◈

Elijah visits the Passover *seder,* but he appears at other times too. He comes disguised as a guest to test people's hospitality, or he comes to reward pious people with his vision or to save those in trouble. Elijah is God's messenger of salvation. This pious couple had resolved never to sell their treasured Elijah's cup regardless of their financial difficulties. But when they could not afford the matzah or wine for the *seder,* Elkana gave in; Penina did not. His faith was weak; hers was strong. Penina trusted that God would provide for their Passover needs—and if not, not!

Penina refused to pawn the symbol of their faith in God's salvation, even to buy matzah, wine, and food for the *seder.* Because of her greater faith, she was, so-to-speak, "awake" when Elkana was "asleep." Because of her trust in God, they received everything they

needed for the holiday. And she merited to see Elijah and to conclude the *seder,* unlike her husband, whose faith had failed and who
dozed off toward the end.

In the Torah, Elkana and Penina, the parents of the prophet
Samuel, are portrayed as an ideal couple of beloveds.[2] So at the gates
of paradise, this latter-day Penina refused to enter without her Elkana
and won him entrance. Penina, who refused to sell Elijah's cup and
refused to enter paradise without her husband, was rewarded for
what the Hasidic rebbes call *aizut d'kedusha,* her holy stubbornness.

Faith means "to the very end"; it means not to give up! Although
life involves many tests, we must trust that God will save us. If we hold
on and trust Him, we will pass the tests and be rewarded—with spiritual consolation and with visions of the divine presence in our lives.

The Screaming Baby

⇒ Rabbi Yaakov Mutzafi often used to say, "The main
thing is faith." And he would tell the following story.

A child was born to a certain family, and the baby
cried morning and evening—not like other infants but
terrible constant screeching. The family took the baby
to doctors, to specialists, but after countless tests,
they could not find the cause of the nonstop crying and
screaming. The parents then went to sages expert in
amulets and *segulot*—mystically potent remedies—but
that too did not help. They actually became disgusted
with their life. Their strange son had no time to eat,
drink, or sleep—he was always screeching and crying!
And of course, this wore terribly on the poor parents!

One day, the mother went to the market and found
a page of a *Chumash* [the Five Books of Moses] on the
street. Being a pious woman, although uneducated and

illiterate, she bent over, picked it up, and said to herself, "Perhaps God, blessed be He, will send a healing to my baby through this holy page!"

When she got home, she cleaned off the page, which was covered with dirt, and put it under the baby's pillow, with the silent prayer, "God in heaven, I don't know how to read or write, but I know that this is a page of the *Chumash* and is holy. May this page be a holy amulet for my son, that he heal quickly from his suffering!"

And that very night, for the first time in the baby's life, he slept soundly and peacefully without any disturbance, without any screeching or crying, so that it amazed everyone. He was quiet for a whole week.

Finally, the child's father asked his wife if she knew what had caused this miracle. She went over to the baby's crib and took out from under the pillow the page of *Chumash,* which she showed to her husband and said, "Is there any amulet in the world better than the *Chumash?* See how great the power of the holy Torah is!"

The husband, who could read and write, looked at the page and turned pale. He began to scream, "What have you done? Do you know what this page is? It's from the *Tochacha* [the Rebuke, a section of the Torah full of fearsome curses against evildoers]!¹ Look what it says here: 'God will smite you with madness . . . you shall be terrified night and day. . . . In the morning you will say, "Oh that it were night!" And at night you will say, "Oh that it were morning!"'"

His wife answered calmly, "My dear husband, how could I know what's written on the page? I'm illiterate.

All I knew was that it's a page from the holy Torah! And
I thought to myself, 'In the merit of the Torah and of
the divine Names written on this page, may God send a
complete healing to our son!' So I put the page under
the pillow, and you see, it helped!"

When Rabbi Yaakov Mutzafi would finish this
wonderful tale, he always said, "How great is the power
of faith that turns God's judgment to mercy and turns
curses into blessings!"[2] ❧

Have Faith!

❧ Rebbe Yisrael of Rizhin once said to his Hasidim,
"The most important thing is to have real faith, even if
the rebbe says the opposite of what seems right to you.
Nevertheless, if you have real faith and do what he says,
you will be saved and helped in the way that you need.
I'll tell you a story.

"In a certain village there lived two Jews, one
an innkeeper, the other a religious-school teacher. The
innkeeper wasn't a Hasid, but his wife was a *Hasidah*
[female Hasid]. The teacher and his wife, however, were
both Hasidim.

"Once, the innkeeper couldn't pay his rent, so the
lord wanted to throw him out of his inn. At the same
time, the teacher was sick. So the two wives came to
me, and each had a *pitka* [prayer request note] written
for her by my aide, as is customary. Since there was a
large crowd pushing to enter my room for an audience,

the *pitka'ot* fell from the hands of both the women, and when they picked them up, the notes were exchanged.

"My aide sent the wife of the innkeeper in first for an audience. When she handed me the *pitka*—which belonged to the other woman—and I saw that it said that her husband was dangerously ill—am I a prophet? I simply thought: Her husband's sick! So I told her to go home and have twenty leeches applied to bleed him for a long while, and God would help!

"This woman went home and her skeptical husband asked her with a mocking laugh, 'What did the rebbe say?' She didn't tell him because she was afraid. On the day that he was going to be evicted from the inn, he spoke to her again, saying, 'I'm ready to do whatever the rebbe said; just tell me the truth.' She told him, and he immediately sent for the doctor, who applied the leeches. Now the innkeeper was a big, strong man and completely healthy, but when they put the leeches on him, he lost so much blood that he became very weak.

"While he was lying in bed, the agent came from the lord to throw him out. But the agent returned and told the lord, 'How can I evict someone out who's seriously ill?' The lord didn't even believe what the man said because he thought, 'I saw him just recently, and he was completely healthy. How could he suddenly become so sick?' So he went to the inn himself and found the innkeeper lying in bed groaning, covered with blood and very weak.

"The lord asked him, 'What happened to you?'

"He answered, 'I'm so broken about being thrown out that I became sick!' And he told the lord that when

he died, all his children would cry and complain to
Heaven that the lord had caused this disaster!

"When the lord heard this, he became full of pity for
the innkeeper and said, 'It's better that I let you remain
in the inn than have your children accuse me to Heaven!'

"Now do you think," the rebbe asked his Hasidim,
"that I had any idea about all this? I didn't know the
pitka'ot had been exchanged. I thought her husband was
sick! But because she had real faith to do whatever I said,
they were saved!

"Now let's go back in the story," said the rebbe,
"to what happened earlier. After the innkeeper's wife
left, the wife of the sick teacher came in and handed me
her *pitka*—which said, however, that the lord wanted to
evict her and her husband from the inn. So I told her,
'Don't be afraid! No evil will rule over you!' When she
returned home, she saw a few people standing near her
husband's bed holding lit candles, as is customary when
someone is dying, because her husband was expiring,
God forbid! She blew out their candles and yelled to
them, 'The holy rebbe promised me that no evil will rule
over us!' And her husband recovered!

"Now did I know about all this? Am I a prophet?
I thought that they wanted to throw her husband out
of the inn. But because this woman had real faith to do
what I said, they were saved!

"So we see," said the rebbe, "that the most important thing is to have real faith, even if it seems that the
rebbe is saying the opposite of what you think is right.
But if you have real faith, you will be saved."[1] ◈

What can those who are not Hasidim and do not visit a rebbe learn from this tale? That when facing a problem, the most important thing is not always to know exactly the right thing to do but to have real faith that God will save you.

The Bris

A *bris,* the ritual circumcision of a newborn boy, is customarily performed in the presence of a *minyan,* a quorum of ten, if possible.

≈ Rebbe Menahem Mendel Taub of Kalev told a moving story he heard from a Jew who arrived in Israel from Russia during the difficult period when Jews were persecuted for religious activity behind the Iron Curtain. The Jew who told the story was part of a secret *minyan* invited to be present when there was a *bris.* Of course, everything was secret because the whole affair involved a lot of danger, even to life. If the authorities discovered that someone had circumcised his son, they immediately began a campaign of harassment, job firing, imprisonment, and exile to a distant region. Those who attended the *bris* were exposed to the same dangers. So they needed to have a *minyan* of men who were completely trustworthy, who would keep the whole operation in the greatest secrecy; and of course, the *bris* itself was conducted in total secrecy.

Once, a high-level official, who was Jewish, came to this *minyan* and invited the men to a *bris* that he was having the next day. When they arrived at the agreed place, he led them to a house in a secluded location and took them to the innermost room in the house.

When they got there, they found tables arranged with all kinds of good food, and the whole atmosphere was very joyful and festive, as if there were no Russians to worry about.

A short while later, they brought in the baby boy and performed the *bris.* But a minute after they returned the baby to its mother in the other room, they heard a shout: "She's fainted!"

They all ran to the room to see what had happened and finally succeeded in reviving her. When they asked her what had happened, why she had fainted, she said, "My baby is already more than a year old. Because of the danger in having a *bris,* my husband and I knew that we might not be able to arrange it immediately. To strengthen our resolve, we vowed not to kiss our precious baby until he was circumcised—although we knew it would be very difficult![1] We hugged him, caressed him, and gave him all our love, but we would not kiss him. We waited with desperate longing for an opportunity to have the *bris*—but the risks were always too great. So now, when you finally brought him in to me and I could kiss him, I smothered him with kisses. And from my great excitement, I fainted!"[2]

A Special Gift

On the third day of Hanukkah, there was a *bris* in Boro Park, Brooklyn. The Bobover Rebbe was the *sandak*—being honored to hold the baby on his lap—and he told this story at the *bris.*

There was a woman in Brooklyn who was married for fifteen years and was not blessed with children. She went from rebbe to rebbe, from tzaddik to tzaddik, from one to the other to ask for a blessing, for them to pray for her, but still she had no child. She did not know what to do with herself.

Being without children, she had a lot of time, and so she became a volunteer in a hospital. And there she discovered a woman who was sick and all alone, who had nobody in the world. For two years, she took care of that woman.

After two years, the ill woman left this world, and the woman without children was with her when she died. The dying woman said to her, "There's no way for me to thank you in this lifetime for what you did for me. But I promise you, the moment I go up to heaven and stand before the Master of the world, I swear to you I will send you a baby."

The Bobover Rebbe said, "The baby that was just circumcised is that baby. He is a gift from that woman."[1] ◆

A Covenant in the Flesh

◆ During World War II, Rebbe Yisrael Spira of Bluzhov was doing slave labor sawing wood in the Janowska concentration camp. A few Nazi guards stood nearby watching like hawks for a reason to pounce. The wicked Nazis had paired the tall rebbe with a very short Jew, which made the inmates' handling of the large saw both difficult and humiliating. With each pull of the saw, the rebbe's short partner had to stretch out and stand on his toes, while the rebbe had to bend down, which caused both of them acute pain and suffering. Meanwhile, the Nazis stood by and watched with enjoyment; this was their cruel entertainment.

Suddenly, there was heard the screech of a truck braking to a stop at the camp entrance. Upon command, a group of pale, weakened Jewish women and children got down from the truck. Then the rebbe heard tormented cries such as he had never heard before, even in the hell of the death camp. The desperate shrieks and wailing were coming closer and closer, as if the weeping was filling up the entire universe and drowning it with painful tears.

"They've brought women and children from the entire vicinity," said an inmate who passed by pushing a wheelbarrow without even glancing in the rebbe's direction. The rebbe was certain that screams and cries from the innocents would shake the world's foundation. But he continued sawing the wood as his eyes became heavier and heavier with tears.

One of the women who had just arrived ran as if insane right up to the rebbe. She was carrying a bundle in her arms, and she demanded, "Give me a knife! Do you have a knife?" The rebbe pretended not to hear and kept sawing, back and forth, back and forth; to do otherwise was risking death. But he whispered to her, "It is forbidden for a Jew to commit suicide! God can destroy, but He can also save. Have faith!"

"What are you talking about?" yelled the Nazi guard as he approached. "What are you plotting, you filthy Jew?"

"This woman was asking me for a knife," explained the rebbe softly, "and I told her that a Jew is forbidden to commit suicide."

"Ah," said the guard with glee. "She wants a knife? My pleasure." He took a knife from his breast pocket and handed it to the distraught woman. She grabbed it from him and started to tremble as if from some wild joy. She unwrapped the bundle of rags she was carrying and put a new baby down at her feet. With intense focus, she bent down, within sight of the crematorium ovens, and her face glowed with fervor as she made the blessing for a circumcision: "Blessed art Thou, O Lord our God, King of the Universe, who has commanded us to perform the commandment of circumcision!" She then swiftly cut the foreskin of her infant.

She rose up with the newborn in her arms, her whole body now expressing a divine triumph. She lifted the infant up as an offering and called out, "Master of the world, You gave me a healthy child. Now I'm giving you back a Jew!"

She returned the knife, dripping with blood, to the astonished Nazi and then handed him her precious child, amid terrible weeping.

A few hours later, this woman and the fruit of her womb went up to heaven as a pure sacrificial offering in the smoke of the ovens.

Whenever the Bluzhover Rebbe told this tale, he would note, "I said to myself when I saw this deed that it will probably shake the foundations of heaven and earth. Next to Abraham's attempt to sacrifice Isaac on Mount Moriah, where can you find a greater act of faith than this Jewish mother's?"

The Bluzhover Rebbe used to say that there were countless stories of the incredible events that happened in the camps, but it was a *mitzvah* to tell this particular tale. He used to tell it at every circumcision, through his tears.[1] ✑

The Clotheslines

✑ This tale is about a woman who lived in the Old City of Jerusalem about a century ago. Washing clothes for a family then was a chore of almost unimaginable difficulty. So after six hours of backbreaking labor, this pious housewife hung her laundry out to dry in the sun, on two clotheslines that were stretched between poles and went the whole length of the courtyard.

That afternoon, one of the women neighbors came into the common courtyard on her way home. For some reason, she saw the two clotheslines with all the laundry hanging from them as hindering her as she walked to her house, as if there was not room enough for her to pass by unobstructed.

Instead of being understanding and stooping for a moment to get through, and keeping her good relations with her neighbor, her *yetzer*—her evil inclination—incited her, and she burst into a fit of anger and revenge.

She ran into her house, grabbed a pair of scissors, rushed back out into the courtyard, and cut the two cords. The laundry, which was now clean and bright after all the first woman's work, fell with a thud into the dirt of the unpaved courtyard.

The woman whose laundry it was heard the sound, rushed out to see what had happened, and was stunned. At that moment, she stood before a test of fire. According to ordinary human nature, she should have started screaming and cursing at her neighbor and her ugly deed. This pious woman's evil inclination was about to explode like a raging fire. But in a sudden blessed moment, she drew strength from the wellspring of her pure faith. After a few tremulous moments, she over-came this painful test, bit her lip, and justified heaven's judgment, saying to herself, "I must deserve this. May it be an atonement for me!"[1]

She quietly picked up the fallen laundry, washed off the dirt, tied the cut clotheslines back together, and took the laundry to the large public courtyard some distance away, where she once again hung it up. In the evening, she brought the dry laundry home, in a good mood; but the incident was not yet finished.

When her husband came home after praying the evening service, she did not tell him what had happened to her in the courtyard! This second test—not to slander or gossip—was perhaps even greater than the first, because the Rabbis teach, "If you are troubled, talk it out to someone." How much greater still was her test, because she could even expect similar incidents in the future from this bad neighbor. But she controlled herself a second time and said nothing to her husband.

No one would ever have known of this whole matter had not the woman who had acted out of control come to her neighbor's house that night, ashamed of her mean behavior, and asked forgiveness for the ugly incident.

The pious woman forgave her wholeheartedly, and during their ensuing conversation, it came out that she had redone the laundry elsewhere and had not even mentioned the incident to her husband. The other woman was surprised to hear this; moved by her neighbor's patience, she exclaimed, "May God help me learn to control myself—as you did—in my moments of testing!"[2] ❧

This story contrasts two women at a moment of testing, when they were spurred to rage. One reacted with anger; the other overcame the temptation and reacted with patience. What was the source of the pious woman's patience? The story credits it to her strong faith. A pious Jew believes that everything happens because of divine providence. Any suffering or mishap that befalls a person comes from the hand of God, to chasten and humble him, and to bring him back to God, if he accepts his affliction with love.

This tale portrays in graphic images the beauty of patience and the ugliness of anger. If everything is from God and for our own good, to help us grow, there is usually no point in blaming other people or raging at how they have harmed us. May we echo the prayer of the chastened woman: "May God help me learn to control myself in moments of testing!" May God strengthen our faith so that we too can attain patience.

The Guest

⫷⫸ One Friday morning, the marketplace was humming with people, both men and women, carrying baskets on their arm and making their purchases in honor of the holy Sabbath. Everyone was buying meat, fish, fruits, and vegetables.

Among the customers was also Hanna Hayya, a granddaughter of the famous Rabbi Yaakov Emden and the wife of a great Torah scholar. This *tzaddeket* was searching everywhere among the fish stands, looking for a big, beautiful fish to provide extra enjoyment on Shabbat. [The kabbalists say that the customary fish course on Shabbat has a special mystical significance.] In one of the stands, she found what she was looking for—a large, fine fish for sale. She happily paid the price and hurried home with the alacrity befitting a *mitzvah*, all the while thanking God for putting into her possession such a nice fish in honor of Queen Shabbat.

Once home, the *tzaddeket* cleaned the fish and prayed, "Master of the world, just as You gave me this beautiful fish in honor of the *Shabbos,* please also send to our home a worthy *Shabbos* guest to enjoy it with us!"

Soon the pleasant odors of her Sabbath cooking filled the rebbetzin's kitchen. The house had been thoroughly cleaned and was now spotless, prepared and ready in honor of Queen Shabbat.

After the noon hour, a carriage pulled up in front of the house, and out stepped a distinguished looking man, clearly a tzaddik, whose face glowed with holiness and purity. Everyone in the house who went out to see who had arrived could tell that this was a great man; it was evident. They welcomed him warmly and immediately invited him to stay with them for Shabbat.

This holy guest was none other than Rabbi Yitzhak of Drohobitch, a disciple of the Baal Shem Tov and the father of Rebbe Yehiel Michal of Zlotchov. The members of the household had never met him, and he did not know them. And during the course of his stay with them on the Sabbath, he never revealed his identity to them.

Rabbi Yitzhak was wondering throughout Shabbat, "Why did Heaven send me here?" At his home in Drohobitch, he had heard a heavenly voice directing him to this town and to this house. But why? Was he to accomplish some special divine task here? He would have preferred to stay at home, where he was able to immerse himself more fully in his divine service. But here he was, and he had no idea why!

Late Saturday, after the third Sabbath meal, the rabbi took a nap and asked a dream question. Before going to sleep, he asked Heaven, "Why was I sent here?" When he woke up after his short nap, he realized that he was not sent to this town and house to accomplish any divine task. "The woman of the house," he was told, "is a great *tzaddeket*. On *erev* Shabbat, she prayed for a worthy guest to be sent to her for Shabbat, to enjoy the beautiful fish she had bought." Her prayer had been answered immediately, and Rabbi Yitzhak was sent to her house because he was a great tzaddik and a guest worthy of her. That was why Heaven had told him to visit this house.

After the *Melave Malka* feast [escorting Queen Sabbath out at sundown], Rabbi Yitzhak took leave of his hosts, who accompanied him to his carriage. And he took Hanna Hayya, the *tzaddeket,* aside and said to her, "Please don't pray that way anymore on *erev Shabbos.* I was forced to travel a great distance to spend *Shabbos* with you, because your prayer was received immediately in heaven. And it was very inconvenient for me!"[1]

This gently humorous tale teaches that Heaven answers the pure prayers of a *tzaddeket* like Rebbetzin Hanna Hayya. If someone truly desires to serve God, he will be granted the opportunity. Heaven therefore fulfilled her desire for a holy guest on Shabbat in order to give Hanna Hayya added spiritual pleasure. Evidently, her wish to serve a holy guest carried even more weight in heaven than the desire of the tzaddik, Rabbi Yitzhak, to remain at home, immersed in his divine service of study and prayer. What can this story teach us? That we too can pray for an opportunity to serve God and our prayers will be answered.

The Sound of Her Blessings

⬅ According to Jewish law, when one hears another person reciting ordained blessings—such as those uttered during prayers or recited over food—one is obligated to make specific responses. Having the opportunity to respond to a blessing is considered precious by pious people.

One morning, a Hasid for some reason entered the dwelling of his elderly rebbe, Rabbi Avraham Yehoshua Heshel Twersky of Machnovka, and saw a strange sight:

the rebbetzin, Havva Bas Tzion, was standing next to her seated husband with a *siddur* in her hand and was reciting with passionate devotion the morning blessings, and the rebbe was fervently answering in response, "*Baruch Hu u'varuch shmo*" – "Blessed is He, and blessed is His Name!" – and "Amen!" for each blessing.

Although women are not obligated to recite the morning prayers, many pious women – particularly a very pious woman like the rebbetzin – make it a point to do so. Yet the rebbe's practice of responding to the rebbetzin's blessings was certainly unusual, and the scene seemed so bizarre to the Hasid that he could not hide his amazement.

Noticing the Hasid's reaction, the rebbe explained, "Know, my friend, that I was exiled for four whole years in Siberia. Most people couldn't even imagine the sufferings of body and soul that the exiles experienced, let alone the sufferings of a devout Jew whose whole being aches for something spiritual, for a little Jewishness; yet we were never able to get even the least bit of Jewish holiness to satisfy our desperate craving!

"I had the good fortune that after much pleading on my behalf, together with large bribes handed out by my close associates, I was given permission to have a visit from my wife, the rebbetzin, the daughter of the Rebbe of Zhurik, for a few weeks. The trip she made from Moscow to visit me in faraway Siberia lasted a full month, with inconveniences and discomforts that can hardly be imagined and require the kind of self-sacrifice that only a great woman like the rebbetzin is capable of.

"How happy I was, then, that after being cut off
for so long from hearing any holy words of prayer or
Torah, the rebbetzin surprised me from the very first
day of her arrival by standing up early in the morning
in order to recite before me the morning blessings,
giving me the great merit and pleasure of responding
fittingly to her blessings.

"Yet this Garden of Eden did not last long because
her visitor's permit soon expired and she had to return
to Moscow. But the sweet taste of her morning blessings stayed with me, and the longer my exile endured,
the greater did my longing increase to hear the morning blessings uttered by such a totally pious woman
from the depths of her pure heart. The moment we were
reunited, we resumed this former custom of ours."

The rebbe concluded, "I have no doubt that our
custom is also considered precious in heaven, because
it symbolizes the age-old yearning of Jews throughout
the centuries to come close to God even when they are
crushed and broken. The gratitude I still feel for the
rebbetzin's blessings during my time of exile is expressed in the poem '*Ribon Kol HaOlamim*' [Master of
All the Worlds] that we recite before the *kiddush* on
Sabbath night: 'I will speak of Your greatness in song,
and place Your presence before me, for You had mercy
on me to redeem me in my exile, and aroused my heart
to Your love.'"[1] ☙

In his Siberian exile, the rebbe was starved for spirituality and holiness. He yearned to see another pious Jew; his heart ached to hear
words of prayer or Torah. And his holy wife knew what he needed

and gave him comfort and consolation with the sweet sound of her morning blessings.

Why was the Hasid shocked? Because such intimacy between a rebbe and rebbetzin is unusual in Hasidic society, and it is uncommon for a man to arrange to respond this way to his wife's blessings. The Hasid probably also sensed that in this scene, the rebbe was the receiver and the rebbetzin the giver and benefactor, contrary to the standard pattern of a rebbe's being a spiritual benefactor to his Hasidim or to anyone else.

The Kabbalah says that all of reality operates according to a pattern of giving and receiving and that typically, men are givers and women are takers. Yet we are told that in the period leading up to the redemption of the world, women will become givers—just as the rebbe was redeemed from his spiritual exile by the piety of the rebbetzin. The mutual dedication to holiness of Rebbe Avraham Yehoshua Heshel and Rebbetzin Havva Bas Tzion foreshadows a future time, the time of the Messiah, when husband and wife will be truly one in their yearning for the One and Only One.

The Water Barrel

At the beginning of her book of memoirs, Raichel Horowitz, the current Bostoner Rebbetzin, tells the following story and attaches a word of wisdom.

⟫ My earliest memories are of Stryzov, a small town in Poland, the "Old Country" for many Jews before the War.

There was a water pump in the middle of the town square where people used to gather. Every day someone—often a public water carrier or the family's gentile maid—had to come and pump water. Then they had to haul it back home and pour it into a big water barrel. That was our water supply for the day.

I remember, when I was a little girl, going over to our water barrel and looking at my face mirrored deep inside.

This is my earliest memory and a symbolic one at that—deep down, we always see ourselves, wherever we look in this world.[1] ⊰⊱

We can add to the rebbetzin's words: if we follow the Torah's path to spiritual insight, we will finally see our deepest self wherever we look; we will see the face of God.

Even Her Taking Was Giving

There is a custom among some pious Jewish families of keeping their home open to anyone who needs strictly kosher food to eat or a temporary place to stay. With all these guests, the family is constantly occupied in feeding them, washing their laundry, and so on. It is a tremendous job, but the family members serve their guests as a vital expression of their religious devotion.

⊰⊱ Hayya Schechter was a pious woman whose home in Tel Aviv was open to all, like the legendary home of Abraham and Sarah. There was never a day when she and her husband did not have guests. Rabbis, rebbes, and simple people alike all ate at their table, and everyone was treated like a king or queen. Some guests lived in the house for months at a time; sometimes there were ten such guests, at other times as many as thirty! And all of them were made to feel as if they were in their own home.

Hayya was always ready to give everything she had to another human being. She had reached perfection in kindness, and her giving was done wholeheartedly and joyfully.

Another aspect of her perfection in kindness was reported by one of her sons, who said that his mother had once sent him to borrow some money from a neighbor. When he returned with the money in hand, she took the envelope with the money in it from him, placed it somewhere, and never even opened it.

Her son asked, "Mother, why did you borrow the money if you didn't want to use it?"

"I did it," she explained, "so that our neighbor won't be ashamed to borrow from us when he's in need."[1] ≈✷≈

Hayya Schechter had an open home, an open heart, and an open hand. The Torah says that God is "compassionate and gracious." The usual English translation of the Hebrew *hanun* is "gracious," but that word is antiquated. A better translation would be that God is what today we call "giving." Hayya Schechter was "giving," and added to that was her refined sensitivity—to act so that no one would be ashamed to take. Like some other holy people, even her taking was giving.

A Reward for Kindness

When Rabbi Yissachar Ber of Radoshitz was a famous rebbe, with people coming to him from near and far to seek his advice and receive his blessing, his wife, Rebbetzin Bailah, once told this story to a gathering of Hasidim.

≈✷≈ When we were young and desperately poor, without a penny to our name, everyone called my holy husband "Berl *Batlan,*" Berl Do-Nothing, because he didn't engage in any business or work; he just sat in the *beit midrash* studying Torah and *davvening* the whole day, or he would be visiting his holy rebbes.¹ This went on for a number of years. We supported ourselves by my washing clothes for rich people. It goes without saying that our livelihood was the barest minimum. Sometimes we had nothing to eat and had to fast for a few days and nights in a row.

One day, my holy husband said to me, "My dear wife, how long should you have to suffer such grinding poverty because of me? Why don't you listen to my advice and free yourself from this humiliation and this misery of starvation? You know that I'm a *batlan,* and I'll never succeed at any business or work. Why should you suffer because of me? I'll give you a divorce, and you can go and marry an established and stable man who'll support you properly. And I'm sure you'll find someone to marry you, because you're an *eishet hayil,* a woman of valor. Then you won't have to suffer hunger any longer; you'll live decently, as you deserve. If I'm lost, I'm lost."

But his words made absolutely no impression on me. On the contrary. I said to him, "Why are you speaking to me like this? Don't you know that my soul is bound up with your soul, that wherever you go, I'll go? As long as my soul is within me, I'll never leave you. Only death can separate us. God will do what is good in His eyes, and I have strong trust that God, blessed be He, will provide for us more generously. He won't abandon us forever. He'll soon make things easier for us. We won't die of starvation, God forbid. He'll see our suffering and have compassion on us. We won't die; we'll live. My trust in God is strong," I said to him, "and I'll tell you why—because of something that happened when I was still a young girl living in my parents' home.

"You know, my beloved husband, that my dear parents lived in a village, and although they were not wealthy and were just people who made an ordinary living, they were totally devoted to the *mitzvah* of hospitality, with all their strength and energy. They were always standing at the doorway looking out at the street—because our house was at a crossroads—to see if any traveler was passing by. If they saw someone, they would take him in and feed him and give him something to drink. Needless to say, our home was known in the whole area as an open house, so there were always guests constantly coming and going.

"My father and mother were always ready to wait on guests and to serve them with all their energy to the fullest extent and to try to please them in every way possible. My mother sat the whole day peeling potatoes to boil, and my father would make borsht. There were always big pots, full of potatoes and borsht, simmering on the oven, so food would be ready and guests would not have to wait to be fed. A tired, hungry, and thirsty traveler would come in and immediately find food and drink ready, to sate his hunger and thirst and to soothe his weariness from the journey. And my parents would welcome guests with warmth and smiles as if they were paying the full price for all this.

"Once, on a market day, my mother and father were
preparing to go to the town on business and would be
there the whole day. Before they left, my father said to
me, 'My daughter, you know how much we trouble ourselves and all the work we do to satisfy all the guests
that pass by and enter our home. You see what we're
always doing for them. Today, too, we prepared food,
and the oven is hot. So if someone comes to our home,
whoever it is, we want you to welcome him warmly and
graciously, to honor him and serve him food and drink,
from everything that's prepared. If you promise us to do
that, we'll leave with a clear mind, and we'll be able to
stay in town as long as we have to, without worrying.'

"'I'll do everything you want, Father,' I said.

"So my parents left, and I stood near the oven to
make sure that the fire didn't go out. A short while later,
two travelers came to our house, looked in, and seeing
that no one was home except me, quickly left. I realized that they ran out because they didn't want to be
alone with me, a girl, in the house [which is forbidden
by Jewish law].[2] I could see from their faces that they
were pious and holy men, and I was pained, because I
realized that although they were tired from their long
journey on foot and also hungry, they couldn't come into
the house to eat the food that was prepared and waiting
for them because of me.

"I ran outside and called after them, 'Wait!' So
they waited. I told them, 'Please, come into the house
and eat as much as you want from the food that's ready

for you. I'll wait outside so you won't violate the prohibition against *yihud* [being alone with a single female].'
They went inside, sat down, and ate while I waited outside. After they had rested a while from their weariness,
they came out and blessed me, saying, 'May you marry
a tzaddik who will light up the whole world with his
Torah and wisdom.'

"When my mother and father came back that
night, I told them what had happened. My father asked
me to describe the two men, and I told him and said I
could see that they were tzaddikim, shining with holiness. He immediately called out joyfully, 'Do you know
who they were? That was the holy Rebbe Elimelech and
his brother, the holy Rebbe Zusya!' My parents were so
thrilled that they had been able to provide hospitality to
these two holy guests. And they were even more thrilled
and happy when they heard the blessing the rebbes had
given me."

Then I said to my husband, "When I saw that the
blessing of those two tzaddikim came true, and I married a pious and holy man like you, should I be divorced
from you now just because we're poor and are having
difficulties? Stop speaking to me about this! I don't
want to hear any more about it, because 'God's salvation
comes in the blink of an eye.'"

[Rebbetzin Bailah concluded her story to the
Hasidim]: When my holy husband heard what I said,
he never again talked to me this way; he only tried to
encourage me with holy words, until God, blessed be He,

had compassion on us and my husband became a famous rebbe and we finally had enough money to live.[3] ⪧

Rabbi Yissachar Ber of Radoshitz was determined to scale the heights of holiness but did not want his pious wife, Rebbetzin Bailah, to suffer for his sake. So he gave her a chance to escape from him. But once he saw that she was his true partner, he only encouraged her, just as she had encouraged him, with words of faith and trust.

Why was she worthy of a holy partner? Because of her holiness, which she grew into under the guidance of her pious parents. What parents she had, with their open home! And how sensitive she was to the plight of the holy rebbes who would not enter her house to eat because of their resolve not to violate the prohibition of *yihud*. Her purity and holiness, her modesty and compassion, won for her the rebbes' blessing to be married to a tzaddik, her partner and equal, because she was a true *tzaddeket*.

One Flesh

According to the Rabbis, a husband and wife—who, the Torah says, "shall be as one flesh"—are each "half a body" and together comprise one body.

⪧ The love between Rabbi Kalonymus Kalman Shapira, the Peasetzner Rebbe, and his wife, Rebbetzin Rachel Hayya Miriam, was evident to everyone who had eyes to see. The rebbetzin was a great Torah scholar and always avidly followed her husband's Torah talks to his Hasidim.

In one of his books, the rebbe notes that his wife would review his writings for him, making comments and posing questions. When she passed away in 1937, he wrote a poignant and moving letter to his Hasidim in Israel eulogizing her.

Among many other praises, he wrote: "She would awake every morning at six and study Torah and pray until ten. She studied *lishmah* [for its own sake], for love of the Torah and God and out of pure holiness. If for any unusual reason she was unable to study, she was unhappy the whole day and said that the day was dark for her. She studied *Tanach, Midrash, Zohar,* and other books of Kabbalah and Hasidism, and she had extensive knowledge of Kabbalah and Hasidism. Many times, I was astounded by her expertise in these subjects. And she did not just study; she labored in divine service, with her heart, body, and mind. . . . Since she knew that the available house money could not satisfy her great yearning to give *tzedaka* and do favors, she borrowed money, paying permitted interest."[1]

Hasidim recall that after the rebbetzin's passing, the Peasetzner Rebbe never again played his violin.

Soon after her death, the rebbe was in a discussion with one of his close Hasidim, and his wife came up in the conversation. The rebbe led this Hasid to a cabinet in his home, opened the drawer, and took out a piece of paper. On it was written a Hasidic talk, but as the Hasid saw, the handwriting changed in the middle of the paper. The rebbe told him that when he was writing this talk, he was suddenly called away for a medical consultation [surprisingly, the Peasetzner had pursued a private course of medical studies with a great doctor until he had acquired expert medical knowledge and was occasionally called for consultations]. When he returned from the consultation, the rebbe saw that his rebbetzin had taken up the pen and finished writing the talk. Holding this paper, which he treasured so much, in his hand, the rebbe looked at his Hasid and said, "You see, this is the true fulfillment of the verse: 'They shall be as one flesh'!"[2] ⬥

The mystics say that husband and wife are "one flesh" because they are soulmates and share one soul. But their oneness can only be manifested when they share their spiritual journey as equals—as with Rebbe Kalonymus Kalman and Rebbetzin Rachel Hayya Miriam.

At His Wife's Death

⬥ When his wife, Sarah, died, the Baal Shem Tov was dejected and forlorn. His disciples assumed that it was because of her death. Since they knew that he was far beyond being sad about anything that could happen in this world—even his beloved wife's death—they asked him about it.

He told them, "I'm depressed by the thought that the great God-awareness residing in my body will one day have to rest in the earth. I expected to ascend into heaven alive in a whirlwind, like the prophet Elijah, may he be remembered for good. But now that my wife is gone, and I'm only half a body, that's impossible. That's what depresses me."[1] ⬥

The holy Baal Shem Tov could not be saddened by anything earthly and would only mourn for spiritual reasons. When his holy wife, Sarah, died, he felt himself spiritually diminished, only "half a person." Yet we know almost nothing about Sarah. If the Besht would make such a comment regarding her greatness and his loss, are we not missing something by knowing so little about her?

How to Accept Suffering

Rebbe Tzvi of Rimanov had been a humble servant of Rebbe Menahem Mendel of Rimanov. Yet when the master died, the simple servant, and not one of the rebbe's sons, became his successor.

◄◙► Rebbe Tzvi the Servant of Rimanov had many children, but only two survived. At the time his eighteenth child passed away, a child of Rebbe Shalom of Kaminka also died. Rebbe Tzvi heard that Rebbe Shalom was very depressed and sent him a letter of consolation. But in the letter he said, "I'm surprised at you that you're so depressed by the death of the child (God forbid, it shouldn't happen!). My eighteenth child has just died, yet I'm not very upset. But I understand your grief because I, too, had to learn to accept suffering—from a village woman.

"This is the story: When my holy master, Rebbe Menahem Mendel, was still living in the town of Pristik, he had a Hasid who lived in the nearby village of Klinkipka. This Hasid regularly visited the rebbe and always arrived carrying gifts. Together with his wife, he visited the rebbe every year at the beginning of the new moon of Elul and stayed in Rimanov through the High Holidays until after *Sukkot*. Now, this Hasid was a fine Jew—pious, hospitable, and charitable—but he had no children. Every time he visited the rebbe, he asked for, and the rebbe gave him, a blessing for children.

"Years passed, and the Hasid was still childless. One year, as Passover approached, the rebbe had no money for his holiday needs. But a few days before Passover, this Hasid came and generously provided the rebbe with everything required—guarded wheat for matzah, chickens, eggs, chicken fat, potatoes, wine—and he also gave the rebbe some money for anything else he needed.

"The rebbe became very joyful and expansive, and he said to the Hasid, 'You've given me new life. May God, blessed be He, give new life to you—a child.'" And so it was. That year, the *Hasidah* gave birth to a daughter. Her husband was fifty, and she was just a few years younger.

"After this, Rebbe Menahem Mendel moved to Rimanov, and the Hasid continued his pious custom of regularly visiting the rebbe. Every year, for the new moon of Elul, he came with his family and stayed until after *Sukkot*. When his daughter was fourteen, the Hasid arranged for her to marry a fine boy, and the Hasid sent a letter to the boy's parents, telling them to bring the youth to Rimanov; he would bring his daughter, and they would make the engagement in the rebbe's presence.

"The other father sent a letter back, saying that he was traveling with his son to Rimanov, as suggested, and asked that the first Hasid bring his daughter there. But for some reason, it was absolutely impossible for the first Hasid to go to Rimanov just then, and so he sent his wife with their daughter. He also wrote to the rebbe, asking if he would be so kind as to arrange the engagement.

"The *Hasidah* and her daughter set out, taking
with them liquor, honey cake and sweets, meat, and
challahs for an engagement party.

"Now, there is a mountain near Rimanov, and
when the *Hasidah* and her daughter were traveling on
it, the girl complained that her head was hurting badly.
By the time they reached the inn to which they were
traveling, the girl was dead. They took her body to the
inn, and the mother immediately sent for the Holy
Burial Society to hurry and arrange for a burial. The
mother herself arranged a feast with the food she had
brought for the engagement party.

"When everything was ready for the funeral, the
men of the burial society wanted to begin the procession, but the woman said, 'Wait a little bit.' She cut the
honey cake into pieces, took some liquor, and went into
the rebbe's synagogue just as morning prayers were
ending. She walked over and put the honey cake and
liquor on a table and called out to the Hasidim:

"'I came to your town to engage my daughter to
this man's son,' she said, pointing to the bridegroom's
father. 'He's just a man, a human being of flesh and
blood. But when I approached the town, a matchmaker
like one I'd never before seen came to me and said, "You
have only one daughter, and you want to engage her to
a mere human being? I have a much better match for
you! The Father is of incomparable lineage. He is so
fabulously wealthy that He has no peer, yet He wants to
make an engagement with your daughter and take her
to live with Him in His mansion! I tell you, living with

Him, your daughter will be well cared for! Furthermore, this In-Law seeks no dowry from you, not does He ask you to provide fancy clothes for your daughter. Just a simple white cotton dress. And He wants not only the engagement but also the marriage to take place this very day." This offer pleased me, and thank God, the match was concluded, and now I'm going to the bridal canopy for the wedding. So I'm asking you all to eat a little, have a drink of liquor, and come with me.'

"When she finished speaking, the rebbe clapped his hands in grief and said, 'I didn't see this at all!'— meaning that he had not foreseen this tragedy with his holy spirit. 'Now we all have to accompany her,' said the rebbe. So he and all the Hasidim accompanied the woman in the funeral procession for her daughter. Of course, when the rebbe joined the procession, the whole town also went with him.

"After the funeral, when the rebbe wanted to return home, the *Hasidah* said, 'I've prepared food, and I'd very much like for everyone to come to my feast.' So the rebbe, all the Hasidim, and the rest of the towns-people went with her to the feast and ate. And this woman served them without the least trace of sadness on her face. On the contrary, she seemed filled with joy.

"When they finished eating and had said the Grace, the rebbe asked for more wine to be brought to the table for him, and he recited the blessings for a mourner over another cup of wine. And he said, 'Because you have not complained (God forbid) against the Holy One, blessed be He, and have accepted these afflictions with love for God

and with joy, I tell you that you will be blessed to have
another child who will have a mere human being for an
in-law! And there will be time enough for this child yet
to be born to have a wedding of the kind you had today
when she is seventy years old!'

"And so it was. The *Haṣidah* had another daughter
that year who lived to the age of seventy. But Rebbe
Menahem Mendel was not at her wedding, for he had
passed away," said Rebbe Tzvi, concluding the story in
his letter. "And I had to perform the marriage cere-
mony. It was from this woman that I learned how to
accept suffering, even the death of a child, with love for
God and with great joy."[1] ❧

Great Love

❧ When his son passed away, the Hafetz Hayim[1] stood
at the deathbed in silence. Then he told this story:

"During the Spanish Inquisition, in 1492, the
bloodthirsty murderers killed two children in front of
their mother. She raised her eyes to heaven and, with a
steeled heart, whispered this prayer: 'Master of the
world, I've always loved You! But as long as my precious
children were alive, my heart was always divided in two.
There was always a place in it for loving them. Now that
they're gone, my heart is totally devoted to my burning
love for You! Now I can truly fulfill the *mitzvah* to "love
the Lord your God with all your heart, with all your
soul, and with all your might!"'

When the Hafetz Hayim finished this story, he said loudly, his voice full of fire, "Master of the world, the love with which I loved my sons, I give to You!"[2] ⋘

The Torah path is to love your children, your parents, your husband, or your wife as an expression of your love for God. But even pious people, like this mother, never succeed fully; their heart always remains somewhat divided between their love for God and their love for other than God. Yet the spiritual goal is to love God with all your heart, soul, and might—to love God, and God alone. Thrown back on God by her tragedy, this holy woman did not mourn or rail against the divine decree; she ascended to great heights and returned her love to the One and Only One.

Centuries later, this moving story served to inspire the Hafetz Hayim when he lost his son.

Tzedaka as a Cure

⋘ Rebbetzin Reizel, the wife of Rebbe Moshe of Zelichov and daughter of Rebbe Yehoshua Asher of Parisov, had a custom of giving away large sums of money as *tzedaka* to poor people without her husband's knowledge.

Once he said to her, "I hear that you're giving away a lot of *tzedaka,* beyond my means and without my knowledge or consent. You should know that this falls into the category of a *mitzvah* performed by means of a transgression, because there's a touch of robbery in giving away money without my consent." But his wife paid no attention to his words and kept on giving as always.

Finally, her husband complained about it to his father-in-law, the holy Rebbe of Parisov, who promised,

"Next time I see her, I'll speak to her about it and tell her that what she's doing is contrary to *halacha*."

Not long after that, when Reizel visited her father in Parisov, he said to her, "My daughter, your husband is upset that you're giving away more *tzedaka* than he can afford. You have no right to be so extravagant."

"Father," she replied, "I've heard that there is a ruling in the *Shulhan Aruch* [Code of Jewish Law] that a husband is obligated to spend money to heal his sick wife, regardless of cost; there's no limit to the amount. When I see a poor man, my pity for him is so strong that my heart breaks and I'm actually sick; my whole body becomes weak. If I'm sick, I have a right to spend my husband's money to heal myself. And when I give *tzedaka,* I'm restored to health. So I have permission for what I'm doing, according to *halacha*."

Her father realized that she was right, and always praised her for these words.[1]

A Fifth

Rabbi Naftali and Rebbetzin Pessia Carlebach (parents of the famous Rabbi Shlomo Carlebach) were not people of means. Torah study was Rabbi Naftali's only occupation, and Pessia, who helped support the family by working as a bookbinder, never had cash to spare. Yet they kept an open house for visiting scholars and made *tzedaka* a household rule. In the days after World War I, when the Carlebach family lived in Berlin, any visiting *rosh yeshiva* or charity collector made for their home, knowing that generous hospitality would be available there—as well as good advice, if required.

The economic recession that hit Eastern Europe in the late 1920s caused great hardship, and starvation menaced the renowned yeshiva of Ponevezh in Lithuania. "If there is no flour, there is no Torah," the Sages declared, and the cessation of Torah study became an immediate danger. In view of the situation, Rabbi Yosef Kahaneman, who was then *rosh yeshiva,* decided to conduct a fundraising tour abroad, visiting one city after another and calling on potential benefactors.

Unfortunately, the Jews of Eastern Europe were not the only ones facing hard times; before long, the recession affected communities elsewhere. The number of people requesting charity multiplied, and for every penny of *tzedaka,* a dozen hands were outstretched. To make matters worse, businessmen in the West also began to suffer. Stock markets crashed, trade slumped, and wealthy folk were impoverished. In desperation, the Ponevezher Rabbi kept trudging around seeking donations, but the money he raised did not even cover his travel expenses.

Eventually, he arrived in Berlin, located the Carlebach family's address, and went straight there in the hope of receiving advice and assistance in contacting possible donors. Rabbi Naftali promptly invited him to have a meal and a rest after his difficult journey. While chatting with his host, the Ponevezher Rabbi told Rabbi Carlebach about the grim situation in Lithuania and mentioned the failure of their brethren in Germany and neighboring lands to give a helping hand. Recently, for example, a Polish-Jewish magnate had sent only meager donations with letters bewailing his own misfortunes; another philanthropist, who had previously covered one third of the yeshiva's expenses, was now barely able to make ends meet. Rabbi Kahaneman discussed these problems at length until his voice gave out.

Hearing their guest's tale of woe as she prepared a meal in the kitchen, Rebbetzin Pessia Carlebach was struck to the heart. "You're going to stay here with us," she insisted, "and tomorrow, with God's help, there may be a solution to your problem."

Bright and early the next morning, when everyone was fast asleep, she got up, gathered all her jewelry and treasured possessions, quietly left the house, and negotiated a loan at the pawnbroker's.

Once back home, she went to the *rosh yeshiva* and joyfully presented him with a substantial check. The Ponevezher Rabbi took a hard, silent look at this check. On the one hand, it would enable him to revitalize the yeshiva and its students; on the other hand, it was not difficult to guess how she had obtained the money, and for fear of endangering her financial situation, he could not bring himself to accept the "poor man's lamb."[1]

"Well," said the *rosh yeshiva,* "this is indeed a house of God, and the benevolence practiced here knows no bounds. But accepting this money would run counter to the Sages' injunction that no more than a fifth of one's means be devoted to charity. Giving *tzedaka* must not turn anyone into a beggar, and your donating this

large sum could easily put your own household's finances
in jeopardy."

"True enough," replied Rebbetzin Carlebach.
"As you say, no more than a fifth of one's assets may
be spent on *tzedaka*. But my object in performing the
mitzvah is also to educate our children. And the Sages
say that for the sake of education, any financial sacrifice is permitted."[2] ≈◈≈

As in the previous tale, when a holy woman wants to give more than
a fifth, she can find a justification. Rebbetzin Pessia Carlebach
wanted her children to learn that wholehearted giving to holy causes
is the Jewish way. She certainly educated her children well by pro-
viding them with such a clear example of pious generosity.

Standing Up for Herself

≈◈≈ A traditional story says that Havva, the wife of
Rabbi Yeshaya Moskat of Praga (a suburb of Warsaw),
gave him trouble from morning till evening. She would
walk around with a *siddur* in her hand, continually
uttering prayers under her breath. In the morning, when
Rabbi Yeshaya came home from reciting his morning
prayers in the synagogue and asked for some breakfast,
Havva signaled to him that she was in the middle of her
prayers and could not interrupt them. In the afternoon,
when he asked for lunch, she explained that she had to
finish saying psalms first. And in the evening, when he
asked for his supper, she told him that she had to finish
reciting *ma'amadot* [selected holy texts] first. Whenever he would ask her for a cup of tea, she excused

herself by saying that she did not concern herself with physical matters.

Rabbi Yeshaya restrained himself in the face of all this, but once said to her, "The Sages say, 'Who is a good wife? One who does her husband's will.'"

Unfazed, she replied, "They also say, 'Whoever is occupied with one *mitzvah* is exempt from the obligation to perform another *mitzvah*.' And I'm always occupied in doing *mitzvot!*"

Rabbi Yeshaya answered gently, "The Torah tells us that the pious Jewish women took part in constructing the Tabernacle in the Sinai Desert. The verse in Exodus refers to '*all the women* whose hearts stirred them up in wisdom.'[1] Elsewhere, in the Book of Esther, the Torah says, '*All the women* should honor their husbands.'[2] The parallelism of expression shows[3] that even pious women who are constantly occupied even in such important *mitzvot* as constructing the Tabernacle are not exempt from honoring and serving their husbands and doing their will at every hour and time."[4] ໑

This tale is told and written from the man's side and does not record Rebbetzin Havva's response to her husband's final comment. It seems unlikely that she agreed with him; if she had, her submission would have been noted. Perhaps her retort was censored or she let him have the last word.

In most traditional tales, women are praised for supporting their husband's spirituality. In this tale, Havva is criticized, albeit gently, for failing to support her husband's religious efforts and insisting on pursuing her own. Despite the intent of the tale itself, which sides with the rabbi husband and seeks to elicit our condemnation of Rebbetzin

Havva's viewpoint, it is exciting to read of a pious woman standing up for herself.

Of course, most of us would agree with her husband's claim that a pious woman should care for her husband and family. But doesn't it work both ways? Shouldn't the husband support his wife and family? Yet there are many traditional tales that praise a pious husband who pursues his own religious goals and neglects his wife and family until they are actually on the verge of starvation!

And shouldn't a husband support his wife's spirituality? Should her fervent piety merely be an annoyance for him—as in this story—because it interferes with his needs? Perhaps they were both wrong in pursuing their spiritual goals separately; but historically, we know that the onus for this is mostly on the husband, because men typically slighted their wives' religiosity. We cannot know the details of the relationship between Rabbi Yeshaya and Rebbetzin Havva, and we are not here to judge between them. But it is inspiring to find a rare tale of a woman standing up for her own piety and spirituality—even if the tale's editor and teller believes her to be in the wrong. We may beg to differ with him about this.

No Joke Needed

Rebbetzin Sarah Rivka Rachel Leah was the daughter of the *gaon* Rabbi Yukel HaLevi Horowitz, the religious judge of Gluga, and the wife of the *gaon* Rabbi Shabtai, the religious judge of Krasni. She was very learned and expert in Talmud and had also written a book, *Tehinnah Imahot* [Supplications of the Mothers].

At a wedding, she met Rebbetzin Dinah, the wife of the *gaon* Rabbi Tzvi Hirsh of Haig. The two women began to engage in *pilpul,* talmudic discussion, and still another *gaon,* Rabbi Tzvi Hirsh of Berlin, who was also present, overheard them and was amazed.

He said to them, "It's customary for Torah scholars to tell a joke before they begin to discuss Torah.
I'd like to hear the joke you told."

Rebbetzin Sarah Rivka Rachel Leah replied, "The
reason the Rabbis instructed Torah scholars to tell a
joke before study was to guard the Torah's holiness.
Torah study is a commandment for men, and the Rabbis
were worried that the *yetzer ha-ra* [the evil inclination]
and the Satan would come and attach themselves to
the study, God forbid. By telling a joke at the beginning
of study, the *yetzer ha-ra* and Satan are 'bought off'
with a superficial share of the outer aspect of the Torah
study, and they depart. The scholars then go on to study
Torah *lishmah* with utterly pure inner motives.

"It's different for us women, since we are not commanded to study Torah. No 'stranger'—no *yetzer ha-ra*
or Satan—comes between us to suck holiness from the
study. This is what Solomon said in Proverbs about
the 'woman of valor': 'She opens her mouth with wisdom.'[1] A woman can immediately open her mouth with
Torah wisdom without needing to tell a joke beforehand.
Although she begins teaching without first telling a joke,
the verse continues: 'and the Torah of *hesed* is on her
tongue.' In the Talmud of *Sukkah* 49, the Rabbis interpreted 'the Torah of *hesed*' [usually translated as "kindness"] as 'Torah *lishmah*'—Torah for its own sake, with
pure motives. So you see that without needing any opening joke, women scholars—unlike men—can immediately
engage in the purest kind of Torah conversation."[2] ⋘

This story is highly unusual in showing two learned women engaging in talmudic discourse. It also shows one of them besting in repartee a male *gaon* who entered the discussion. I sense, in the story, that the rebbetzin was slightly irritated at the nature of the rabbi's intrusion, whereby he reduced the women's talmudic discussion to "a joke."

According to the Kabbalah, the Evil Side can suck life—draw energy and power—from the Side of Holiness; for example, a person who is proud at teaching Torah provides energy not to Good but to Evil. One traditional antidote to this potential problem is to "give the Satan his share." That is, one distracts the Evil Side by giving it a little "offering" and thereby pushing it away. There is a psycho-spiritual reality behind this customary practice: A person's lower nature is satisfied by being even slightly acknowledged and does not act up to disrupt holy efforts; it is effectively suppressed.

Rebbetzin Sarah Rivka Rachel Leah used this concept of giving the Satan his share to explain why the ancient Rabbis ordained that a joke be told at the beginning of a session of Torah study. Male scholars might be inclined to be lightheaded during their studying, which would empower the Evil Side. But when they tell a religious joke at the beginning—and are seemingly engaged in action lacking seriousness—that impediment is gotten out of the way, and pure study can ensue.

However, the Rabbis also teach that there is a particular resistance to divine commands, which is not the case when a person acts freely without being commanded. Therefore, the rebbetzin explained, since women are not, according to the traditional view, commanded to study Torah, they do not need to tell a joke.

By this profound thought, the rebbetzin avoided entertaining the rabbi, whose question was perhaps less than respectful to the learned women. In fact, the rebbetzin was probably obliquely rebuking him for being lightheaded in asking to hear a joke. (The Rabbis say that lightheadedness, frivolity, leads to lewdness.)

Otherwise, this exchange could be read differently—that the rebbetzin's answer was itself a joke. In either case, her response was sharp and quick-witted.

It is notable that the unusually named Rebbetzin Sarah Rivka Rachel Leah—who bore the names of the four Matriarchs—had written a book of prayers for women called *Supplications of the Mothers*—or one could translate the Hebrew as *Supplications of the Matriarchs*. We can reasonably suppose that her parents, who gave her this unusual name, were strongly attuned to the holiness of the four Matriarchs and of later *tzaddikot!*

The Boldness of Rebbes

⟨◆⟩ Rebbe Baruch was a great rebbe in Medzibuz. Now, the custom among the Hasidic rebbes in Volhynia was that on specific Sabbaths, Hasidim visited their rebbe and ate at his table; but on other Sabbaths, the rebbes did not conduct public meals. Rebbe Baruch's custom on those Sabbaths was to eat his meals with his wife, Rebbetzin Yitta, and his four daughters—Hanna Hayya, Raizel, Edel, and Pessia; he had no sons.

On one of those Sabbaths, Rebbe Yaakov Yitzhak, the Seer of Lublin, was visiting Rebbe Baruch, and having women at the table greatly displeased him, because in Galicia and Poland, Hasidim did not eat together with the women. Rebbe Baruch engaged in conversation at the table with his wife and daughters, which also displeased the Seer.

At the second Sabbath meal, Rebbe Baruch's aides seated the Seer opposite one of the daughters, and she annoyed him by looking in his face, for he avoided inti-

macy with women. Then Rebbe Baruch entered a trance
and made a soul ascent into heaven while sitting at the
table. The Seer of Lublin also made a soul ascent, and
so too did the Rebbe's daughters. [During a soul ascent,
the soul exits the body and ascends into heaven to receive mystic teachings.]

Rebbe Baruch proceeded to direct matters through
his *yihudim* [mystical unification meditations] by moving his snuff box, which he held in his hand. When he
stretched out his snuff box, his daughters elevated
higher than the Seer of Lublin.

When they all returned to the normal plane of
consciousness, the Seer of Lublin was angry, thinking,
"Why did he draw down such high souls into female
bodies?" [According to mystic teaching, great tzaddikim
can draw down the souls they choose for the children
who will be born to them. The Seer considered it improper that Rebbe Baruch drew down great souls into
"mere" female bodies.]

One of Rebbe Baruch's daughters did not cease
from staring in the Seer's face, because due to the
daughters' souls, they were bold like rebbes. The Seer
of Lublin then decided to remind them that they were
women, so he projected his negative energy, and immediately, the offending daughter began to menstruate
and ran away from the table. Rebbe Baruch realized
what had happened and angrily called out, "Who dares
disturb my Sabbath table?"[1]

This is a striking story. And we can appreciate aspects of it for reasons different from those intended by the teller—most important,

because it shows the boldness of the rebbe's daughters, who did not back down from confronting the Seer and indeed held their own. Undoubtedly, they were raised to be bold by their father and mother, who seemed to have had different, more open ideas about women than the Polish and Galician rebbes did. Rebbe Baruch's daughters even engaged in a competition in soul ascent with the Seer, the greatest rebbe and mystic in Poland, and they in fact won, although the story says they were aided by their holy father. The tale, which appears in the traditions about Rebbe Baruch and is favorable to him and his ways, remains cautious about overtly criticizing the holy Seer of Lublin. The mystic competition finally ends in a draw when Rebbe Baruch's daughter is forced to flee, but Rebbe Baruch himself complains about the Seer's tactics, although without touching on the pertinent issue—the involvement of women together with men in religious life.

In fact, one need not judge this issue, because there is more than one way in spirituality, and separation of the sexes can promote holiness. It is not as if the Seer was simply "wrong." The true issue is not the separation of the sexes but the development and encouragement of women's spirituality. And clearly, Rebbe Baruch and Rebbetzin Yitta did encourage their four daughters—Hanna Hayya, Raizel, Edel, and Pessia—to be great women, like the four Matriarchs—Sarah, Rebecca, Rachel, and Leah.

Thank God!

Elisheva Schechter was a pious Israeli woman who passed away at the young age of thirty but whose life inspired many people. She had tremendous faith and trust in God. The Rabbis say that one should thank and praise God for everything that happens, for "bad" as well as for good, because the truth is that even what seems bad is for good. Therefore, pious people always have the words *Baruch HaShem*, "Thank God," on their lips.

◈ The words *Thank God* were always part of Elisheva's speech, whether she was discussing the good or the difficult, for what is "bad" is really only "difficult."

When one of her children was ill and Elisheva came to the school where she taught, looking as tired as she felt, a fellow teacher asked her if she had slept that night. She answered, "Thank God, I didn't sleep at all!"

On another occasion, during an especially busy time at school and at home, when someone asked her whether it was hard for her to manage, she gave her typical answer: "Thank God, it's hard!"[1] ◈

Serving a Torah Scholar

◈ Rebbetzin Sheina Hayya, the wife of Rabbi Yosef Shalom Elyashiv, self-sacrificingly took on herself the yoke of caring for their house as well as raising their children during all the various difficult circumstances and situations so that her husband would not be disturbed in his holy Torah study.

She was content with a minimum in her small and cramped apartment. They did not even have a bath, just a small tub, and no washing machine; until her last years, she did her laundry the old way, by hand. When she became weak toward the end of her life, her daughters took her laundry to do in their homes. But the rebbetzin would not allow them to take the rabbi's laundry. She insisted on doing it with her own hands because, she said, she did not want to lose the *mitzvah* of serving a Torah scholar.

Rebbetzin Sheina Hayya did not have an electric coffeemaker and troubled to make coffee in a small kettle. In her old age, someone gave her a coffeemaker as a gift, so the rabbi could make himself coffee when he wanted and she would not need to bother herself. But the rebbetzin refused to accept the gift, saying, "Do you want to take this *mitzvah* from me also?"[1] ❧

In Judaism, it is considered a spiritually potent practice to personally serve a Torah scholar. The Rabbis say that serving a Torah scholar is even more beneficial spiritually than studying Torah from him. Why? Because humbly submitting to him by serving him is like submitting to God and opens one to the scholar's transformative influence and to a great divine influx.

A pious woman like Rebbetzin Sheina Hayya, whose husband was a Torah scholar, derived spiritual benefit from her loving and devoted service to him.

Finally, we can note that piety or holiness are not always or even often expressed in "great" deeds. The rebbetzin's piety was in doing her husband's laundry with her own hands and insisting on making his coffee. The Rabbis teach that "deeds have significance according to the intentions that motivate them." Many women do their husbands' laundry and make them coffee, and the Rabbis tell us that by serving our family, we fulfill the commandment to love our neighbor as ourself. But when a pious woman does these deeds with a clear intent to serve God, they have even greater spiritual power to elevate her to holiness.

Her Share in the World to Come

❧ Before he became famous, Rabbi Hayim, the Tzanzer Rebbe, was very poor. His wife, Rebbetzin

Rachel Feigeleh, would buy everything on credit and pray that somehow there would be money to pay the shopkeepers. So one *erev* Shabbat, she tried to buy challahs for Shabbat, but the merchant refused. "You owe me too much already," he said.

She begged him, "Please give me challahs for Shabbat for my holy husband."

The merchant was adamant. "Absolutely not! You owe me for months and months. No more credit for you!"

The rebbetzin began to cry, "Please, please, I can't have an empty table for Shabbat. I'll give you anything! I'll give you my share in the World to Come!"

This merchant was no fool. He thought, "This pious woman's share in the World to Come?" "For your share in the World to Come," he said, and handed her two challahs.

Rachel Feigeleh took the challahs and said, "And some cheese, too!"

That Friday evening, the Tzanzer sat at the table, glowing in the light of the Shabbat candles. Rachel Feigeleh came in and placed his soup before him. As she walked away, Rabbi Hayim, who had noticed that something was bothering her, spoke up and said, "My dear wife, what's wrong?"

The rebbetzin started to cry. "For years, I've served you faithfully despite our great poverty. I never complained because I knew that in caring for a man as great as you, even if we had nothing in this world, I would be rewarded in the World to Come. But today, in order to have challahs on the table for Shabbat, I sold my share in the World to Come, and now I have nothing."

"My dear wife," said the Tzanzer, as he hugged her, "be assured that you have a share in the World to Come. You saved my life. When I was coming home from synagogue, I was sure that I would die from starvation. But the food that you put on the table has kept me alive, and for this, your share in the World to Come is even greater than before."[1] ◅◈▻

The tale's humor has the rebbetzin not undervaluing her share in the World to Come by demanding "cheese too!" Rachel Feigeleh rose to great heights of devotion by her self-sacrifice to serve and support her husband. Indeed, one of the most exalted titles that a Jew can aspire to is to be a servant of the servants of God.

After the Fact

◅◈▻ Rabbi Avraham, the brother of the Vilna Gaon, lived in the town of Kaidan, and one of the families there concerned themselves with his upkeep, taking care of his needs and his family's needs while he sat and studied Torah.

Once, some people came from Vilna and suggested that he move there. "It's a bigger city," they said. "We'll arrange to take care of you and see that you have a larger income and live in better conditions."

"You have to speak to the rebbetzin," he replied.

They went to Rebbetzin Hinda and told her about their offer, but she completely refused. When they asked her why, she said, "A few years ago, we had no

money to allow my husband to sit and study Torah,
so we sold our apartment and moved to a smaller place
that we could afford. Now, three times a day, I pass by
our old apartment and feel elevated, knowing that we
gave it up so that my husband could study. And I'm not
willing to give up this pleasure!"[1] ❧

Rebbetzin Hinda fully shared in her husband's devotion to study
and enjoyed contemplating, after the fact, their decision to move to
smaller quarters. Her attitude illustrates a trait we might not otherwise have thought of: pride and joy in a great deed years after its
performance.

How to Give Birth

❧ Just after Rebbetzin Leah Schwadron had given
birth to one of her children, her husband, Rabbi Sholom,
the Maggid of Jerusalem, asked her, "How do you feel?"

She answered, "The Sages, of blessed memory, say
that the key of childbirth is not given into the hand of
flesh and blood; it is in the hand of the Holy One, blessed
be He, alone.[1] I feel as if I'm in the hand of God."[2] ❧

The Rabbis say that God may delegate authority over events in the
world so that prophets or tzaddikim occasionally have the power to
decide and decree, for example, matters concerning livelihood,
health, and children; the tzaddikim decree and God fulfills. But, say
the Rabbis, the power to decree that a woman give birth is withheld
from any human being's control; it remains in God's hand alone.

When someone fully believes in the Torah and the words of the
Sages, the divine teachings penetrate his consciousness so that he
actually feels and experiences that in which he believes. Rebbetzin

Leah could take comfort and experience the ultimate consolation in her labor: She felt that she rested in God's hand.

Facing God

⋘ Rachel Gittel, the daughter of Rabbi Simha Zissel Ziv, the Elder of Kelm, once refused to be anesthetized when her life was in danger and she had to undergo major surgery because she wanted to remain clear-headed during the procedure. Confronting death, she wanted to face God and did not fear the pain. During the whole operation, she never gave voice to her pain.[1] ⋙

The duty of a Jew facing death is to call out the *Sh'ma*: "Hear O Israel, the Lord our God, the Lord is one!" The Rabbis say about God's word to Moses that "no person can see My face and live": "At death one can see God's face."[2] Can one easily pass on this promise? How can a person see his Maker's face while anesthetized and asleep? But how many of us have the courage of a holy woman like Rachel Gittel Ziv?

The Passing of a Woman Who Had the Holy Spirit

⋘ At the foot of the Alps in Switzerland, along the shores of the Rois River, lies the town of Lugano. In this quiet place, the Jewish community dwelt in untroubled peace and tranquillity.

Among the special Jewish families that lived here was the family of Rebbetzin Toiba and Rabbi Shimshon Rafael Erlanger. Their home was a radiant source of love of God, love of Torah, and love of kindness. Their doors were always open wide, and their home was a regular meeting place for Torah sages and scholars.

Great rabbis testified that Rebbetzin Toiba, a woman of exalted soul, had through her piety attained the holy spirit. Her whole being was permeated with an elevated spirituality. One of her exceptional traits was that she was utterly scrupulous about slander, *loshon hara*. She never spoke or listened to a negative word about any human being. Her whole house was suffused with an atmosphere that said, "The Holy One, blessed be He, is in this house."

But sadly, this *tzaddeket* did not live long. She passed away in 1938 at the age of forty-one, in the month of Tishri [in which fall the holidays Rosh HaShanah, Yom Kippur, *Sukkot, Hoshanna Rabba*, and *Simhat Torah*]. Before her passing, her greatness and holy spirit became even more evident. As with some other very holy people, she knew the exact day of her death. Weeks before her passing, she told her husband that on a certain day and date, her obituary and eulogy would appear in the newspaper; she was correct.

Her illness worsened during *Sukkot*. Mustering extraordinary powers, she asked to take in her hand the willow branches on *Hoshanna Rabba,* the final day of *Sukkot.* She beat them on the ground, as is customary, while reciting the appropriate liturgical verses, and gave them back to her husband, saying, "Please place these with me in the grave. This is the last *mitzvah* I'll perform in this world of deeds."

As her end approached, everyone in the house was troubled. On *Simhat Torah*, her husband sat beside her, gazing at her and praying for her recovery and speaking to her words of support and comfort. At this time, everyone else was in the synagogue dancing with the Torah scrolls. Rebbetzin Toiba, whose love for the Torah effaced her ego, asked her husband to go to the synagogue to celebrate with the Torah because, she said, despite her illness, nothing should eliminate the joy of the Torah; and it would please her if he went.

Her condition steadily worsened, and it seemed that the end was near. On Sunday morning, her husband asked her, "Are you afraid of death?"

She replied, "Have these ears ever listened to *loshon hara*? Have these lips even once spoken *loshon hara*? Why, then, should I be afraid of death?"

Two days later, she passed away. On her tombstone is engraved: "Even the dust of *loshon hara* was hateful to her"—not even the slightest bit of slander or other negative speech soiled the purity of her soul.[1] ❧

Speech is a world in itself, and whole books have been written about how a Jew should speak. Pious people, such as Rebbetzin Toiba, cultivate purity and kindness in speech. The rebbetzin's remark that she did not fear death because she avoided speaking badly about others tells us that this precious trait is a key to attaining higher spiritual levels. Her comment seems to say, "If you have this, you have the rest." The psalm says, "Who is the person who desires true life, who covets long life that he may enjoy good? Keep your tongue from evil and your lips from speaking guile. Depart from evil and do good; seek peace and pursue it."[2] Rebbetzin Toiba fulfilled the verse, so she merited the holy spirit and a "long life" of goodness and peace in the World to Come.

My Time Has Come

◀◐▷ The famous Rabbi Moshe Sofer, the Hasam Sofer, said about his mother, Rebbetzin Reizel Sofer, that "the Lord God did not do anything great in the world that He did not reveal in a dream to my mother."

Once, when her son was explaining what an elevated soul she had, he said, "If my mother had lived in ancient times, she certainly would have been among the prophetesses."

Reizel Sofer was holy and pious. When she was about to give birth to her son, the Hasam Sofer, she sent a message to the rabbi of her city, Frankfurt-on-Main, begging him to order that they delay beginning the Friday night *Kabbalat Shabbat* service in the synagogue until she delivered so that she would not desecrate the Sabbath by giving birth. The rabbi acceded to her wish. [Customarily, they would begin welcoming the Sabbath somewhat early, and then those attending her in childbirth would have been required to do various kinds of work desecrating the day of rest. She asked that the prayer service wait until the last permissible time so that she might give birth before Shabbat.]

She always prayed three times a day with a congregation [which is not required of women]. Even on her last day on earth, Sunday, 17 Adar 1922, she went to the synagogue for the early afternoon prayers.

Afterward, as she was returning home, she called to her daughter-in-law, Hulda, and said to her, "My daughter, my time has come to pass from this world. Call the pious women to come and be present when my soul leaves. And bring me the shroud that I prepared so that I can put it on."

Hearing these words, her daughter-in-law was struck with dread and asked her in a quivering voice, "What is this all about?" But her mother-in-law did not answer and asked her a second and a third time to do as she requested.

Finally, the daughter-in-law did what the rebbetzin wanted.

In the presence of the pious women who came quickly, Reizel got into bed, said a few prayers, and immediately returned her soul to her Creator.[1] ◄◈►

Her great son said that Reizel Sofer was worthy of being a prophetess. How often one reads that a rebbe or rabbi said that his mother, wife, or sister had the holy spirit or would have been a rebbe if she were a man—yet we know almost nothing about most of these great women! We must appreciate holy women while they are alive, not only after their death, and learn from their wisdom and teaching.

The Dress

◄◈► Rebbetzin Hendel, the wife of Rebbe Zusya of Hanipol, once gave a roll of fine cloth to the tailor to make a dress for her. She and her husband were quite poor, and acquiring a new dress was a rare occasion. When the tailor finished his work, he brought the dress to the rebbetzin. As he placed it on the table, he let out a deep sigh.

"What's bothering you?" she asked.

The tailor said, "My daughter is engaged to a young man, and when he saw me sewing a woman's dress, he assumed it was for his *kallah,* his fiancée. When he found out that it wasn't, he became dejected and disheartened. The whole thing is painful for me."

Her compassion aroused, the rebbetzin took the dress and handed it to the tailor, saying, "Give it to your daughter."

When she told her husband, Rebbe Zusya, about this later in the day, he asked her, "Did you pay the tailor for his work?"

"What do you mean?" asked the rebbetzin with surprise. "I gave him the dress as a gift! How does pay come into this?"

"This poor tailor worked the whole week," said her husband, "to make you a dress, not a dress for his daughter. He was expectantly looking forward to the minute he'd finish so he would have money to buy food for his family. Now what will they eat? Because you gave a gift to a *kallah,* is it permitted to withhold a laborer's pay?"[1]

The rebbetzin did not hesitate. She went immediately to pay the tailor for his work.[2] ✍

How beautiful when husband and wife are true helpmates in goodness.

The Homely Lesson of a Patch

❧ Rebbetzin Batya Karelitz of the renowned Karelitz family (the famous Hazon Ish was her brother), told of her visit as a child to her pious grandmother, Bubba Yuspa—Grandma Josepha—who taught her how to patch a worn garment. At that time, her grandmother also taught her a lesson in religious values.

"One should not be ashamed to wear patched clothes," her grandmother said. "On the contrary, one should feel good about it. Do you know why? Because God gives us everything we have. But all these wonderful things are not presents forever. No! He entrusts them to us for safekeeping only. At any moment, without warning, He may take them all back. So it's a sin to show neglect for anything God Himself entrusts to us. A patch, Batya, not only prolongs the life of a garment, but the patching demonstrates how much we appreciate everything that God entrusts to our keeping!"[1] ❧

Few people today wear patches on their garments. Patches have largely disappeared in our wealthy society. But Bubba Yuspa's lesson still applies. God gives us everything we have. Every object that comes into our possession is a gift from God and should be treated with reverence. The mystics teach that a spark of divinity is in each thing in the world, and therefore every object, every possession, should be properly honored. By prematurely discarding an old item to replace it with a new one, we show disrespect for the holy spark that resides in that object. How long should we keep a garment or other item? Each of us should decide with wisdom; there is no rule. The only rule—which we can learn from Bubba Yuspa—is to show proper care and respect for your possessions.

Rebbetzin Malka of Belz

Rebbetzin Malka of Belz presents a rare case of a holy woman who was famous in her own time and about whom there are a significant number of stories.[1]

More Than a Helpmate

⋘ Malka was a great *tzaddeket* who helped her husband, Rebbe Shalom of Belz, become a great tzaddik.

After their marriage, the young couple, Malka and Shalom, lived in her parents' home. Every night, before midnight, she woke him up and said, "Shalom, get up from your bed to serve God. Open your eyes and see that all the laborers have already risen to go to work. You too must rise for your holy service of God!"

Like some other pious people, Rabbi Shalom made great efforts to conceal his piety—his devotion was for God, not to appear devout in other people's eyes. Every night, he pretended to the others in the household [mainly his parents-in-law] that he was sleeping in his room. But Malka helped him climb down to the street through the window.

Then he would go to the *beit midrash* of Rabbi Shlomo Lutzker of Skohl, with whom he would study the entire night. Before dawn, he returned home, and Malka let him in through the window. No one else knew of this. Then he would lie down to sleep for a short while. Just as he had closed his eyes, his father-in-law would awaken and get up. When Malka's father would see that his son-in-law was still asleep, he would grow very angry at the young man. He was supposed to be a scholar! Why did he not rise early to study? The father-in-law would knock on his door and tell him, "How much longer will you sleep? When will you get up?" The pious Rabbi Shalom would then get out of bed and go to study with his father-in-law. This was his regular custom.

One day, his father-in-law announced that he could no longer support him. His son-in-law would have to find some way to make a living. Rabbi Shalom was ready to go to Leipzig to buy merchandise, but Rebbetzin Malka sold her pearls and earrings so that he could continue for a while longer to study Torah undisturbed.[2]

Later, Malka stayed awake for one thousand nights consecutively with Rabbi Shalom. She held the candle and provided light for him for all those thousand nights so that he could achieve true piety and attain his great spiritual levels. And if he slept for more than the length of time it takes for a small Hanukkah candle to burn, she would wake him.

Rabbi Shalom became a great rebbe in Belz.

Rebbe Meir of Premishlan once made a pun about Malka's name, which means "queen." He said, quoting Genesis 14:18, *"Malki tzedek melech shalem"*—literally, "Malkitzedek, the king of Shalem" but also understandable as hinting that: "Because Malka is a *tzaddeket,* Shalom can be a *melech* [king]."

Malka too had a deep appreciation for her holy husband. She once said to him, "I think you will be the Messiah."[3] ☙

We have all heard the saying that there is a woman behind every great man. Rebbe Meir of Premishlan testified—in his typical joking way—that this was the case with Malka and her husband Shalom. The image of her holding the candle for him is, it seems to me, purely metaphorical, although we can believe that they stayed up together: the candle hints that she provided him with light that aided him in his spiritual pursuits.

Malka gave up her possessions and chose a life of deprivation and difficulty so that her husband could perfect himself in Torah and become a great man. But she too attained perfection. Rebbe Shalom of Belz became holy because of Rebbetzin Malka's help. She became holy by helping him and by joining her spiritual journey with his.

Sitting with the Rebbetzin

≪◈≫ When Rebbe Baruch of Gorelitz visited Belz for the first time with his father, Rebbe Hayim of Tzanz, they found the Belzer Rebbe sitting at a table with Rebbetzin Malka. It was very unusual and irregular in Hasidic society for a husband to sit familiarly with his wife; it was considered improper and even uncouth. But after they ended their visit and left, the Tzanzer asked his son, "How did the rebbe and his wife appear to you?"

"Like Adam and Eve before the Sin," he replied.

"That is the way they appeared to me too," said Rebbe Hayim. Then he asked, "And how did the room they were sitting in appear?"

"Like the Garden of Eden," answered his son.[4] ≪◈≫

Because of their high spiritual level, Rebbe Shalom and Rebbetzin Malka were considered by discerning spiritual people to be exempt from normal standards of behavior. They could be intimately together,

even in public, without a doubt arising about their holiness and purity. It was rare in Hasidic culture for a rebbetzin to be held in regard
equal to that of her husband. She would usually be invisible, in the
shadows. Rebbetzin Malka was by her husband's side, shedding the
light of holiness.

Rebbe Shalom and Rebbetzin Malka are, then, a model—for our
generation and for the future—of a holy couple. If husband and wife
together seek the highest, they can aspire to the holiness of Adam and
Eve in the Garden of Eden before the Sin, when man and woman were
equal. That is the Torah's ideal; that is the true Jewish goal.

Good Advice for Healing

≈❧ Rebbe Shalom of Belz was famous as a miracle-
working healer who sometimes laid hands on the sick.
Once, a sick man came to visit the rebbe when he was
sleeping. Rebbetzin Malka asked him what his problem
was, and he told her that he had a great deal of pain in
his foot. The rebbetzin advised him to light a candle
in the synagogue every day. [It is a pious custom and
an act of penance to honor the synagogue by lighting
candles there, to symbolize the light of God.]

The man did as she suggested and was healed.

When the rebbe heard about this, he asked the
rebbetzin, "From where did you take this advice?"

She replied, "Didn't King David, the Sweet Singer
of Israel, say, 'A candle for my foot'?"[5] ≈❧

The rebbetzin was a holy woman who, like other rebbes and holy
people, considered a thought that fell into her brain, especially a
verse from the scriptures, as divine inspiration. This does not mean
that she believed that this prescription would be effective with every

person in every situation, just that it was what God wanted this particular man to do at that moment.

The story shows that basically, Malka was on the same level as her husband and was like a rebbe in her ability to offer miracle-working advice. When her husband was asleep, she could take care of business.[6]

How to Eat

◄◊► Malka had a custom to personally distribute kasha—buckwheat groats—to the Hasidim during meals on Shabbat. Her motive was undoubtedly spiritual, and indeed, holy power may be "transmitted" through food.

Once, when she was serving the kasha, she saw a young man who ate it hurriedly, in a gluttonous manner unbefitting a Hasid. The rebbetzin called him over and said to him, "Do you know how many prayers were sent into heaven on behalf of this food? At seed time, the seeds were praying that they be received into the earth and sprout. Then they pray that if heaven decrees a blight to afflict the sprouts, they be spared. Later, at threshing time, when many grains are simply lost and others carried off by the wind, they pray that nothing be lost. Still later, the grains pray that they come into the possession of a Jew—who will elevate them by making a blessing when eating them. Then they pray that they will become a food to be eaten on Shabbat, for this will cause their fixing—their *tikkun*—and elevation. But if, after all this, one eats in a lowly way, one spoils everything, for a grain of kasha can only receive a fixing when eaten in a way befitting a human being!" ◄◊►

Holy, meditative eating is an important Hasidic practice whereby both the person and the food are elevated spiritually. Rebbetzin Malka's words to the Hasid make clear that that is the way she ate—with sanctity and dignity. She poetically described the kasha seeds and grains as praying. I have little doubt that she also prayed a great deal while making the kasha and while distributing it to the Hasidim—to fulfill her goal that the Hasidim and the food they ate be elevated by their eating.

How Much to Eat

⋘ On another Shabbat, when Malka was distributing kasha, she noticed a certain Hasid who came back for seconds—which she gave to him. When he came back a third time and asked for more, she also gave it to him and said not a word about it. But when he came back for the fourth time, she whispered, "My whole life I'm repenting because I once overate. But if you need more food, here—I give it to you wholeheartedly!" And she gave him the kasha without making it noticeable what she was doing, so as not to embarrass him. ⋘

Holy people do not easily forget even their rare, minor sins because of their desire to serve God perfectly. Yet it is also the sign of a great person not to hold others to the same strict standards as those to which he holds himself—and to be lenient with others, as Malka was with this Hasid.

A Questionable Rebbe

⋘ A rebbe with his Hasidim once came to visit the Belzer Rebbe for Shabbat. The Belzer was in doubt as to how to act toward him, since he did not consider this man to be a real rebbe and had even criticized him publicly. Should he honor him—because, after all, he is a "rebbe" who has followers who are here with him—or should he ignore the man? The Belzer asked Rebbetzin Malka's advice.

"Act friendly toward him," she said. "If the Holy One, blessed be He, covers up for him and doesn't expose his faults, you should too."[7] ❧

Malka Saves the Poultry

"God issues a decree of misfortune, and the tzaddik annuls it," says the Talmud. A *tzaddeket* can also annul a heavenly decree, as in the following story about Rebbetzin Malka of Belz.

❧ One day, a certain Hasid was traveling to Belz from a distant town in Galicia to see Rebbe Shalom. On the way, he spent Shabbat in Premishlan. Naturally, he considered it improper not to visit the famous tzaddik of Premishlan, the holy Rebbe Meir. "You certainly didn't travel intending to visit me," observed Rebbe Meir when he saw the Hasid's unfamiliar face. "You're on your way to Belz, I'm sure. When you get there, tell them that Meir likes to eat capons." Rebbe Meir—like a few other tzaddikim—always referred to himself in the third person, to avoid using the arrogant word *I*.

The Hasid was unaware of the meaning of Rebbe Meir's words, but he hastened to deliver the message. Thinking that which particular food Rebbe Meir preferred was a matter for the rebbetzin, he went to Malka.

"All right," said Malka when she heard the message. "Then we'll transfer the decree to the unclean, nonkosher birds!"

Malka's words were equally incomprehensible to the Hasid. Only later did he understand their meaning, for soon afterward, all the crows and owls in the area began to die off, as though shot by an unseen hand.

What had happened was this: a decree had gone forth in heaven that a fatal disease would attack the poultry that year. Rebbetzin Malka was concerned about all the Jews who eat chicken, especially on Shabbat, so she mystically altered the decree to fall only on capons, because few people ate them in any case. Clearly, she had forgotten that the holy Rebbe Meir of Premishlan had a taste for them.

He too knew of the heavenly decree and was also aware of what Rebbetzin Malka had done. Hence his message—which prompted Malka at the last moment to intervene in heaven a second time and so prevent the heavenly decree from afflicting the capons. Now it would fall only on unclean, nonkosher birds, such as crows and owls.[8] ❧

This story shows that a tzaddik or a *tzaddeket,* like Rebbetzin Malka, can alter heavenly decrees—sometimes by transferring them to other parties. It also deals with the problems that may arise when tzaddikim have different opinions about a specific event or matter. There is also a humorous aspect to heaven's willingness to accommodate even the personal tastes of a tzaddik—such as Rebbe Meir's fondness for capons—because, it may be assumed, everything he does has a profound spiritual or even mystical reason.

It is said that this lower material world is the world of effects and the higher world is the world of causes. When a person rises spiritually until he enters the world of causes, he, like Rebbetzin Malka, can effect changes in the natural world. Regardless of what one believes about the traditional claim that tzaddikim can alter natural events, it is certainly novel and refreshing to see that a holy woman is put on this exalted level.

They Are Clapping in Heaven

⋙ There was once a serious epidemic that caused its victims to fall into a coma. People from the affected area went to Rebbe Meir of Premishlan and asked him what he saw in heaven. Was some sin of theirs causing it? What could be done to remedy the disaster?

Rebbe Meir said that he was forbidden to tell them what he saw, but "when a certain woman named Yenta lights the *Shabbos* candles, the angels in heaven are clapping."

They understood the hint that this Yenta's prayers could help them, so they went to her and told her that Rebbe Meir had sent them. She prayed, and the plague ceased.[1] ⋙

Rebbe Edel of Brody

Edel of Brody was the daughter of Rebbetzin Malka and Rebbe Shalom of Belz.

Her Greatness

⋙ Edel was her father's favorite child, more beloved even than his son, Rabbi Yehoshua, who succeeded him as rebbe. When Edel was young, Rebbe Shalom would place his yarmulke and *tefillin* [phylacteries] on her head. Later in her life, he would say about her, "My Edel is only lacking the *shtreimel*."[1] He meant that she lacked only the outer mark of a male rebbe, the customary fur hat; otherwise, she is like a rebbe.

Years later, a certain man was about to travel from Belz to Brody, where Edel lived with her husband, Rabbi Yitzhak. Rebbe Shalom said to him, "Please deliver this little bundle in which I've wrapped a silk shawl as a present for my daughter."

The man brought the bundle to Rebbetzin Edel. When she untied it, he saw that there was no silk shawl in it but a silk curtain for the holy Ark in the synagogue.

When he later went back to Belz and to the rebbe, he said, "Holy Rebbe, you made a mistake. You said that there was a silk shawl in the bundle, but there was a silk Ark cover."

The rebbe laughed and said, "Was I wrong? Isn't my Edel a *sefer* Torah?" [a Torah scroll that must be covered with an Ark cover].[2] Edel's rebbe father considered her Torah knowledge and holiness to be equal to that of a Torah scroll.

Rebbe Shalom regretted that Edel had not been born male. He used to say, "The Hidden Light that was to illuminate the whole world[3] is hidden in my daughter Edel. If she were a man, there would be no tzaddik as great as she, and she would certainly have brought the redemption of the whole world. But it was the work of the Satan that she was not born male."

In truth, Rebbe Shalom was troubled about this all his life, and even on his deathbed, when his daughters were asked to leave the room so that their wailing would not disrupt his passing, he said, "Let Edel stay here, because she's not my daughter but my son."[4]

After her father's passing, Edel settled in Brody and set up her own Hasidic court. Many Hasidim came to her holy meals from all around, and they praised her Torah teaching, her responses to *pitka'ot,* and her profound wisdom and understanding. Most people called her "Rebbetzin Edel," but some called her "Rebbe Edel." She was given great honor.[5] ❧

Rebbe Shalom saw his daughter Edel's greatness and expressed his esteem by saying that she lacked only the *shtreimel,* that she was full of divine knowledge like a Torah scroll and could wear the Ark cover like a shawl. It pained him deeply that her light was hidden because of the limitations of his era, which could not accept that women's light be revealed. But when the Hidden Light of women's holiness is manifested, the redemption will come. It jars one today that the rebbe wished she had been a son, considered her a "son," and lamented that the Satan had conspired for her to be a female, for if she had been born a male, she would have brought or been the Messiah. But although the rebbe expressed himself this way because of the limitations of his time, his words also attest to Edel's greatness.

Healing by Faith

❧ A man from Brody was sick with a disease of the lungs and chest, and the doctors said his condition was hopeless. At one point, blood came gushing out of his throat; the doctors said that it was the last remaining piece of his lung, and the moments of his life were numbered.

In a great tumult, his family rushed to Rebbe Edel and told her what the doctors had said.

She replied, "Something like this happened when my holy father, Rebbe Shalom, was alive.

"He said, 'First of all, I don't believe what the doctors said—that he has no lungs left. Second, even if he has no lungs, who says that a person needs lungs? The One who said that we need lungs to live can also say that he can live without lungs!'[6] And that man was restored to health.

"I hope to God that this man too will be restored to health." And so it was, for he was healed and lived for many years after this event.[7] ≈≫

Telling the tale of a miracle that happened in a comparable situation is a mystic technique used by some Hasidic rebbes to produce a similar miracle. Such a tale is like a prayer. Rebbe Edel also offered a brief explicit prayer at the end of the miracle tale she told. She, like her father, did not believe the doctors' negative prognosis. She believed that God rules nature and that if He wills it, a person can live even without lungs. One need not take her remark literally—as if she believed that God might cause this man to live without lungs—but as an expression of total faith—that God could do that if He wanted to. Her prayer, her story, and her faith effected the miracle, and the man lived.

Sadly, we know nothing about Rebbe Edel's relation to her holy mother, Rebbetzin Malka of Belz. Both were clearly exceptional women. Having such a wife and daughter, Rebbe Shalom of Belz could obviously appreciate holy women. With a mother like Rebbetzin Malka and a father like Rebbe Shalom, it is no wonder that they produced a daughter like Edel. In our time, when women are asserting themselves as true equals and spiritual partners with men, there is reason to hope for exceptional children. One such child, God willing, will bring the redemption.

Doubtfully Kosher

⊸ A Hasid of Rebbe Yisrael of Rizhin was once traveling to be with his rebbe on Shabbat when he was delayed on the way and had to spend Shabbat with Rebbe Meir in Premishlan. When he saw the awesome divine service of the Premishlaner, it pleased him so much that he accepted Rebbe Meir as his spiritual master.

After Shabbat, he went to the rebbe and gave him a *pitka* and a large *pidyon* [soul-redemption donation] of one hundred and fifty rubles. The rebbe said to him, "Undoubtedly, you prepared this *pidyon* money for the holy Rizhiner Rebbe!"

"Yes!" replied the Hasid. "But I want to give it to you, Holy Rebbe, and when I'm in Rizhin, I'll give the same amount there too!"

Concerned about taking a *pidyon* originally intended for another rebbe–his good friend, the Rizhiner–Rebbe Meir convened a *beit din* [religious court] of three rabbis to decide whether he was permitted to accept the money. They ruled that it was permitted.

But then Shlomtcha, Rebbe Meir's rebbetzin, walked in and admonished her husband, saying, "You wouldn't eat meat on which a *shayla* [question] was asked of a rabbi! Why will you take money on which a *shayla* was asked?"

Needless to say, Rebbe Meir refused to accept the money.[1] ᐁᐁᐁ

Many scrupulously pious Jews will not eat meat whose kosher status is doubtful and about which a question was asked of a rabbi, even though the meat was finally declared kosher. Why, asked Rebbetzin Shlomtcha, would her husband not be equally strict about which money he accepts? It is often easier to be exacting about religious ritual concerns than about money matters. Shlomtcha needed only to "remind" her holy husband with her pointed remark.

A number of tales and comments connect Rebbe Meir of Premishlan with holy women—this tale about his wife; the following tale about his daughter, who became a rebbe; his remark that Rebbe Shalom of Belz owed his greatness to his wife, Rebbetzin Malka; Rebbe Meir's awareness that Rebbetzin Malka could change a divine decree against the poultry; his comment about the angels clapping in joy at Yenta's candle lighting; and his appreciation for Rebbe Pessia Leah of Zablitov (see "The Future Redemption"). Some men, it seems, can see women's greatness.

Rebbe Miriam Hayya of Shatz

Preparing the Coffee

ᐁᐁᐁ Miriam Hayya was a daughter of Rebbe Meir of Premishlan, who treated her as someone with an elevated soul and revealed to her many awesome secrets that cannot be fathomed by the ordinary human mind.

Once, when Miriam Hayya was still a girl, another tzaddik visited Rebbe Meir, who pointed to the tray of refreshments on the table and said to his guest, "Do you see how my daughter arranged this tray? I tell you, the only thing she's lacking to be a rebbe is the fur hat,

the *spodek!*[1] Notice the kabbalistic intentions she had
in arranging the tray: she put the milk, which is white
and sweet, to the right, which signifies the divine cosmic quality of *heśed* [gentleness]. The black coffee is
dark and bitter, so it's on the left, which signifies *gevurah* [severity]. She put the sugar below them and in the
middle, because it signifies the quality of *tiferet* [beau-
tiful balance]!"[2] ◄◙►

In the kabbalistic Tree of Life, the ten *sefirot* (divine emanations) are
arranged in three columns—right, left, and central. Someone who
knows kabbalistic secrets arranges all things in their proper places.
One mystic goal is to properly balance *hesed* and *gevurah* in *tiferet*.
A kabbalist tries to sweeten (ameliorate) *gevurah* with *hesed* because
an excess of *gevurah* produces adverse events—*dinim* (judgments)—
in a person's life.

◄◙► Because Miriam Hayya, even as a girl, knew about
these hidden matters, she merited performing the task
of preparing her father's coffee every day. One day,
one of her sisters said to her, "Why don't you let me have
the *mitzvah* for once?" So she let her sister prepare the
coffee that day. But when her sister poured the coffee
and offered the cup to her father, he pushed it away and
refused to drink it. He explained to his surprised daughter, "If you want to serve me coffee, you have to know
how! Your sister, of her own, knows that first, one puts
in the coffee, which signifies *dinim;* then one sweetens
it with milk, which signifies *heśed.* But you put them in
topsy-turvy! You first poured in the milk and then the
coffee, so the judgments are floating on top!" ◄◙►

Every act a kabbalist performs—even one that might seem trivial—
has cosmic significance: How the items are arranged on the tray,
whether coffee or milk is poured into the cup first, and so on—all
these actions have reverberations and ramifications that produce
great effects in the larger web of spiritual causality. Yet even as a
girl, Miriam Hayya was an accomplished kabbalist and understood
what was required in every situation.

A Miracle-Working Partner

◈ Miriam Hayya was married to Rabbi Yoel, who became a Hasidic rebbe during the lifetime of his father-
in-law, Rebbe Meir of Premishlan. When Rebbe Meir
passed away, Rebbe Yoel moved to Shatz in Romania.
Even during Rebbe Yoel's lifetime, the secret became
known that the Rebbetzin of Shatz had the power to
perform miracles and that she was a full partner in the
prayers and blessings that Rebbe Yoel offered on behalf
of his Hasidim. In a letter to one of his Hasidim, he
wrote: "I and my wife always mention you for good and
for blessing in our prayers." ◈

How She Became a Rebbe

◈ After Rebbe Yoel passed away, the rebbetzin became
a rebbe in every regard. She also had a female aide.
     Rebbe Miriam Hayya had a cane that belonged
to her holy father, Rebbe Meir of Premishlan, who be-
queathed it specifically to her. From the time that she
inherited it, an air of mystery surrounded that holy
cane, and many stories were told about it. Rebbe Hayim

Mordechai of Nadvorna reported that before Rebbe Miriam Hayya replied to those who spoke to her, she rested her head on the cane; then she answered them. He connected this to the statement in the Jerusalem Talmud about the famous Rabbi Meir the Miracle Worker of ancient times: "The cane of Rabbi Meir was in my hand, and it taught me wisdom."[3]

Rebbe Yisrael of Vishnitz once visited the "rebbe rebbetzin," accompanied by two colleagues—another Hasidic rebbe and a great Torah scholar. During their conversation with her, he asked, "From where do you derive your great power to do miracles?"

The rebbe rebbetzin answered humbly, "For that, I have to thank Leibke the Thief!" Then she told this tale:

"On *erev* Yom Kippur, the custom was for all the Jews in Premishlan to pass before my holy father to receive his blessing of *gemar hatima tova,* 'May your heavenly decree be sealed for good!' One year when I was still a little girl, I was standing in his room at that time. One of the men who entered was a certain dubious character named Leibke, who had a reputation as someone who makes his living by taking others' property. He tried to avoid stealing from Jews, but that didn't excuse his crooked ways. When his turn in line came to be before my holy father, he put out his hand to shake my father's hand and receive a blessing, but my father quickly pulled his own hand back and refused to bless him.

"But Leibke was stubborn and began to cry a flood of tears, as he pleaded and begged the rebbe to bless

him like all the other Jews. He even argued that he was
not to blame if this was the livelihood that heaven had
decreed for him! But my father denied that, saying that
every Jew can choose for himself a decent and upright
way to make a living and that heaven will provide for
him! In the end, after much begging and crying, my father softened and had pity on Leibke. My father covered
his holy hand with a cloth and then held Leibke's hand
and gave him a blessing. [Some exceptionally holy people may experience great pain when coming into physical contact with a grossly sinful person; that is why the
rebbe covered his hand.]

"When I saw my holy father bless this thief," said
Rebbe Miriam Hayya, "I immediately went over to him
and said, 'If a person like this succeeded in receiving
a blessing from you now, it must be a time of special
grace. So I want you to bless me too!'"

"'What blessing do you want?' he asked.

"'That my blessings be fulfilled!' I said.

"And he blessed me!" concluded Rebbe Miriam
Hayya.

It is told that Leibke completely repented after
he received Rebbe Meir's blessing, and that after Rebbe
Meir's death, he was found more than once crying his
heart out on the rebbe's grave.

In 1978, Rebbe Miriam Hayya's grave was opened
and her remains moved from Shatz in Romania to the
Mount of Olives in the Holy Land. ✧

Miriam Hayya asked that her blessings come true, which is the power
of a rebbe. That is how she merited to do miracles and became a

rebbe herself. Why would a little girl ask for that, for the power of blessing? Perhaps because she realized that it was the outward sign of her father's greatness.

But in explaining how she became a rebbe, Miriam Hayya humbly compared herself to an unworthy thief who, so to speak, stole a blessing from her father, the rebbe. Yet despite her holy humility, even as a little girl she was sensitive and realized that it was a time of special grace—when even a thief was accepted—and she was bold enough to ask for what she wanted. May we also be alert to times of grace and know what to ask for at the right moment.

Rebbe Sarah of Chantshin: A High Soul

⋘ Rebbetzin Sarah, the wife of Rebbe Hayim Shmuel of Chantshin, was a great personality in her own right. When she was a little girl of about nine, her mother presented her to a great Hasidic rebbe, Rebbe Yossel, the "Good Jew" of Neishtadt, and told him that her late husband, Rabbi Yehoshua Heshel (a disciple of the Seer of Lublin), had said that their daughter Sarah had an elevated soul.

That evening, when the mother went to put Sarah to bed, she could not find her. She looked everywhere and finally found her hidden away in a corner, crying. When her mother asked why she was crying, little Sarah said, "I heard you say that I have a high soul, and I was praying to God that I at least return it to Him in purity and not blemish it!"

As a rebbetzin, Sarah took care of her rebbe husband's household; she also gave him moral and emotional support. And she was famous for her deeds of kindness and charity. Many times, she pawned her few valuable possessions to borrow money to give to poor people. [How noble, not only to give everything you have to the poor and needy, but even to pawn your valuables to have money for them!]

The rebbetzin was also famous for her piety. Even in her husband's lifetime, he occasionally sent Hasidim to her for her blessing. It is not surprising, then, that after his death, Hasidim began to travel to Chantshin to give Rebbetzin Sarah *pitka'ot* and to seek her blessings. Three times a day, she prayed with a *minyan* that assembled in a room next to hers. When they took the *sefer* Torah from the Ark, they brought it to her to kiss.

When she was almost one hundred years old, she was already a famed and revered rebbetzin who wore the crown of a good name. Once, when her granddaughter came to visit her, a long line of Hasidim was waiting to seek her blessing. Suddenly, the granddaughter saw her grandmother, the *tzaddeket,* crying.

She asked, "Grandma! Why are you crying?"

"Because," the *tzaddeket* answered, "when I was a child, I was told that I have a high soul. So I'm crying and praying to my Creator that I not taint it, and return it to Him in purity!"

For more than ninety years she held on to the same holy thought![1] ❧

Why does a person cry like this? Because he yearns to serve God. Because he longs to fulfill the deepest potential of his soul. When someone has an elevated soul, he is expected to attain great things in the service of his Creator. Did Rebbe Sarah cry all the time? Probably not. Hasidism teaches the way of joy. But there are times, the rebbes say, when we must cry, if we want to attain something spiritually, if we truly yearn to be close to our Creator. The holy Rebbe Sarah was weeping in front of her many Hasidim and her own granddaughter. What was the message they received when they discovered the reason for her tears? What is the message we receive when we hear the tale? May we use the talents and abilities God has given us to our full potential. May we fulfill our purpose in this lifetime.

Sarah Shneirer

Sarah Shneirer was the great founder of the Beis Yaakov movement of religious schools and seminaries (teachers' colleges) for girls and young women.

Tzedaka *in Secret I*

◅◈▻ Among the many blessed deeds of Sarah Shneirer, her kindness and *tzedaka* particularly stood out. And she was always careful—as the Rabbis instruct—to give *tzedaka* secretly, so as not to embarrass the poor person.

Once, she became aware of a certain man who was experiencing great poverty. Passover was approaching, and he was at a loss for what to do; he had absolutely no money and had made no preparations for the holiday.

This man's suffering pained Sarah Shneirer deeply and gave her no rest. She took fifty gulden and began to consider how to get the money to him. It was not simple either, as this man had once been well off and had lost his money, so he would be terribly embarrassed to accept charity.

Sarah went to a well-known community worker, who was an acquaintance of the man's, to ask for his help. "I know that you pray in the same synagogue as so-and-so, who badly needs this money," she said. "Please take this fifty gulden and slip it into his pocket secretly when his coat is on the wall during services, when he's saying the *Shemoneh Esreh* prayer with his eyes closed and won't see you."

When the destitute man put on his coat after the services and found the money in his pocket, he lifted his eyes to heaven to thank God for sending a messenger to save him from his desperate situation.[1] ☙

The man was thankful not only for the money but also for the way it was given and his having been spared embarrassment. Undoubtedly, Sarah Shneirer's sensitive and thoughtful act also inspired him, renewing his will to live and giving him strength to face his difficulties.

Tzedaka *in Secret II*

☙ Sarah Shneirer was devoted not just to every one of her Beis Yaakov students but also to every needy and unhappy person. She spent countless hours trudging from one Jewish home to another to raise charity money for those who required it so badly.

Her acts of charity, which exerted a powerful influence on her students, were typically done quietly and secretly. But from time to time, she would send one of her students out on a mission in order to arouse their feelings of pity and sympathy and to inspire them with a readiness to extend help to any needy soul. At every

opportunity, she emphasized to her students the importance of doing acts of *tzedaka* secretly.

Every *erev* Shabbat, Sarah would give one student
a large sum of money and send her out to distribute it
according to a list of addresses. One *erev* Shabbat, there
was an additional address on the list—a man whom
everyone thought was well off. To the great surprise of
the student, this man was slated to receive double the
normal amount. When the student returned from her
mission, she spoke to Sarah Shneirer about this and
could not contain her admiration at her teacher's generosity to this man.

"I think you're too impressed," said Sarah with
calmness and humility. "After all, isn't he a better
person than me? Who am I? And what big favor am I
doing him?" Then she said, "There's something else you
should know: giving *tzedaka* secretly doesn't mean just
that the poor person doesn't know who gave it or that
other people don't know about it. Giving *tzedaka* in
secret means that it's a secret even from the one who
gives it, and he doesn't think of himself as having done
the other person a favor."

And indeed, with utter simplicity and innocence,
Sarah Shneirer then turned her attention to other matters and completely forgot this whole incident.[2] ≪≫

Alive

Someone once entered Sarah Shneirer's home to ask her about something and witnessed the following exchange, which he later reported.

᷿ It was two in the afternoon. Sarah Shneirer was sitting at the table about to eat her lunch and had just made the blessing over the bread. Sitting next to her were two women, and it was clear from their faces that some catastrophe had just befallen them and they were pouring out their hearts to her.

I was waiting in the kitchen, where Sarah's elderly mother was warming a glass of milk for her daughter. Her mother told me that her daughter hadn't had a bite to eat yet that day. She then began to sigh deeply and said, "They don't let my daughter live. They're wearing her down! She has no time to eat, and even when she sits down to eat, they sit next to her and tell her their troubles!"

In the other room, Sarah overheard her mother's words. She immediately got up, came into the kitchen, and said, "Mother, please don't worry! Everything will be fine, with God's help! They're letting me live. See, I'm alive. I'll live even after I'm dead! These women need my help. I'm going with them now because it's already late for what needs to be done to help them. I'm not hungry, so don't worry about me. Goodbye, Mother!"[3] ᷿

Sarah Shneirer's mother complained that people did not let her daughter live, but Sarah assured her that doing good gave her life in this world and life in the World to Come, as the Rabbis teach: The righteous are called "alive" even after their death.

Good Pay

The same man wrote the following story:

◈ It was the night of *Simhat Torah* 1933, at 10 P.M.
I was lying in bed falling asleep when suddenly my wife
came into the bedroom and woke me up. "Mrs. Shneirer
is here," she said. "She wants to talk to you." I immediately got up, dressed, and went out to the living room.
Sarah Shneirer apologized for coming so late and then
told me why she had come. One of the women teachers
in the school urgently needed our help.

After this, she turned to my wife and said, "If they
wake a doctor in the middle of the night, to save the life
of a sick person, do they also have to apologize to him
and ask him to forgive them? Of course not, because the
doctor gets well paid for what he does! And kind deeds
are so precious, their value simply can't be measured;
they're worth more than all the money in the world!
So please don't be upset that I asked you to wake your
husband. God will pay him well, and the merit of this
mitzvah will protect us all." She then got up, wished us
hag ḳame'ach, "a joyous holiday!" and left.[4]

With exceptional sensitivity, Sarah Shneirer apologized not only to
the husband but also to his wife for asking her to wake him up. Her
apology explains her own motive for running around late at night to
help people: Kind deeds are so precious! And the chance to do a
favor for someone made it, for her, a truly joyous holiday.

The IOU

◈ A poor Jew once came to Sarah Shneirer and complained to her about his difficult situation. His daughter had reached marriageable age, but he did not have

the money or means to marry her off. Sarah listened to him and shared his pain, but she too had no money then. Yet her heart would not let her send him away empty-handed. She did not excuse herself by telling him about her poor financial situation. Instead, she took out an IOU from her desk drawer and wrote out and signed it for the sum of several hundred gulden. The man left her home relieved and elated. But Sarah began to worry about how she would cover the amount of the note when she did not have a penny to her name.

After some thought, she put on her coat, fixed her scarf on her head, and went to the home of one of Cracow's wealthy men, a certain Reb Shalom, who was famous for his tireless activism on behalf of the Jewish religious community. Sarah knocked lightly on the door, and Reb Shalom himself opened it. Seeing this exceptional visitor, he quickly invited her to come in and to sit down and then he asked her the reason for her visit and how could he help her.

Sarah did not delay; she immediately got to the point.

"I came to do some business with you, Reb Shalom. The Holy One, blessed be He, put a *mitzvah* of charity in front of me, and I took care of it. Now I want to sell the reward I earned in the World to Come for this *mitzvah,* for several hundred gulden. Would you like to help me find a buyer?"[5]

At first, Reb Shalom looked at her with disbelief. "What is she talking about?" he wondered. But he knew Sarah Shneirer and knew that she was not joking. So he questioned her until she told him the whole story. She then asked for his advice on how to cover the IOU.

Reb Shalom was very moved by everything she said. "People are right," he thought, "when they say that this *tzaddeket* is a very special woman." He then told her that he himself would pay off the note and took it from her.

Some time later, Sarah ran into Reb Shalom at a Beis Yaakov function and asked him about this matter. He told her that he had already taken care of it. She then took out her diary and showed him that she too had fulfilled her promise. In her diary, she had recorded that he had acquired the *mitzvah* and its reward in the World to Come.

"Oh, no!" protested Reb Shalom. "You signed the IOU. I just paid it off. The *mitzvah* is yours!"

"Oh, well," she said with a smile, "then the Holy One, blessed be He, will just 'pay off' the reward of this deed to you too. And His IOUs are always good."[6] ᦸ

Sarah Shneirer sold the *mitzvah* she had done. The Rabbis say that the spiritual reward of a *mitzvah* is inestimable. How much so is that true of a *mitzvah* done by a *tzaddeket* like Sarah Shneirer! What would the reward of a *mitzvah* done by her be worth in monetary terms? What would its price be?

By her wisdom and goodness, Sarah Shneirer won Reb Shalom's heart and was even scrupulous enough to write down her sale of the *mitzvah* to him. He was so impressed by her that later he could not accept that he had "bought" her *mitzvah*. But if Sarah Shneirer sold the reward of the *mitzvah*, why was *she* doing it? What was her motive? The answer is that her actions were simply for love of God. Because of this, she so inspired Reb Shalom that he too wanted to act only from love and could not even imagine receiving a reward for his act of charity.

The Quality of Voice

❧ One day, Sarah Shneirer was sitting in her room at her Beis Yaakov school but went out after hearing raised voices in the hall. When the children saw their teacher, they immediately became embarrassed and quieted down. Sarah asked them to come closer and gestured for them to sit down on a nearby bench. She then sat next to them and told them this story:

"There was a certain vegetable seller in Lublin named Reb Avraham. He would call out to advertise his produce: 'Jews! Come and buy vegetables, every kind!'

"Once, a certain tzaddik was walking through the market and happened to hear this Reb Avraham touting his vegetables. The tzaddik stopped, listened carefully, and said to himself, 'The voice is the voice of Jacob— I hear holiness in that voice.'

"He investigated, and it was clear to him that this Reb Avraham the Vegetable Man was one of the thirty-six hidden tzaddikim."

Sarah Shneirer finished the story, looked at her students with a gentle smile, and said, "You see, children, we learn from this tale that a person's voice reveals a lot about his character and what's inside him. And whether someone speaks loudly or softly tells even more about him.[7] ❧

According to Jewish legend, there are thirty six "hidden tzaddikim" for whose sake the world remains in existence. In the story Sarah Shneirer told, a "revealed tzaddik," meaning someone whose holy qualities are known, was able to identify a "hidden tzaddik" by the sound of his voice, despite the latter's appearance as a common vegetable seller. Although in the Book of Genesis, the righteous Jacob appeared before his father Isaac disguised as his lowly brother Esau, Isaac still recognized his voice as "the voice of Jacob." Regarding Sarah Shneirer's final remark, perhaps even when Reb Avraham called out about his vegetables, his voice was relatively soft.

Sarah Shneirer wanted to quiet the students down and teach them to be refined and not raucous. But being a gifted teacher, she also wanted to use the opportunity to teach them that a person's voice tells much about him. Loud speech is a sign of pride; soft speech indicates humility. Such character traits can be heard in a person's voice by someone on a high spiritual level. Certainly, Sarah Shneirer's own voice was soft and gentle when she gave this lesson, for, as the Torah says, "The words of the wise, being softly spoken, are heeded."[8]

A Favor

❦ Aside from the heavy burden that Sarah Shneirer took on herself, of establishing a network of Beis Yaakov schools and teachers' colleges in Poland, she was also actively involved in doing deeds of kindness on a large scale. Although she was occupied and even overwhelmed with pedagogical matters during the day, at night she worked with tremendous zeal to help sick and needy people. Still later, in the small hours of the night, she would sit at her desk and send off countless letters to her many students—to strengthen, encourage, and inspire them to labor for the sake of the Torah. Finally, every night before she went to sleep, she sat down and made a "soul accounting" of all her actions during the day. Like other holy Jews, she gave every minute of her life and every ounce of her energy to serve God and help people; she knew no rest.

One of the students whom she raised in her own home tells the following tale:

"Once, at 2 A.M., Sarah was sitting at her desk absorbed in her thoughts, making her soul accounting for that day. I begged her to go to sleep already. After much pleading on my part, she said to me, 'How can I go to sleep when the whole day I didn't do a single favor or kind deed for anyone? How can my soul appear before the Heavenly Court empty-handed?' And she began to sigh deeply. She was upset because she had not had an opportunity to do a favor for someone that day.

"I couldn't bear to think that after a full day of working with all her energy for others, she would sit at her desk like this late at night, troubling herself! So I said to her, 'Mrs. Shneirer, would you like to do a favor for someone right now?'"

"'Yes!' she said with fervor and enthusiasm. 'I'm ready! Quick, tell me who or what!'

"'Do a favor for all your devoted students!' I said.

"She jumped up as if ready to go anywhere needed. 'What, what?' she cried out. 'I'll do anything for them, with all my heart and soul!'

"'Do a favor for your students who'll be learning Torah and religious character lessons from you tomorrow: go lie down in bed right now and go to sleep, so you'll be awake and fresh tomorrow and be able to teach them with a clear head!'"

Sarah embraced her student and exclaimed, "You've given me life by what you've said!" and she immediately began to call out the bedside *Sh'ma* before sleep.[9] ⋙

A Devoted Heart

⋙ Sarah Shneirer once lay down to rest in the afternoon and fell asleep. As the time for the afternoon prayers approached, her students were confused, uncertain what to do. Should they wake her or not? They knew that she was strict about not missing any of the set times for prayer. Nevertheless, they did not want to wake her because they knew that she had not slept the whole previous night and was awake writing letters of instruction and encouragement to all her Beis Yaakov schools.

Meanwhile, dusk was coming on, and a debate ensued among the students. Some of them argued that they should wake her anyway because she would be very angry with them for allowing her to sleep through the time of prayer. Others maintained that it is forbidden to deprive her of such needed sleep. While they were still disputing the issue, Sarah opened her eyes, ritually washed her hands,[10] and stood up to recite the afternoon prayers.

The students were of course happy to see their problem resolved by itself. Afterward, they told her about their confusion and about the debate they had

had about the issue. Sarah said to them, "You worried unnecessarily because in any case I would wake up on time. When a Jew sleeps like a Jew, it's impossible for his sleeping to cause him to be late for prayers. If his heart is truly devoted and dedicated to his Creator, then it acts as his clock to wake him from his sleep, so that he is on time for prayers. For a real Jew, even sleep is a form of divine service, whose purpose is to renew him and give him new energy to serve the Creator."[11] ✺

Under All Conditions

✺ Sarah Shneirer tried never to be late for prayers and never to miss reciting her prayers. She also did her best to pray with a congregation in a synagogue.

On a Shabbat morning during the summer when she and her seminary students were at the Beis Yaakov camp in the country, the skies darkened with dense clouds, and rain began to pour down. The rain did not let up for a minute. The girls decided that this time, they would not go to the synagogue but would pray in the dormitory.

Meanwhile, the rain came pouring down even more strongly, and it started to hail, which only increased the girls' determination not to venture outside.

Then Sarah appeared, dressed in her Shabbat clothes, ready to go to the synagogue, as on every Shabbat.

With all kinds of reasons, the girls tried to persuade her not to go outside in such a storm, but all their arguments were in vain. Sarah would not even consider staying; she was determined to go to the synagogue.

"No, girls!" she said. "Today is Shabbat. We can't pray here; we must go to the synagogue. Congregational prayer is so important and precious to me. Come, let's go pray!"

In the midst of her words, her eyes suddenly began to sparkle, and with a smile wreathing her face, she added, "You remember the verse 'To the House of God let us go with aroused emotion [b'ragesh]'.[12] The Hebrew letters of the word b'ragesh can be interpreted as an acronym standing for *barad, ruach, geshem, sheleg*—hail, wind, rain, snow—meaning that we have to go to God's House under *all* conditions, even when it's raining or snowing or there's hail or a storm outside!"

When she finished speaking, she joined arms with the girls, and together they all walked to the synagogue, with joy and zeal, in the rain, wind, and hail.[13] ❧

From Heart to Feet

❧ When Sarah Shneirer was a young woman, she fled from Cracow to Vienna, where she lived for a period of time during the First World War. Although she was a pious girl who was on fire to save the precious daughters of Israel from assimilation, she was earning a living as a seamstress, but her deeper purpose was to make garments of light for her Jewish sisters.

In Vienna, she met a certain Rabbi Fleish, whose talks and teaching inspired her and helped her find the path to achieve her goal. She became a regular attendee at Rabbi Fleish's synagogue. No circumstance or obstacle could keep her away—not a heavy snow or any other turmoil or tumult, such as the kind that regularly occurred on the streets during the war. Sarah Shneirer always attended her classes with the rabbi, regardless.

One day, when she was sitting in the house absorbed in her sewing, she found that she could not thread her needle. She tried many times, without success. This was quite surprising to her because she was usually quite adept at handling a needle and thread.

Suddenly, she felt an inner impulse directing her elsewhere. She put down the needle and thread, got up from her sewing, left the house, and walked to the synagogue, where she found Rabbi Fleish beginning a lecture.

Only then did Sarah remember that the lecture had been set for that time. She had been so immersed in her sewing that she had totally forgotten!

Yet her legs had carried her by themselves to the synagogue, to the place for which her heart yearned. At that moment, she remembered the saying of the Sages: "To the place that a person wants to go, Heaven leads him."[14] ✍

In the *Midrash*—an ancient collection of rabbinic comments on the Torah—the Sages say that the Patriarchs (and certainly also the Matriarchs) reached a level of holiness so complete that their body, of itself, did God's will without requiring any conscious decision or direction. They also said that when King David left his house to go somewhere, his feet of themselves led him instead to synagogues and houses of Torah study. Sarah Shneirer's heart was so devoted to God that despite her absorption in her sewing and outward forgetfulness, her heart was so on fire for God that it led her feet to the place she wanted to go. May our hearts reach the purity of that fire.

(For another tale about Sarah Shneirer, see "A Fence to Wisdom" earlier in this book.)

Why Did the Milk Boil Over?

⚬ Rabbi Isser Zalman Meltzer was once sitting with his students in his yeshiva, which was adjacent to his house, as they occupied themselves in Torah study. Suddenly, knocking was heard on the door, and in the doorway stood Rebbetzin Baila Hinda, Rabbi Isser Zalman Meltzer's wife, who said to the rabbi, "The milk boiled over!"

The rabbi immediately got up and left the room to go with his wife. Now, traditionally, Torah study must not be disturbed except for the most urgent matters. Rabbi Isser Zalman knew that if his pious wife interrupted their studying in the middle of the session, there must be an important reason. So he immediately got up and went with her, to learn what the problem was.

This occurrence seemed very strange to the students, who were astonished by it. They thought, "The rebbetzin has never disturbed the rabbi in the midst of Torah study. Why did she do so today? And what did she mean by 'The milk boiled over!'? Merely because the milk boiled over, she interrupts the rabbi's session? And why did the rabbi immediately get up and leave? What's going on here? Is there some secret involved?"

Nevertheless, the students continued their studying. "The rabbi will certainly come and explain everything," they thought. "But for now, let's not waste any time. . . ."

After half an hour, the rabbi returned to the yeshiva, sat down, and said to his students, "I know that you're all wondering why I ran out in the middle of the lesson when I heard what the rebbetzin said. I'll explain. When the rebbetzin heated the milk this morning, it suddenly boiled over. She was surprised. Why was she so distracted that she was not paying attention, something that had never happened before?"

(Milk was very expensive in those days. But every day, Rebbetzin Baila Hinda boiled some milk for her husband to drink so that he would get strength from it, for he expended so much energy in his Torah study. And because the milk was so dear, she was always careful to see that it not boil over and some be lost.)

"Although she was standing right next to the stove to watch," continued Rabbi Isser Zalman, "the milk boiled over. The rebbetzin said to herself, 'Certainly Heaven is alerting me to something by this. I'm being sent a hint to search my deeds. Did I unintentionally overlook something and, because of that, the milk boiled over?'

"Suddenly, she remembered the milkman! This milkman had delivered milk to our house for many years," explained Rabbi Isser Zalman. "When he became old, he could no longer work and make deliveries. For a long time now, my wife has been going to his house every *erev Rosh Hodesh* [eve of the New Moon]¹ to give him charity to support him for the whole month.

"She suddenly remembered that a few days had passed since *Rosh Hodesh* and she had forgotten to bring the milkman his money! The milk boiling over reminded her of the milkman! So she immediately came in to tell me, 'The milk boiled over!' And the two of us went to his house to give him his money and to apologize to him for our oversight."[2] ✑

A holy person searches the events of his life for divine messages and hints. A *tzaddeket* may ask herself why she cannot thread a needle (like Sarah Shneirer in the preceding story) or why the milk boiled over, as here. This anecdote also shows that Rebbetzin Baila Hinda had no qualms about interrupting the holy Torah study of her husband and his students because the situation involved another person's welfare and feelings. The rabbi, far from disapproving of her interruption, went together with her to deliver the money and to apologize to the elderly milkman. One has to understand the tremendous importance of uninterrupted Torah study to pious people such as the rabbi and rebbetzin to appreciate the exception they made here. Why did Rabbi Isser Zalman tell his students this whole story? Not only to explain the unusual actions of himself and his wife in interrupting Torah study but also to teach them all these profound lessons—of charity, kindness, and sensitivity.

Sensing Others' Troubles

✑ Esther Rivka Blumenkranz was an eminent pious woman of the old Jerusalem whose door was never locked but was always open wide. Together with her husband, Asher Nisan, she provided a refuge for many people, who found in her home warmth and a tower of light that was suffused with the love of kindness, because she always

welcomed them with a warm smile. New immigrants of
that time found a welcoming first stop at her house when
they arrived in Israel. Her home was also a meeting place
for Torah scholars and a place where rabbis and Hasidic
rebbes were often given lodging. How fittingly symbolic
that her door was never closed except during the cold
days of winter. The rest of the year, a person never even
had to open the door; it was always open.

Just as her door was always open, so was Esther
Rivka's kind heart always open. She constantly thought
about ways to be kind and knew another person's problems even before they were verbally expressed. The
Torah calls this *maskil el dal*–sensing a poor person's
troubles and offering help in a way respectful of the
other person's feelings.

Near Esther Rivka's home was a Talmud Torah
school where a certain poor man worked. The man had
had a hard life but was honest and upright. He married
a crippled woman who also knew suffering. Their wedding was small, simple, and humble. During the cere-
mony beneath the bridal canopy, the bride burst out in
tears when she thought about the poverty that awaited
them in their home. The poor man whispered in her ear,
promising her, "We'll be happy." And they did lead a
happy life together. This man, like many others, found
peace and security in the Blumenkranzes' open house.
They always welcomed him there warmly and regularly
gave him hot drinks and much friendship.

Since his wife could not go to the market to shop,
he would go, and when he went, he would borrow Esther

Rivka's shopping basket, which he always returned the next day. Once, he did not return the basket on the following day. Esther Rivka's special sense told her that if he did not return the basket, it meant that something was wrong with him. So she went to his house to see what was the matter and why he had not come.

When she arrived, she found the couple sitting in their house, broken and in despair. She could see the hopelessness in their eyes, which made clear how great a disaster had befallen them. They told her that all the members of their family had been invited to go on a trip with a relative who was visiting from abroad, except for them, with the excuse that the walking would be too difficult for his wife (she may be crippled, but she could have gone)! They felt that no one needed them or valued them at all. They were so dejected and depressed that they did not even have the strength to leave their house!

The visit of this *tzaddeket,* Esther Rivka, restored this hopeless couple to life and gave them the feeling that someone was thinking about them and valued them and worried about them, that they still had a hold on life in the dark world in which they felt themselves to be. From the moment she entered, their faces changed from sadness to joy, and they were revived. The kindness and sensitivity of this woman who thought about others gave new life to two Jewish souls.[1] ❧

Do we pay attention to the hints and signs that tell us that others near us need our help? Whom do we know that may be sitting now lonely and despairing, hoping that someone remembers them and calls or visits? May we be alert to sense other people's secret suffering and be inspired by this tale about Esther Rivka to help them in a sensitive way.

Pawn

&> Rebbetzin Miriam, the wife of Rebbe Mendel of Vishnitz and the daughter of Rebbe Yisrael of Rizhin, was a great person in her own right. Aside from her Torah knowledge, she was famous for her generosity and *tzedaka.*

Once, a formerly rich widow, who had lost her money, came to Rebbetzin Miriam and asked her help in marrying off the widow's daughter. The bridegroom was threatening to call off the wedding because the widow could not pay the promised dowry.

At that moment, the rebbetzin did not have the money needed. So she pawned all her jewelry and gave the money to the widow.

The next day, she told everybody that all her valuables had been stolen so that no one would know the good deed that she had done.[1] &>

Most people would consider the lack of money as a sufficient excuse to exempt themselves from giving *tzedaka*. Not so someone who yearns for goodness, like Rebbetzin Miriam of Vishnitz. When she did not have the money, she pawned her valuables, like the holy women in several of the tales in this book. The Rabbis teach that the greatest charity is done in secret. Rebbetzin Miriam concealed her deed even from her family.

Coins That Sparkle

In Eastern Europe about two hundred years ago, a Jew who rented a tavern or other property from a landowner and could not pay the rent was thrown with his family into a pit until someone redeemed them.

◅❧ Rabbi Shneur Zalman of Liadi, the first Lubavitcher Rebbe, was once involved in collecting money to redeem someone from captivity. He assessed sums for various Hasidim, among them a certain Reb Gavriel, who was assessed a large amount of money for this important *mitzvah.*

When Reb Gavriel told his wife, the *Hasidah* Hanna Rivka, about the large sum he had been assessed, she went and sold all of her diamonds as well as some of her other jewelry.

She then took the coins, polished them until they sparkled brightly, and sent them to the rebbe, saying, "Among the donations to build the Tabernacle in the desert, there was gold, silver, and copper. But the only things that sparkled were the polished metal mirrors given by the women."[1]

When Rabbi Menachem Mendel Schneersohn, the Lubavitcher Rebbe, told this tale, he explained, "The particular merit of an *eishet hayil,* a woman of valor, is that when she does something, it shines and sparkles. This is so for all matters relating to the home—such as hospitality and the children's education. Although they can also be taken care of by the husband, only when they are done by the wife are they accomplished in the manner of shining sapphires, without any blockage of

the divine light, which shines forth.[2] Moreover, through
the aspect of "a woman of valor" that is in every individual [whether man or woman], meaning the aspect of
accepting the yoke of heaven, the act is elevated; it shines.
This is a preparation for the Time to Come, when all
actions will be elevated.[3] ❧

There is a traditional concept of doing a *mitzvah* beautifully—wearing
a beautiful *tallis,* beautifying one's *sukkah,* and so on. By giving charity in such a beautiful way, Hanna Rivka showed that she was more
concerned about the beauty of devotion than about the beauty of her
personal appearance. The righteous women mentioned in the Torah
who donated their mirrors to build the Tabernacle also placed devotion to God above vanity about their looks. Hanna Rivka reminded the
rebbe that although donations to the Tabernacle in the desert involved large amounts of precious metals, only the metal mirrors given
by the women sparkled. Why? The metal of the mirrors sparkled because it was finely polished. That polishing signified the preciousness
of the *mitzvah* to the giver. Hanna Rivka gave a large amount of money
without begrudging it and considered the *mitzvah* of charity so precious that she actually polished the coins.[4] When a person does
mitzvot and makes contributions to help others in this selfless way,
he also polishes his own soul.

A Disregard for Wealth

❧ Hayya was the daughter of pious and wealthy parents. In her father's house, she was accustomed to great
luxury: she ate on silver plates with golden utensils. She
could have married a rich young man, but she had the
opportunity to marry Rabbi Mordechai of Nadvorna [who
eventually became a famous Hasidic rebbe]. When she
was told of the awful poverty in his parents' home—that

they ate from crude clay dishes and did not own a house or furniture, that everything was the exact opposite of what she was used to in her father's home, she nevertheless chose to pass over the wealth and everything else for his sake, because she knew that nothing material was equal to his Torah knowledge and divine service, as the psalm verse says: "The Torah of Your mouth is better than thousands of gold and silver [coins]."[1]

She had a total disregard for wealth. On one occasion, a Hasid who had been saved by her husband, the Rebbe of Nadvorna—meaning by his blessing, prayer, or his practical advice or help—brought many very expensive gifts of silver and gold to their home as a token of his reverence for the rebbe. When he found that the rebbe was traveling and not at home, he gave the gifts to the rebbetzin.

As soon as this Hasid left, a poor man entered and anxiously told the rebbetzin that he desperately needed help for his marriage expenses. The rebbetzin hardly hesitated: she took all the gifts that she had received minutes before and gladly gave them to the poor man.

When her holy husband returned and heard what she had done, he too was happy, because he too had an open heart and an open hand.

The Nadvorner Rebbe once said, with tongue in cheek, to his daughter-in-law that his rebbetzin used to be a good woman but now she no longer gave a piece of bread to a poor man. When his daughter-in-law looked puzzled, he explained to her that now his wife was so holy, she gave away the whole loaf.

From time to time, people came to the rebbetzin for her blessing and were saved through her.[2] ⋙

It is one thing to choose spirituality over comfort and wealth. It is yet a higher level to transcend these concerns completely, as the rebbetzin did. The rebbe's joking comment about his wife expressed his recognition of her spiritual level: she had formerly been good; now she was actually holy. Most of us are so far from this holiness that it is easy to be stunned by the mere contemplation of her deed. How can a person so utterly disregard wealth?

A *Glass of Water*

The Torah says that the reward for fulfilling the *mitzvah* of honoring one's parents is "length of days," long life.

⋙ Rabbi Yitzhak, the Vorker Rebbe, visited his mother, Yutta, once a year to fulfill the commandment to honor one's mother. His father had already passed away. His mother still lived in his distant hometown, Zelushin, so he could visit only once a year.

Whenever he went to visit his mother, he would sit at the table with her on the holy Sabbath. During one visit, he was sitting together with his mother, and the many Hasidim from the surrounding area who had gathered to be with him crowded around the table. His mother asked him, "Yitzhak, could you please bring me some water?"

Immediately, a Hasid jumped up to bring the water. Devoted Hasidim are always ready and quick to serve their rebbe, since it is taught that serving a holy teacher does more to elevate a person spiritually than even learning his teachings.

But Yutta did not drink the water; she left the glass untouched in front of her on the table. She said, "Yitzhak, I asked *you* to get me the water."

The rebbe got up and went quickly to bring his mother the water.

She then said, "The truth is, I'm not thirsty. I only asked you to get me the water so you could have the merit of doing the *mitzvah* and gaining long life."

Then she turned to the Hasidim and said, "You don't merit to have sons like my Yitzhak by making noodle soup!"[1] ⤬

The rebbe had traveled a distance to fulfill the commandment to honor one's mother—by a visit. His pious mother, Yutta, wanted to give him a further opportunity to fulfill the *mitzvah*—by personally serving her. Just as there is a spiritual reward for personally serving one's rebbe, there is a reward for serving one's parents. The Torah specifies that the reward for honoring our parents is long life.

Loving service to a parent by even the least act, such as bringing a glass of water, extends the parent's life. A parent lives longer when loved and honored by his children. A child also lives longer when he honors his parents—because his vital energies are being properly channeled.

Hasidism explains the Torah's reward of "length of days" for honoring parents in still another way, saying it means that each day will be long because we will live so fully. We are only really alive when we are in touch with our soul. We are so much our parents that only someone who honors his parents can be truly in touch with himself; if you despise your parents, you are despising yourself. For a person who becomes more spiritually "whole" by honoring his parents, each day becomes "long" because it is full of real life; he is more in touch with his soul. Rebbe Yitzhak of Vorki's mother, Yutta, gave him a chance to honor her because she wanted him to live long both physically and spiritually.

This tale also teaches us that sometimes we can give to someone by taking from him, by allowing him to help us and do us a favor. It is often a sign of affection and regard to ask someone for a favor, since you do not ask a favor of someone you dislike. One way to begin a friendship is to ask an acquaintance for a favor.

In her final words, Yutta wanted to explain to her son's Hasidim her peculiar action in asking for water and not drinking it. She expressed herself humorously, but she wanted them to realize that all of her actions vis-à-vis her holy son, when he was a child or now, were intentional and deep, to seek his good in every possible way.

In the Merit of His Mother

⁂ When Rabbi Meshullam Feish Levy, the first Rebbe of Tosh, was a young man, he visited the Tzanzer Rebbe to see if Rabbi Hayim could be his rebbe, his spiritual master.

When he greeted the Tzanzer with a handshake and the customary blessing of "*Shalom aleichem*," the Tzanzer grasped his hands in his own and exclaimed excitedly, "Holy hands! I feel great holiness in these hands! Tell me, where are you from?"

Rabbi Meshullam said, "From the village of Yazeps in the province of Bohemia."

The Tzanzer replied with surprise, "Bohemia is impure, and Yazeps is the most impure! Where did you get your holy hands from?"

"My mother is a good Jew," said the young man.

He attributed everything he had attained spiritually to the merit of his pious mother, Zelda, who was a great *tzaddeket*.[1] ⬥

A Mother's Tears

⬥ Dobrusha, the mother of Rabbi Yisrael Meir, the Hafetz Hayim, was a great *tzaddeket* and exceedingly modest. She was exacting in performing the *mitzvot* and a book of *tehinnot* [supplications] or the Book of Psalms never left her hands for almost the whole day.

Years after her passing, they found in her house her old Book of Psalms, which they brought to Rabbi Yisrael Meir. When he took it in his hand, he poured kisses on it and, with tears in his eyes, turned to the people there and said, "Do you know how many tears my mother, of blessed memory, shed over this Book of Psalms? Every day before dawn, she prayed from it, weeping, that her son grow up to be a good and faithful Jew!"[1] ⬥

Be like My Mother

⬥ Rebbe Yisrael Ber of Vilednik lived about a hundred and fifty years ago when divorce was almost unheard of; it rarely happened. One day, the rebbe was told that the wife of one of his Hasidim had moved back to her parents. He was heartbroken. He called the woman and said, "Your husband loves you dearly. He's reciting psalms in the synagogue the whole night and praying that you come back to him. I'm begging you to return to your husband; he loves you."

"Rebbe," she said, "please understand, I didn't leave my husband because I don't love him! On the contrary, I love him so much! But God didn't bless us with children. And a house without children is more in ruins than the holy Temple. A house without children's laughter, without the crying of children, is so lonely, so empty, I couldn't bear it anymore! So I went home. Rebbe, if you want me to go back to my husband, bless me with children." She was a clever woman, so she added, "Rebbe, bless me to have a son like you."

The Viledniker smiled and said to her, "I'll be happy to bless you to have a son like me, but you have to promise me something. If you will be a mother like my mother, then you'll have children like me.

"Let me tell you about my dear mother, the holy and pure Perl Gutta, of blessed memory. My father left the world when I was only seven. And I had a brother five years old. My mother took care of us by herself. She was so devoted to us! She was so pious and holy!

"Every morning, she went down to the cold basement even during the most frigid days of winter to say the morning blessings. One is not allowed to say holy words in an unclean place, and my mother wasn't sure that the house was clean enough to say the blessings, but she knew that the cold basement was clean!

"She once asked me to hand her a holy book. I knew she didn't read Hebrew, so I was surprised but asked her which one. She said, "Any one." She took the book in her hands, kissed it passionately, and said, 'Holy letters! I'm begging you to pray to God in heaven that my son Yisrael Ber grows up to be a pious Jew!'

"Once, my mother was very sick. But she rolled out of bed and crawled over to the table on which there were some Torah books. She took a book in her holy hands and cried out, 'Master of the world, Father in Heaven, I'm very sick. But You know that if I won't take care of my children, nobody else will care for them. I can't read Hebrew! But for the sake of these holy books, for the sake of the holy letters, Master of the world, make me well!' I swear to you, she got up and she was well!

"One more story about my mother. Can you imagine how many tears my mother shed, how many prayers she offered, when she kindled her Sabbath candles? When I was a little boy, I was certain that the only one who prayed more than my mother was the high priest on Yom Kippur in the holy of holies! One Friday, she was crying so much, she bent over the candles and her tears fell on them. When she opened her eyes, it was already the Sabbath, and her tears had extinguished the candles. My mother said, 'Master of the world, holy Father in Heaven, I can't bear it without the light of *Shabbos*! Master of the world, how can I have *Shabbos* without my *Shabbos* candles! But it's already *Shabbos,* so I'm begging You, Master of the world, please . . . You, You Master of the world, rekindle my *Shabbos* lights!'" The Viledniker said, "I swear to you, I saw a hand come down from heaven and kindle those *Shabbos* lights!"[1] ⚜

Ungrammatically Correct

≈⊗≈ Rebbetzin Hayya Mushka, wife of the third Rebbe of Lubavitch, Rabbi Menahem Mendel, was forever reciting psalms, but with many mispronunciations.

Once, she commented to her son, Rabbi Yehuda Leib, "You know, it's strange. By now I should know the whole Book of Psalms by heart. I've been reciting the psalms every day for many years now."

"True," said Rabbi Yehuda Leib, "but each time you recite them with new mistakes."

The rebbetzin related this exchange to her husband, adding that perhaps she had better stop her custom of constantly reciting psalms, rather than distort the holy words.

"No," insisted Rabbi Menahem Mendel, "continue to recite as before."

Later Rabbi Menahem Mendel admonished his son and instructed him to ask his mother for forgiveness. "What do *you* know?" he told him. "My success at the St. Petersburg conference in frustrating the czarist plan to forcibly assimilate the Jews was in the merit of your mother's psalms!"[1] ≈⊗≈

What pious humility that Rebbetzin Hayya Mushka was ready to cease reciting psalms rather than mangle holy words! Yet her rebbe husband knew that her ungrammatical psalms were more spiritually potent than his own Torah expertise and holiness.

Which Blessing to Give

✦ The Hafetz Hayim's wife, Frayda, was a very pious woman who ran a small store so that her husband could study Torah undisturbed. Frayda was uneducated and did not even know how to write, but she was very intelligent and goodhearted to those who were suffering. She made do with little and never asked anything of her husband except for him to perfect himself in Torah and divine service.

The Hafetz Hayim used to say to his son, Arye Leib, "I have your mother to thank for the little Torah I've acquired, because she is satisfied with the minimum and has never asked me for new clothes, a nice house, and so on."

"I remember," writes Rabbi Arye Leib, "when my mother went with me to a clothing store to buy a new suit for my wedding. This storekeeper had a habit to always bless the customer when he was measuring the garment. So he blessed me that I wear the suit with success, that I become rich and successful in business. My mother became angry and said to him, "Who asked you for this blessing? Bless him to be a great Torah scholar and to be pious!"[1] ✦

Every mother wants blessings for her son or daughter. But which blessing she desires makes an impression on the child. Having a mother with these spiritual values forms a lasting imprint. Rabbi Arye Leib never forgot this incident and reported this tale many years later. And he became a pious Torah scholar in part, certainly, because of his holy mother, who was not ashamed to scorn materialism.

The Secret of the Yarmulkes

About a hundred years ago, the house of the *tzaddeket* Rebbetzin Leah was located in one of the poor lanes of Jerusalem. Like many other Jerusalem families in those days, her family lived in poverty and deprivation. But Leah knew how to knit fine-looking yarmulkes, and she was able to support her family. How were her yarmulkes different from others that were sold in the market, so that the mothers of Jerusalem ran to buy hers? The pious women saw that Leah's children were well behaved and succeeded in their Torah studies more than other children. They were truly pious, like little tzaddikim, and all the other women of course envied her. This was not the bad envy but the good kind, which the Rabbis call "envy among scribes" and which leads a person to strive for greater piety. What mother would not want her children to be pious and pure like Rebbetzin Leah's children?

When the other women would ask her, "Rebbetzin Leah, what is your secret? How did you succeed so well with your children (may there be no evil eye!) that they're so good?" Leah the *Tzaddeket* would answer humbly, "My children are like all children. Are there any children that don't sometimes misbehave?"

Possibly, her secret and the secret of her children's piety and goodness would have remained concealed, except for a particular incident that happened. One of her children was playing with a friend in the common courtyard. The mother of the other boy was sitting nearby, cleaning beans and inspecting them for insects, when she overheard Leah's son say to her son, "Exchange yarmulkes? No! Why should I do that? I don't want to exchange my yarmulke for one bought in a store, even for a minute!"

"What makes your yarmulke so special that you don't want to trade with me?" asked the neighbor's son.

"Of course, my yarmulke's special!" said the boy innocently, his big eyes flashing. "Do you know what my mother told me when she gave it to me? She said that every yarmulke she makes has four rows of knitting. And for every row she knits, she recites a psalm. And when she finishes knitting the yarmulke, she sheds tears into it and prays, 'In the merit of the psalms that I recited while knitting, may my children and all Jewish children be pious!'"

The neighbor took in every word that this exceptional boy spoke. In just a few hours, every woman in the Jerusalem neighborhoods knew Rebbetzin Leah's secret, and they ran to her to buy her yarmulkes for their children. What mother wouldn't give her last few coins for her child to be pious?[1] ❦

According to the Jewish tradition, all work should be holy work in the service of God. A devout person has divine intentions as he labors. How much more should that be true for people producing religious articles. Religious objects are not like ordinary objects. A yarmulke, for example, has a vibration that affects its wearer. There is a difference between a yarmulke made by a pious person who has prayerful, holy thoughts while making it and a machine-made object or an object created by a person without pious thoughts and motives.

Religious people who want the true benefit of a yarmulke, *mezuzah,* or any other holy item are willing to pay for the careful labor of pious people, for what they create radiates holiness. Rebbetzin Leah's yarmulkes were actually holy vessels to transmit her prayers and her tears for the spiritual growth of Jewish children.

Pure Thoughts

⪧ In the days of Rebbe Yisrael of Rizhin, there was a very sharp Torah scholar named Rabbi Reuven Odesser. Once, he was not able to understand a particular passage in the writings of the Rambam [Maimonides]. He asked all the Torah scholars of his generation about it, but no one could answer his question.

One day, some of his colleagues jokingly said to him, "Go and ask the Rebbe of Rizhin." Now, it was well known—and a joke to the Torah scholars—that Rebbe Yisrael, the famous Rizhiner Rebbe, did not know how to study Torah on the level of expert scholars, and in fact, he was never seen studying. Regardless, Rabbi Reuven thought, "Why not?" and went to visit the Rizhiner.

He took the book with him and read the difficult passage aloud to the Rizhiner. The Rizhiner said to him, "Read it again." Then, in the middle, he said, "Stop there! Now everything will be clear."

Rabbi Reuven had not been reading it correctly; realizing that there was a break in the middle changed everything.

Then the Rizhiner recited the whole passage of the Rambam by heart, correctly, until Rabbi Reuven's

eyes lit up with wonderment and delight. He was astonished. "Why do people say that you don't know how to
study?" he asked.

"For that you have to ask my mother," replied the
rebbe.

Rabbi Reuven's curiosity was aroused. He went
into the room of the rebbe's mother and asked her,
"How is it that your son the rebbe is able to understand
and explain the Torah so well when no one ever sees
him studying?'"

"Do you know how to study?" asked Rebbetzin
Havva.

"Yes," he said.

"*Nu,* so tell me: the Sages say that an angel teaches
the baby in the womb the whole Torah. They also say that
after it's born, an angel taps it on the mouth, and the
child forgets what it learned. Are these two different
angels or one?"

Not knowing what to answer, he said to her, "You
tell me!"

"They're two angels," said Rebbetzin Havva with
authority. "But how is the second angel, that makes the
baby forget, created? [According to the Rabbis, certain
angels are created by the deeds of human beings. Today
we might say that our deeds create "vibrations" that
later affect us and others.] It's created from the last
thought the parents have at the moment of conjugal
union. Believe me when I tell you that neither I nor my
husband had any low or unworthy thought at that moment; so with us, that angel was not created at all. That

is why my son, Yisrael, remembers everything he
learned from the first angel."[1] ⋙

To remember God at the moment of greatest physical pleasure
means that one remembers Him at every moment. A couple who
achieves that—like Rebbetzin Havva and her husband, Rebbe
Shalom of Prohobitch—is destined to have holy children.

Guarding His Studying

⋙ One winter Shabbat night in Jerusalem, a mother
and her son were sitting together at the table—Rebbetzin
Leah Atiya and her only son, Ezra, a yeshiva boy. The
rebbetzin had been widowed now for a number of years,
so the two had eaten only a meager Shabbat meal.
Rebbetzin Leah was a great *tzaddeket* who was totally
devoted to her son's Torah study. After Ezra sang
zemirot [Sabbath table hymns] and spoke words of
Torah before his mother at the table, he opened up a
volume of the Talmud and began to study.

In those days, there were no electric lights; only
candles or kerosene lamps were used. On the widow's
table, a kerosene lamp provided light as Ezra studied
Torah with diligence and zeal. His whole being was
absorbed in Torah study; he was full of fervor when he
immersed himself in the Talmud's holy pages.

His mother sat opposite him, her heart happy and
expanded within her. If not for his Torah study, life
would have no taste for her. She watched her precious
son, who devoted all his time to God's Torah, turning

nights into days. Watching him study, she felt enveloped in a great and boundless joy.

This was not the only Shabbat night that the mother sat opposite her son and felt joy in his studying; this was her custom every Shabbat. This *tzaddeket* knew the *halacha:* "A person must not read on Shabbat night by the light of a candle, lest he inadvertently move the oil toward the candle in order to increase the light"— thereby doing work on the holy day of rest. She knew that on Shabbat night, it was forbidden for her son to sit alone studying by the light of the lamp, lest when immersed in study, he unthinkingly move the lamp toward him to increase the light. So she sat opposite her son every Shabbat night for hours so he could study.

Although weary, she pushed off sleep. She never said to him, "I'm tired. I worked so hard today." On the contrary, she tried to look alert and would say to him, "Don't worry about me. I slept well the whole week, and I'm not tired at all. It gives me great pleasure to see you studying. Please don't stop. . . ." Because of his mother's words, Ezra would continue studying with great zeal and devotion. He knew that his diligence gave her great joy and *nahas* [gratification].

One Shabbat night, Rebbetzin Leah was very fatigued. She sat opposite her son as always and guarded his studying so that he did not accidentally move the lamp. Her eyelids involuntarily closed from time to time as she dozed off, but she tried to overcome her tiredness and drowsiness, although this night it was difficult for her.

Suddenly, Ezra lifted his head up from the Talmud and, noticing that his mother had dozed off, immediately closed the book. "I'll stop now," he thought; "it's forbidden to study if my mother's not awake." In her sleep, the mother sensed that her son had closed the book because she no longer heard the chant of his studying. She immediately opened her eyes and said, "Please forgive me, my son; I dozed off a little, but I'm awake now. Continue studying. I'm not tired anymore."

"Please, Mother," said the boy, "you're tired; go to sleep now."

But she refused and begged him, "Please, my son, it's too early to sleep. I just dozed off a bit. Don't stop studying. I promise you that as long as I'm alive, I'll guard your Torah studying every Shabbat night. I wouldn't be able to sleep if I thought that because of me, you couldn't study Torah." Ezra knew that if he stopped studying because of her, he would cause his dear mother real grief, so he opened the book and immersed himself once again in the sea of the Talmud. The mother, whose fatigue seemed to have disappeared, guarded his studying and watched him so that he not move the lamp.

The *tzaddeket* Leah, who totally devoted herself to her son's studying and denied herself sleep for his sake, merited to see him become a great and awesome Torah scholar and sage. He was Rabbi Ezra Atiyah, one of the greatest Torah giants of earlier generations.[1] ◄◊►

This poignant tale shows how a devoted mother has a full share in her studious son's Torah knowledge. Many parents make great sacrifices for their children. They work hard to provide a good secular education for their children so that they will be able to make a good living. But for Rebbetzin Leah Atiya, sacrificing so that her son would know Torah, so that he would know the meaning of life and be connected to the living God, was even more important.

Revelations

According to Jewish tradition, since Elijah the Prophet ascended into heaven alive and never died, he can return to earth to make visits. It is said that he mystically appears at two events: during the Passover *seder* and at a *bris.*

Toward the end of the *seder,* the door of the house is opened, because Passover night is said to be a time when Jews have miraculous protection from their enemies. According to legend, Elijah the Prophet enters then to drink wine from the special cup set out for him on the table. Everyone rises and recites the verse that begins "Pour out Your wrath . . . ," invoking God's anger against persecutors of the Jewish people.

Elijah, who was zealous for God's covenant with the Jewish people, also visits every *bris,* and the *sandak* sits in the Chair of Elijah, holding on his lap the baby boy to be circumcised.

When the *tzaddeket* Sarah Devorah was married to her second husband, Rebbe Asher of Karlin, she took with her her daughter Leah, who was then a little girl. Leah's grandfather, Rebbe Aharon of Karlin, was very fond of her.

One Passover night, the whole family was reclining at the *seder* table. When they opened the door to recite *Shfoch hamatcha,* "Pour out Your wrath," from the *Haggadah,* little Leah cried out, "Look at the old man who's come!"

The next day, when the Hasidim came to know
of what had happened, they began to ask the little girl
what the old man had looked like—the one she had seen
the night before. They pointed out many men to her and
asked, "Did he look like this man? Or that man?"

The girl answered, "He was very, very handsome!"

A year later, Leah's mother gave birth to a baby boy.
Rebbe Elimelech of Grodzitsk, Leah's other grandfather
(the mother's father), also came to the *bris*. When they
brought the baby into the synagogue, it was full of people. The little sister, Leah, was also there, standing near
her grandfather, Rebbe Aharon. Suddenly, pointing to
where no one was standing, she called out, "Grandpa,
look! There's the old man again!"

Rebbe Aharon bent over and whispered into the ear
of his in-law, Rebbe Elimelech, "Our little granddaughter's already had a revelation of Elijah twice!"[1] ◈

According to the mystic tradition, some Jewish mystics merit "revelations of Elijah," who appears to them and teaches them the Torah's
secrets. But even to see or greet Elijah is considered a great honor
and a sign of spiritual attainment. This little girl Leah must have been
very special—very pure and of great faith—to have had these two revelations of Elijah at the Passover *seder* and at her brother's *bris*.

Maxine

Stories about visions of Elijah are not only a thing of the past. The
following contemporary story was told by Rabbi Shlomo Carlebach.

◈ A few years ago, on the day after Passover, I had
the privilege of giving a concert for Hadassah [a Jewish
women's organization] of New England. The concert

was wonderful, but when I spoke about Judaism, the women seemed uninterested in spiritual things. Sometimes, you say something and you don't even know why you said it. I said to them, "My dearest ladies. I don't know if you saw Elijah the Prophet. To tell you the sad truth, I didn't see him either. But I swear to you, the children saw him. What a privilege to be mothers of children who saw Elijah the Prophet."

Afterward, one of the women came up to me and said, "Do you know what you said? I can testify to it. My husband is a psychiatrist. Passover night, we have a little *seder*. This year my husband called me up on the phone to tell me, 'All this hocus-pocus is getting on my nerves.' Now, we have a little girl, Maxine. He said, 'Maxine will ask me four stupid questions and I'll have to answer. It's stupid, the whole thing makes no sense. Let's just eat dinner and that's it.' So I said, 'You're right. I don't care so much either.'

"About three o'clock in the afternoon, my little girl Maxine came home from school. Her eyes were glowing with joy. She said, 'I can't wait for my friend Elijah the Prophet to come visit me. Do you know Elijah the Prophet is coming tonight to see me?' I realized that I couldn't do this to her. I called my husband in his office and said, 'Listen, we have to have a little *seder* because Maxine is so excited about it.' He said, 'OK, we'll have a little *seder*; she can ask the Four Questions, I'll mumble a few words. But that's all.'

"My husband came home annoyed and said, 'Maxine, let's go. Ask the Four Questions.' She asked

them, he mumbled a few words, and then we ate dinner.
Then my husband said to Maxine, 'Now go to sleep so
you'll get to school tomorrow on time.' She said, 'Daddy,
Elijah the Prophet is coming to see me.' This was too
much for my husband. He said, 'We are not old-fashioned
Jews who believe in fairy tales. We are modern Jews.
We don't believe in fairy tales. Go to sleep right now.'
My little Maxine ran to the window. In her whole life,
she never cried so much. I walked up to the window and
said, 'Maxine, why are you crying so much?' She said,
'Mommy, can't you see Elijah the Prophet standing by
our door, crying?'"

[Rabbi Shlomo Carlebach concluded:] I just hope
that wherever this little Maxine is now, she still waits
for Elijah the Prophet. So many of our children are so
holy. They are all matzah children.' Sadly enough,
we put *chametz* [leavening] into them. Our excuse is, we
want them to rise. We want them to be higher, more
civilized. That is not what we need. We all need to be
matzah *Yidden,* Jews who have real faith.' ⬧⟶

Usually, Elijah the Prophet appears to mystic adepts. But he also
appears to children because of their matzahlike humility and innocence. (The flat, unleavened matzah is often considered a symbol
of humility.) The Rabbis said that after prophecy ceased in Israel,
children were still receptive to divine communication. How can we
attain spiritual insight? How can we open our eyes to see the divine
reality? One vital aspect of the mystic path is *temimut,* pious simplicity. When we are as childlike as a little girl like Maxine, we too
will see the Truth.

Two Cups

⚛ Rabbi Shalom Sharabi, one of the great kabbalists of the nineteenth century, made *aliyah,* moving to Jerusalem from Yemen.[1]

When he was a young man, he sat day and night studying Torah. A poor devout woman, simple but good-hearted and refined in soul, was a maid in his home. She helped the rabbi's wife, Hanna, with the housework and did so willingly and lovingly. Occasionally, she prayed from the depths of her heart, thanking God for giving her the honor of serving in a holy house like this, where the *Shechinah* was present.

From time to time, she served Rabbi Shalom Sharabi himself. She would make him a cup of coffee, which he enjoyed and which kept him alert as he studied Torah late at night. She would quietly bring the cup in to the tzaddik, leave it on the table near him, and exit quickly and quietly so as not to disturb his holy thoughts.

One night, the rabbi was sitting studying as always when this maid opened the door and brought in two cups of coffee on a tray. She gently put the tray down on the table and turned to leave.

But the rabbi asked her to wait and said, "Why did you bring in two cups today?"

Trembling, with her eyes lowered in embarrassment, she haltingly explained, "I heard two voices in your room, and when I peeked in, I saw a very dignified guest—whose face was so glorious, it shone—sitting next to you. So I decided to bring in a second cup for him. But I don't know where he's gone now."

Rabbi Shalom Sharabi was very moved that this maid had seen what others could not see. He stood up and said to her, "Know that you've merited to see today while awake the one about whom it is said: 'Happy the person who sees him even in a dream.' So you are worthy to know that this was Elijah the Prophet, may he be remembered for good, who regularly visits me to teach me. But I must ask you, my daughter, not to reveal this to anyone." Rabbi Shalom was anxious lest his revelations of Elijah become public.

The maid was thrilled and excited by the rabbi's words—at knowing that she had merited this exalted experience. But she was bold too, and said, "I'll keep this secret—if the holy rabbi will please grant my wish by promising me, in writing, that I be permitted to serve him in the next world too."

The rabbi agreed, wrote her a note, and told her, "Guard this note well, and when your time comes, leave instructions that it be buried with you." She took the note and left.

In 1871, the rabbi's wife, Rebbetzin Hanna, passed away. According to the rule of the kabbalists at that time in Jerusalem, a Torah scholar was forbidden to live without a wife. So after the mourning period, Rabbi Shalom Sharabi married the maid, this *tzaddeket.*

But she too did not live long, and she passed away during Rabbi Shalom's lifetime. On the day of her death, men from the Holy Burial Society came to take her body for burial, but a miracle took place: Her body became so heavy that it was immovable. Confused, they went to Rabbi Shalom and asked him what to do. After pondering the situation briefly, he told them, "Certainly, this *tzaddeket* doesn't want to leave the house without the note I gave her. So search for the note, put it in her hand, and everything will be fine."

They found the note and put it in her hand. Then Rabbi Shalom Sharabi whispered something in her ear. They then lifted her with ease and carried her to the cemetery, where they buried her with great honor.

She is buried in the section of the cemetery reserved for the pious, her grave being next to that of the holy Rabbi Shalom Sharabi. On her gravestone there is no writing, not even her name.[2] ◄❧

This maid saw Elijah the Prophet because she was spiritually elevated by her household work, just as the rabbi was elevated by his divine service of Torah study. Her pure devotion to God, expressed in her devotion to the rabbi, led to her mystical experience. Indeed, she found her service in this house where the *Shechinah* dwelled so spiritually rewarding that she even wanted to serve the rabbi in the next world.

The tale ends with the somewhat surprising note that her gravestone has no name. Undoubtedly, those who saw her unmarked grave next to the grave of the great kabbalist, Rabbi Shalom Sharabi, were surprised. Presumably, the lack of a name on the stone relates to her humble status as a maid. But who can know the true explanation? Her grave in Jerusalem symbolizes all those holy women whose names have been lost.

Pessia Carlebach and the Gentile Maid

⮞ Rabbi Naftali and Rebbetzin Pessia Carlebach, the parents of the late, famed Rabbi Shlomo Carlebach, lived in Vienna. They had a gentile maid, and Rebbetzin Pessia Carlebach noticed that various items seemed to be disappearing from the house. She also saw that when the maid left on Friday before Shabbat, she always carried a suitcase. One Friday, Rebbetzin Pessia asked the maid, "What's in that suitcase?"

"Nothing," said the maid.

"I must look," Pessia said. Inside there were items the maid had stolen from the house.

Rebbetzin Pessia said to her softly, "You're only seventeen. If you're stealing now, what will become of you? Once you start stealing, you won't be able to stop, and eventually you'll end up in prison. If you need something, don't steal. Ask me, and I'll give it to you."

The maid, who was frightened at being caught, was very touched by Rebbetzin Pessia's mild reaction and gentle words. She became attached to her heart and soul and said, "I would die for you."

Two weeks after this happened, the Nazis entered Vienna. They immediately arrested every Jewish girl over fifteen on the pretext that they would have to clean the barracks being prepared for the German soldiers. But something else might also be required. The Carlebachs were terribly afraid for their sixteen-year-old daughter, Shulamith. Their gentile maid went to the

Nazi officer in charge and said to him, "You don't have to arrest her. I'll go in her stead."

The Nazi said to her, "You, an Aryan girl, are ready to go in place of this Jew?"

She said, "These Jews are good people."

This maid was actually beautiful. He said to her, "If you go out with me tonight, I'll let her off. I have to bring her in, because of my superiors, but I'll immediately let her go home." The maid went out on a date with the officer. The next day, they arrested Shulamith Carlebach but soon brought her home on a scooter. The German officer then became a boyfriend of the maid.

Some weeks later, he told the maid that they were going to arrest Rabbi Naftali Carlebach in two days. They would almost certainly kill him because he was a rabbi. But their policy was that if they came to arrest someone and he was sick, they waited until he was well and then arrested him. So if the rabbi could manage "to be sick," he would buy time to arrange a way to escape.

Rabbi Naftali asked his doctor for some kind of pill to make him seem sick, and the doctor complied. The next day, fifteen German soldiers with guns drawn came to the Carlebach home, and when they went in to the rabbi, they saw that he was in bed. He actually appeared very sick. "He's sick," the one in charge said; "we'll come back later."

After that, the Carlebach family arranged an escape—all because of Rebbetzin Pessia's compassion, which had transformed the young gentile maid.[1] ◈

He Who Would Live Should Die

⊸ Miriam Levy was in Florida for a brief vacation and, walking along the boardwalk, saw a group of elderly ladies sitting on two benches. On the spur of the moment, she said "Hello" to them, and one of the women returned her greeting and moved over to make room for her on the bench. She introduced herself as Sima Rachel Neiman, and told Miriam that all of them, who were residents of Miami Beach, were Hungarian survivors of the Holocaust. Now they spent their days trying to help the sick and the old. Miriam asked Mrs. Neiman, "Where do you find these needy people?" and she answered simply, "They have my telephone number."

Miriam was impressed by Mrs. Neiman and asked her if they could meet again. Although she was interested in Mrs. Neiman's charitable work, she sensed that her experiences during the Holocaust would be intriguing, and they proved to be so. This is Mrs. Neiman's story:

"In 1944, when I was a young girl, I was deported to Auschwitz with my family. There were seventy other Jewish men and women in our transport. Stuffed into a cattle car, we had hardly any food or drink for four days and four nights. When the train finally stopped and we emerged, there was a Nazi standing there. I had no idea at that time that it was the monstrous Dr. Mengele who was directing the elderly people and the children to the left, and the young and healthy-looking people to the right. I can still see his finger pointing and hear his cruel voice: '*Recht—links—recht—links.*' I wanted to stay with my grandmother and my younger brothers and sisters, so I went with them to the left side, not realizing, of course, what this meant. Suddenly, I saw that one of my younger sisters had been sent to the right side—the only one from my family—and she looked so alone and frightened, so I quickly moved to the right side to be near her. Dr. Mengele did not notice this. This action saved my life. Because of it, I am alive today and have lived to have children and grandchildren.

"My sister and I were sent to a work camp in Auschwitz. I had taught myself to speak a very good German and, since I was blond and blue-eyed as well, the guards did not believe that I was Jewish. They thought I was a political prisoner and offered me extra privileges if I would agree to be a block supervisor, but I refused. I told them that I was a Jewish girl and I wanted only to be with my fellow Jews. I felt that it would be better to die than to be known as a German girl. *If you want only to live, then you die, but if you are ready to die for a cause, then you live.*

"I decided that I would try to help others as much as possible. I volunteered to go to the so-called kitchen very early in the morning and bring back the food, which was kept in very large containers that served two hundred people. I had to push these containers with superhuman strength to bring them into our camp. While I was in the kitchen, I used to grab a little pot of coffee when no one was looking and bring it to the weaker people, who waited for me anxiously. The people were so happy to see me with the coffee that they could not control

themselves and would push to get to me. There was a
woman in our barracks who had warned me that if I woke
her up too early in the morning—by bringing in the coffee
and causing a commotion—she would punish me. One
morning when I came in with the coffee, she took some
excrement from a nearby trough and threw it at me. It
was freezing cold and I rushed to a place where there was
some water, washed my dress as best as I could, and
then, in the soaking wet dress, had to stand in line until
we were all counted. It was a miracle that I survived.

"There was a man from our town, a friend of my
father's, nearby—just two strips of barbed wire separated
us. I passed by there one day and he called out to me.
He was ill with malaria, he told me, and asked if I could
somehow get him more food. I went to all the women
from our town and they each donated a spoonful of their
meager rations. I collected enough to fill a cup. I managed to bring this cupful of extra food to him every day.
One day an SS officer caught me and shouted, "What are
you doing here?" I told him that the man was hungry,
and that I was bringing him food. He could have killed
me, but he only snarled, 'Verschwinde!—Get out of here!
Aren't you afraid to die?' But again God performed
miracles for me and kept me alive.

"I had one possession that I prized over everything else—more than food or clothing. It was a small
siddur that my father had once given to me. It had the
Book of Psalms in it and, on the inside cover, a list of
all the festivals of the year and their dates. It also contained the weekly Torah readings and the Haggadah of

Passover. I had smuggled it into the camp at the risk
of my life and kept it hidden during the entire day.
Although my group knew about the *siddur,* everyone
kept my secret. At night, after we had been counted and
were supposed to be sleeping, I would take it out and recite psalms aloud in Hebrew, translating each sentence
for the others in my barrack. This gave all the women
courage and inspiration, and kept us going.

"One night, when I looked at my *siddur,* I realized
that it was the day before Passover. I told the others that
we would be having a *seder* the next night. They didn't
understand how I could say such a thing, since we
didn't have any wine or food for Passover, but the next
night we all gathered together and sat in a circle on the
floor. I then told them that we would have to imagine
everything that I would read to them from the *Haggadah.* First, we lit the candles in our imagination.
Then I made *kiddush* and we pretended we were drinking the wine. We pretended to eat the matzah and the
other special foods, and I read the *Haggadah* to them
and explained each paragraph for those who didn't
know it. I'm sure that everyone of us who was there at
that time will never forget that Passover *seder.*[1] ⚜

The Rabbis taught, "He who would live should die, and he who would
die should live." The Torah says, "Charity saves from death." Sima
Rachel Neiman illustrated the truth of these teachings. But even if she
had died for her kindness, she still would have lived, for only goodness is true life. She led a Passover *seder* in Auschwitz where much
was imagined. But the *seder* of that group of Jewish girls was more
real than any at which most Jews will ever recline.

Golda and Miriam

⧽ During World War II, two sisters and a brother
were arrested in their small Polish town and sent to
Auschwitz. The two girls were named Golda and Miriam,
and the boy, Shmuel. At Auschwitz, the men and the
women were separated; they were in two different parts
of the camp kept apart by barbed wire fences.

Golda realized that her brother, with the other
men, was being forced to perform hard slave labor for
the Nazis and that he might not survive, eating only the
subminimal rations provided. So each day, she threw
her bread ration over the fence to her brother. Her sister Miriam and their friends each took a little portion
of their ration and gave it to her so she would have
something to eat. This went on for a few weeks.

But Golda began to feel guilty at having her sister
and their friends deprive themselves of even a small portion of their food because she wanted to help her brother.
Finally, she decided what to do: She began to stand on the
bread line twice. This was of course risky and also dan-
gerous. But everything went well for two weeks.

Then, one day, as she came for the second time
to the table where the bread was distributed, a husky
female German camp guard whom they called Berta the
Brute yelled at her, "You filthy Jew! You're a thief! You're
on the line a second time. I recognize you. I saw you
here earlier!" She then punched Golda in the face and,
when she fell down, began to beat her with a whip.

Miriam and all the other women were watching, terrified. With every blow that fell, Golda screamed, and her sister Miriam screamed silently. Then Miriam remembered a tale she had been taught in the former good days in her Beis Yaakov school, about a man who had been sentenced to be executed by the king for breaking into the palace. His best friend, who knew that the charge was false and that he was innocent, confessed to the crime to save him.

Miriam, who looked somewhat like her sister, jumped forward and yelled, "Leave her alone! It was me; I did it!"

Berta then left Golda and turned her attention to Miriam. She began to pummel and whip her.

But then Golda got up and began to scream, "No! She's lying. It was me! She's only saying that to save me!"

Once again, Berta turned back to Golda. But then Miriam yelled, "No. She's lying!" Each sister was yelling.

Berta looked from one to the other, as if confused and stunned. And she turned and began to walk away. The women who were nearby said that they saw a tear running down her cheek.

The truth is that if the God-people would love each other as they should, with a fiery love, then a spark of compassion might ignite even in the dark hearts of the anti-God people.[1] ❧

I Don't Kneel!

⊷ The following tale was told by Tillie Farkash, originally of Transylvania, who survived Auschwitz and
other concentration camps during World War II and
made her way to Jerusalem.

"I was nineteen when we were taken to Auschwitz.
On the first day, when a selection was made and my
mother was sent in one direction, I wanted to go with
her, but the Germans gave me a blow and I couldn't follow her. I know that she was killed on that first day;
and my father too, with my brother beside him. So many
people died there and in the other camps.

"In Auschwitz, we were kept—one thousand
women—in one barrack. We had no beds, just the floor
to sleep on. Every morning, we were summoned outside
for roll call so that our oppressors could see if anyone
was missing or had tried to escape. We had to stand
outside the barrack in rows of five—one row after the
other—five, five, five, five. We had no coats, no warm
clothing, nothing—and we had to stand outside in the
cold, even when it was raining or snowing. It was forbidden to move from the row.

"Mengele would come, or Grayze. Did you ever
hear of Grayze? She was like Mengele, but a woman, a
German, in charge of the camp. She was very beautiful,
very elegant, dressed in the German uniform. When
Mengele didn't come, she came.

"Everyone feared her, like—I don't know what!—even
more than we feared Mengele. She was very cruel, and

she always came with two big dogs. We stood in the rows outside while she watched as the rows were counted.

"One morning, it was discovered that two girls were missing from the camp, and we were ordered to fall on our knees and to wait until the camp was searched. We fell on our knees.

"But one woman, of about thirty, the daughter of the Rabbi of Budapest, refused to kneel. She was standing at the end of her row, and she just refused to kneel. 'I am a Jew!' she cried out. 'I don't kneel to anyone!' In Yiddish, she cried, '*Ich bin a Yud. Ich k'nee nisht. Ich bin a Yud!*'

"So Grayze ordered the dogs to attack her and the guards to beat her. They tore her apart in front of our eyes. She cried '*Ich bin a Yud!*' a thousand times until she died.

"I didn't know her name. How could I know it? We were a thousand women and girls in one long barrack, and we called each other by first names. There were so many with the same name—Leahs and Rachels and Miriams. No, I didn't know her name, but I knew that she was the daughter of the Rabbi of Budapest, and she refused to kneel, and she cried out, '*Ich bin a Yud!*' – 'I am a Jew!' a thousand times until she died."[1] ❧

A Mother's Passion

❧ Many years ago in Vilna, the following story was told before the great and famous rabbi, the Hazon Ish:

A young widow named Devorah Shulman had overcome many obstacles to send all her sons to study

in holy yeshivas. One day, one of them came home from
the yeshiva and told his mother that he did not feel it
was his place or in his future and did not want to go
back. The mother was shocked at hearing this. She
mustered all her powers of persuasion and tried to make
her son understand that there is no life without Torah
and that someone not fully committed to God's Torah¹ is
not really living. But her words made no impression
on him.

The mother refused to give up. She took him outside for a walk, to have a heart-to-heart talk with him.
She continued to try to persuade him to reconsider,
with words that touch the heart, but all to no effect.

Meanwhile, as they walked, they passed beyond the
city limits and came to a river, where they went up onto
the bridge. Suddenly, the mother changed her soft tone.
She grabbed her son's hand and said fiercely, "Listen to
me! If you return to the yeshiva, good. But if not, I'm
going to throw you into the river! Because what reason
is there for living if one is not studying in a yeshiva?"

Certainly, the mother would never—God forbid!—
consider throwing her beloved son into the river! But by
expressing her feelings in this most forcible way, she
accomplished her purpose—to reach her son's heart—
more so than by any mere words of explanation she
could have used. He immediately returned to the yeshiva,
to the great relief of his happy mother.

After hearing this tale, the Hazon Ish praised the
young widow's awesome self-sacrifice in her dedication

to the Torah and said that now he could understand
how she had merited to send all her sons to yeshivas
despite the many obstacles she faced.[2] ❧

Dear reader, if this tale caused you difficulty, please pause and pon-
der it! If you are shocked by this mother's action, consider the depth
of her devotion to the Torah and to her son. One need not even believe that she was "right." But by doing what she did, she reached her
son and moved him in a way that pleas and gentle persuasion could
not. Rabbi Noson Tzvi Finkel, the Elder of Slobodka, said that the mind
can be persuaded, but the feelings must be jarred by rebuke. Only
when someone's feelings are stirred will he be moved to take action
and change his ways. This tale again and again refers to the son's
heart and to the mother's heart. The Rabbis say that what comes from
the heart enters the heart. This moment was a turning point in her
son's life. If this mother acquiesced in her son's immature decision,
his life might have been irrevocably changed. She would not allow
that to happen, if she could help it. She truly believed that a life lived
according to the Torah is the only true life. How could she permit her
son to risk dying spiritually because of a lack of understanding? So
she showed him how deeply her passion for the Torah reached. Her
fiery words exited her heart and entered his, and he was convinced,
to his eternal good. At that critical moment, she made the spiritual
transmission to her son.

Training Her Sons

Some pious people recite every night at midnight a lamentation to
mourn the destruction of the Temple, the "exile" of the Divine Presence from the world, and the "exile" of one's own soul. The absence
of the *Shechinah* is the cause of all the cruelty, injustice, and oppres-
sion in the world and the lack of love. Such mourning for the state of

the world and one's own spiritual failings leads to the rebuilding of the Temple and the final triumph of goodness.

◄◊► Rebbetzin Hinda, the wife of Rabbi Yitzhak Isaac Eichenstein, was famous for her holy and pure divine service, like one of the rarest few of the spiritual elite. She arose every night at midnight to sit on the ground and recite *Tikkun Hatzot,* the midnight lamentation service. She also always woke up her children at midnight, even when they were little, and put them next to her on the floor. Although they cried, she paid no attention, in order to train them to wake at midnight to say *Tikkun Hatzot.*

Rebbetzin Hinda used to feel the brow of her five sons when they came home from synagogue to see if they were wet from perspiration. If not, she rebuked them for not praying with devotion and fervor, as she wanted.

Once, in his old age, Rabbi Yitzhak Isaac, asked his rebbetzin, "We've gotten old. With what merits will we ascend to our Father in Heaven?"

She replied, "'We will go up on the highway [*b'mesilah*]'[1]—the letters of the word from the verse hint at the names of our children: Berish, Moshe, Sender, Lippa, and Hirsh. In the merit that we raised five such holy sons, we'll go up into heaven." All of her five sons became Hasidic rebbes.

When Rebbetzin Hinda passed away, her son Rebbe Tzvi Hirsh of Ziditchov went down into the grave before they placed her in it, walked around, back and forth, and said, "Mother, I'm making your bed carefully, so you can sleep well in it!"[2] ◄◊►

The Future Redemption

◄◙► Rebbetzin Pessia Leah, the wife of Rebbe David of Zablitov and the daughter of Rebbe Moshe Leib of Sassov, was a religious personality in her own right. She was famous for her righteousness as well as for her scholarship. Words of Torah that she passed on in the name of her father after his death became widely known. The miracle-working tzaddik, Rebbe Meir of Premishlan, who had been a disciple of her father and knew the rebbetzin from her childhood, greatly honored her by frequently sending Hasidim to her with his greetings.

After her husband's death, she conducted herself like a rebbe, taking *pitka'ot* and *pidyonot* [donations] from Jews who came to her for blessings. Miracle stories were told about her. She would give *lekach* [honey cake] to those who came to ask her for a blessing for success. As she gave it, she would say, "*Lekach* equals *hatzlacha* [success] in *gematria* [Jewish numerology]."[1]

Once, when she was visiting her brother, Rebbe Shmelke, in Sassov, she wanted to meet his son-in-law, Rabbi Shlomo Shapiro (later the Rebbe of Munkatsh), whom she did not know. She went to his home but did not get to see him because he had just left for Zlotchov. As soon as she entered his house, however, she said to Rabbi Shlomo's rebbetzin, her niece, "'*Ein zeh ki im beis Elokim,*' 'This is none other than the house of God,'"[2] for here someone is busy studying Torah at night just as in the daytime. Last night, too, your husband studied Torah all night." And that was actually

true, and she could detect the fragrance of Torah study
because of her high spiritual level.[3] ≈≈

The Rabbis say that a special divine grace rests in a place where Torah
is studied at night. According to the Jewish mystics, someone who
fulfills the Torah on the outer level of the Tree of Knowledge of Good
and Evil—what to do and what not to do—has no fragrance. But someone who fulfills it on the inner, spiritual level is fragrant. Isaac said
about Jacob, "See, the smell of my son is like the smell of a field
that God has blessed."[4] The Rabbis said this was the fragrance of the
Garden of Eden, of the Tree of Life.[5] Later, after waking from his dream
of the ladder that went up to heaven, Jacob said, "This is none other
than the house of God!" A house devoted to God—where Torah is
studied at night—is fragrant. Rebbetzin Pessia Leah, so holy herself,
could smell that special and precious fragrance of holiness. The Rabbis say that the Messiah will have an acute sense of smell for spiritual matters. But some holy people have that sensitivity now too.

Hasidim said that Pessiah Leah's name was given to her by her
father, Rebbe Moshe Leib of Sassov, because the first letters of Pessiah Leah are those of *Pesah L'atid,* "the future Passover," and hint
at the words of the Rabbis, "In the month of Nisan the Jewish people
were redeemed from Egypt, and in Nisan they are destined to be redeemed in the future."[6] The Rabbis also said that the redemption
from slavery in Egypt was due to the merit of the pious women. Perhaps the name that Rebbe Moshe Leib gave to his daughter hints that
like the first redemption, the future redemption will also be in the
merit of the holy women.

Waiting for Redemption

≈≈ The most pious people look forward expectantly to
the final redemption.

The life of Rebbetzin Hayya Ruchama Kupshitz
was full of deep faith and pure piety. In her home, all of

her family expectantly awaited the final redemption
each and every minute. Rebbetzin Hayya Ruchama had
in her house a drum that she kept ready to greet the
Messiah. She guarded this drum her whole life. She used
to say, "Just as Miriam the Prophetess went out with
drums and dancing at the splitting of the Red Sea, so
too at the future redemption the women will go out
with drums and dancing."

Once, Rebbetzin Hayya Ruchama's son fell down
and split his lip. The rebbetzin had just given birth to
another baby, so a neighbor was going to take the boy
to the hospital to sew up his lip. The rebbetzin asked
her to wait for a minute and said, "Please be careful
that they do a good job and don't leave any sign of a
defect. My son is a *kohen* [priest], and I don't want him
to be excluded because of a physical defect from serving in the third Temple."[1] ⋘⋙

Certain physical defects disqualify a *kohen,* a Jewish priest, from
serving in the Temple. To the rebbetzin, the future redemption and
the appearance of the Third Temple were such an imminent reality
that she expected them at any moment.

In the Cave of Machpelah

⋘⋙ Fruma Riveleh, the wife of Reb David of Kaminka,
was a very holy woman with a special merit and power.
In those earlier days, many women died in childbirth
because the doctors in the little villages were inexpert.
Everyone in the vicinity knew that if Fruma Riveleh

walked in where a woman was having childbirth pains, the woman would be fine and the child would be born easily.

Later, she and her husband moved to Israel, and they were so poor that Reb David could barely make a few coins for challah for the Sabbath, but they managed. The rebbetzin wanted to hide her holiness, so she would secretly find out if there was a woman who was in childbirth pain, and she would just drop in to visit. Slowly, people began to notice that as soon as she came, the pain would end and the baby would be born with no problem. People wanted to pay her, but she would protest and try to cover up the whole thing.

In those days, Israel was under Turkish rule, with a pasha as governor. At one time, the pasha's daughter was having trouble giving birth and was about to die. The pasha called all the doctors. He also had Jewish friends who said, "Don't waste your money on doctors who can't help. There is one woman here in Jerusalem, and if you can get her to come to your place, you won't need doctors." So the pasha went to her himself because he did not want his daughter to die. He knocked on the door of the broken-down house of Fruma Riveleh and asked her to please come and save his daughter's life.

As soon as she walked into the palace, the baby was born. The pasha wanted to pay her. Even though she was very poor, she refused to take money for her special ability received from God. The pasha spoke to all his Jewish friends. "Do me a favor. Talk to this holy woman. I want to reward her to show her my thanks."

The Cave of Machpelah, where Adam and Eve, Abraham and Sarah, Isaac and Rebecca, and Jacob and Leah are buried, was controlled by the Muslims, who had decreed that any Jew who entered could be killed because it would be a desecration of the holiness of the place if a Jew showed his face there. So Fruma Riveleh said to the pasha, "If you want to reward me, let me enter the Cave of Machpelah to pray at the graves of the Patriarchs and Matriarchs."

"When do you want to go?"

"In three months," she said.

For hundreds of years, not one Jew had been allowed to go there, so she wanted to pray in the name of all of Israel. She thought, "Maybe I can bring the Messiah. I have to pray for the whole world." So she prepared herself. She was holy anyway, but she prepared herself to the utmost.

In the meantime, all the doctors were burning with resentment and jealousy because for all their importance, they could not get the baby out, and this simple woman just walks through the door and the baby is born. They heard that the pasha had given her permission to go to the Cave of Machpelah. Now, many steps led down into the cave. The doctors went to the Muslim who was in charge of the cave and said to him, "You know the pasha only told her she could go into the cave. He never said anything about coming out." They bribed him generously to do as they wanted.

Fruma Riveleh went to the cave with a letter from the pasha giving her permission to enter. She went in and began to pray. After a few hours, she wanted to leave, so she knocked on the door, but everything was closed and dark.

She began to cry and beg, "Please let me out. I'm dying here!" She realized that she had been locked in on purpose, but what could she do? She went back down the steps and started praying again, reciting psalms. Her husband, Rabbi David of Kaminka, was a direct descendant of King David, who knew the names of all his ancestors from King David to himself. So Fruma Riveleh was trapped there in the dark, weeping, just about to faint, when suddenly she saw a great light. Someone was coming with a crown on his head, and he said, "I am your children's great-grandfather, King David. Come with me and I'll get you out."

She realized her opportunity, so she said to him, "I want you to give me something to remember you." She thought, "When I'll say King David saved me, who will believe me?"

So King David gave her a little Book of Psalms; then he opened the door and let her out. The strangest thing is that when he let her out, the door was not in Hebron, where the Cave of Machpelah is located. He opened the door and she was standing right in front of her own home in Jerusalem, and she had the Book of Psalms in her hand.

The little Book of Psalms was handed down from generation to generation. Someone once visited the Tzanzer Rebbe, and he had it in his possession because he was one of the great-grandchildren of Rabbi David and Fruma Riveleh of Kaminka."[1] ⊰⊱

Sukkot Stories

The two main *mitzvot* of the holiday of *Sukkot*, the Festival of Booths, are dwelling in a temporary *sukkah* [booth] rather than in one's home, and ritual waving during worship of the Four Species—*etrog* (citron), *lulav* (palm), *hadasim* (myrtle), and *aravot* (willows). Eating, studying, and even sleeping in an impermanent *sukkah* remind a person that what truly protects one is not the structure but God Himself. There is a similar lesson about the relative value of material possessions versus spirituality in the custom of pious people to spend large amounts of money on the most beautiful *etrog*. It is one of the wondrous peculiarities of traditional Judaism that some pious people spend enormous sums on a perishable fruit, used for ritual purposes for one week only. The money is spent in a spirit of self-sacrifice and devotion, for the sake of *hiddur mitzvah*—doing a divine commandment in the most beautiful way.

She Did Not Taste the Sukkah

⊰⊱ The *tzaddeket* Gittel was a daughter of Rebbe Yisrael of Rizhin and the mother of two tzaddikim, Rebbe Lev of Azsherne and Rebbe David of Radakhov-Brod. Hasidim considered her to be a person who had reached exalted spiritual levels.

One *Sukkot,* she went to her brother, Rabbi David Moshe, in Chortkov. She lit the holiday candles in the *sukkah.* Later on, she complained to her brother that

she had not "tasted" the *sukkah*. Her brother investigated and found that the overhead thatch had not been
arranged properly (and hence the *sukkah* was not
kosher).¹ ❧

A holy person "tastes" the sweetness of a *mitzvah*, of truly doing
God's will.

Visions in the Sukkah

❧ When Rebbe Yosef of Yampola, son of Rebbe Yehiel
Michal of Zlotchov and Rebbetzin Yenta Rechil, com-
memorated his mother's *yahrzeit* [the anniversary of
her death] he told his Hasidim the following story:
   "Once, on the night after Yom Kippur, my father
refused to eat. He refused to eat the next day too. My
mother asked him why he didn't want to eat anything—
after all, he had been fasting for so long. My father
answered, 'How can I eat when I don't have money to
buy a *lulav* and an *etrog* for *Sukkot*?'
   "My mother took pity on him and said, 'I still have
a little of the money I received when I sold my jewelry.
I had set it aside as a gift for our son's future bride.
But now that I see that you're so downhearted that you
don't even want to eat or drink because of this, take the
money and buy a beautiful *lulav* and *etrog*.'
   "With great joy, my father went off to buy the *lulav*
and *etrog* and left us brothers to construct the *sukkah*.
   "On the first night of *Sukkot*, my father called
my mother into the *sukkah* to hear *kiddush*. When she
entered the *sukkah*, my mother began weeping and

sobbing. My father didn't ask her why she was weeping because he was so involved with *kiddush.*

"In the morning, my father went to the *mikveh* [ritual bath] and then entered the *sukkah* and recited the blessing over the *lulav* with great joy. He again sent for my mother to come to the *sukkah* and say the blessing over the *lulav* and *etrog.* And again, when she entered the *sukkah,* she began to weep nonstop. My father asked her, 'Why are you crying when you come into the *sukkah?*'

"'How can I not cry?' said my mother. 'Every year when I enter the *sukkah,* Elijah the Prophet appears to me. That makes me joyful. It's my consolation in this life of poverty. But I haven't seen him this *Sukkot*, not last night or this morning. It seems that he won't appear because of my misdeeds. So how can I not weep?'

"My father answered, 'It was not your wrongdoing that caused this but mine.'

"'No,' said my mother. 'You're a true tzaddik. It was my transgressions that caused it!'

"But my father promised her that from that day and forward, every time she came into the *sukkah,* Elijah the Prophet would appear to her, as he had before. And so it was.

"My father later told me that he realized that it was his fault in having gone to buy the *lulav* and *etrog* and allowing us boys to build the *sukkah.* Because we had not taken certain subtleties into account in building it, Elijah could not enter. My father immediately rectified the problem, and Elijah entered the *sukkah* and appeared to my mother as he had in previous years."[2] ◈

If we saw Elijah or had other powerful mystic experiences, we too would be consoled for any poverty or other deprivation that we endured. May we merit to have the strong belief that produces such revelations.

A Sukkah *of Peace*

⫷ Rebbetzin Miriam Sofer of Hungary was a great figure in the famous Sofer family. After surviving Auschwitz, she moved to Israel, where her husband, Rabbi Yohanan, started a yeshiva—Yeshiva Ohel Shimon. Having been spared from extermination in the death camp, she had decided that her mission in life was to be compassionate and bring joy to those devoted to God.

One of the yeshiva students once came to her home to help decorate the *rosh yeshiva*'s large *sukkah.* The student exerted himself to hang various decorations to fulfill the commandment to beautify a *mitzvah* and to make it a beautiful *sukkah.*

When he was about finished, Rebbetzin Miriam Sofer walked in to thank him for his efforts. After expressing her appreciation and satisfaction with a flood of compliments, as was her way, she more carefully looked around to see what he had done. She then very tactfully asked, "Would you please move this decoration here, facing the entrance, and put this one next to it, and this other one next to that?" She said she knew it was bothersome, but she still asked, would he please do it, if it wasn't too much trouble?

The student was surprised, wondering what the fuss was about, and asked, "What difference does it make if this decoration or the other one is here or there?"

"This ornament was made by a certain student," she said, "and that one by another student. Both of them usually visit our *sukkah* during the holiday. The first thing they'll look for when they come in is their decoration, and if they don't see it immediately in a prominent place opposite the entrance, it will lessen their holiday joy. If their decorations are put in an out-of-the-way place, it might cause them some resentment, and since the *sukkah* is supposed to be a '*sukkah* of peace,' it's only right that it act to increase peace and remove any annoyance."[3] ≈◊≈

"*Sukkah* of peace" is a phrase in the Sabbath prayers, meaning that God creates a place of peace. It was always Rebbetzin Miriam Sofer's way to create and increase peace by being sensitive to others' feelings and to what was important to them.

A Brilliant Female Scholar

≈◊≈ One evening, when Michal Zalman returned from studying at the yeshiva, his older sister approached their father, Rabbi Yaakov Moshe Shurkin, and said, "Daddy, please teach me some Talmud! I want to taste the sweetness of Torah study!"

Hearing this, her father's face became white. He took ten dollars from his wallet—a lot of money in those days—and gave it to her, saying, "Buy yourself a new dress."

She went away happy, but her brother asked their father, "Why did you buy her off? Why shouldn't she study Torah?"

His father looked at him and said, "I'll tell you a story of when I was young.

"When I was studying in Radin at the Hafetz Hayim's yeshiva, the Russian government issued a decree to conscript young men into the army. But you could bribe your way out of it—to change the name of the family. I had to get the money myself, however. With the blessing of the Hafetz Hayim, I set out. I went from town to town. In each town, I met with the rabbi and discussed Torah with him so that he saw I was a scholar and would then help me solicit donations from the townspeople.

"Once, I arrived at an isolated village where the very old rabbi was an awe-inspiring *gaon*. In the midst of our Torah discussion, he took out a gigantic handwritten manuscript that was a commentary on a well-known book about all the 613 *mitzvot*[1] and showed me the comment there on the subject we were discussing. The reasoning in the manuscript was brilliantly clear, and the proofs presented for its conclusions were strong and convincing. Impressed and astonished, I asked, 'Rabbi, is this your manuscript?'

"'No,' he replied. 'It's my daughter's.'

"Seeing my surprise, he explained, 'When I came to this village, I was all alone. There were no other scholars here to discuss Torah with. But I had my daughter, who is brilliant and talented. I taught her, and the two of us studied together. This manuscript is hers.'

"I couldn't contain myself and kept repeating, 'Incredible! Incredible!'

"Just then, his daughter entered the room. Now, the rabbi was very elderly, and his daughter had white hair and walked bent over, leaning on a cane. The rabbi began to weep. The daughter left.

"When she had gone, I asked, 'Why are you crying?'

"'Let me tell you the end of the story,' he said. 'When she was of an age to be married, I asked the heads of all the yeshivas to send me their best student for consideration as a groom for my daughter. I promised I would support the boy while he lived in my home, and when my time came, he would replace me as rabbi here.

"'So the top student from the famous Mir Yeshiva visited. He and my daughter met, and they liked each other. Then they began to discuss Torah. My daughter asked him, "How do you interpret the comments of the Rambam [Maimonides] about the 'uncleanness of the abyss'?" He was speechless. He had never even heard of this obscure concept. "You're the best student in the Mir Yeshiva?" she said. That was the end of that. Then the best students from the famous Telz and Slobodka yeshivas came, and the same thing happened. Those students too were turned away, married others, and had families. But my daughter remained alone in my home—as you saw her now—with her cane and her manuscript!'

"That," said Rabbi Yaakov Moshe, concluding the story to his son, "is why I gave your sister money for a new dress. I don't want her to end up like that old woman."[2] ❧

How sad that this brilliant female scholar (and how many more like her?) remained unmarried because of the unfortunate social situation! Even in today's secular society, women sometimes hide their education and intelligence to avoid alienating overly sensitive young men. (Note that the young woman's condescension was fairly typical for scholars of that time and should not be taken as an excuse for her difficulty.) If the rabbi who told this tale wanted to protect his daughter, why did he not teach her Torah and tell her to hide her knowledge? How sad that such stories become excuses for denying girls the sweetness of Torah study instead of educating young men to value scholarly women!

Hadassah Linder

Hadassah Linder was an Israeli *tzaddeket* who lived in Jerusalem and passed away not long ago in 1999.

What Is Important

Reciting psalms is a central practice of many pious Jewish women. Pious women also avoid gossip, slander, and idle talk. They devote every minute of their lives to spiritual pursuits; where is there time for idleness?

&> Hadassah Linder was utterly devoted to the Book of Psalms. She recited psalms daily at every opportunity with great devotion. She was always careful never to miss her regular sessions of psalm saying, especially on the Sabbath.

She once confided to her daughter, "This Shabbat, I didn't recite psalms as usual."

"Why? What happened?" asked her daughter.

Her mother told her that on Shabbat afternoon, she had received a visit from a certain lonely woman who loved to make idle conversation. Hadassah never conversed idly, certainly never at the expense of her psalm saying, especially not at the expense of Sabbath psalm saying. But on this occasion, she made an exception. "My psalms are important," she explained, "but talking with this woman who enjoys it so much, even though it's idle conversation, is more important; it tips the scale."

So Hadassah gave up her psalm saying to make this lonely woman's time with her pleasant. This woman never knew the sacrifice Hadassah made for her sake.[1] ⊰❦⊱

In the Taxi

⊰❦⊱ The Rabbis say, "Let the poor be members of your household." Hadassah fulfilled this teaching literally. She had an open house and was continually feeding countless guests, putting others up, and so on. Some of those she took in were broken, homeless, mentally unbalanced people. She constantly helped and benefited a poor, embittered, and emotionally disturbed woman named Massouda. Hadassah always invited Massouda to family celebrations, as if she were one of the family. Whenever one of Hadassah's children or grandchildren got married, the bride went in a taxi that would take her to the hall, and Massouda went in the same taxi.

On the occasion of one family wedding, some of the other regular guests who frequented Haddasah's home asked to ride in the taxi together with the bride. Hadassah happily complied. One after another, they entered the taxi while Hadassah herself walked on foot to the wedding hall (although she was fasting, as was her custom on the wedding day of her children, grand-children, or great-grandchildren). "Let these broken people enjoy themselves," she said. "It makes no differ-ence to me how I get to the wedding."[2] ❧

Patience

Hadassah was generous in making loans, without any deadline for repayment, to poor people who regularly visited her home or who had become members of her household, so to speak. And she gave charity to everyone who asked her.

❧ Once an embittered poor person who had received some money from Hadassah's hand ripped up the bill in front of her because the amount did not please him. Hadassah did not think twice but began to search around the house for a larger bill to give him. When she discovered that there was no larger bill available, she ran to the neighbor's to ask for a loan to give to that troubled poor man.[3] ❧

A Single Bagel

❧ One Thursday, while Hadassah was baking cookies for Shabbat, Massouda stood nearby, viewing, inspect-ing, and choosing which cookie would be hers. Every

tray that came out of the oven first passed her inspec-
tion until she found what she wanted. But here special
care was necessary. If anyone commented on her
behavior, she would angrily throw all the cookies to
the floor and yell, "I don't need them! I don't need your
favors!"

One Thursday, a special tray of bagels was baked
in honor of Massouda because she had asked for them.
The bagels came out just as she desired, and she was
very happy about it. She carefully put them all, one by
one, into a bag, and Hadassah was glad to see Massouda
so satisfied.

"Massouda," said Hadassah, "would you like to give
me a bagel?"

Massouda thought it over for a second and replied,
"No! You don't deserve it. But I'll give one to your husband." And she took out a bagel for him.

Hadassah learned an important lesson from this.
That evening, when her children returned from school,
she said, "I have a valuable story to tell you today." She
told them of what had happened with Massouda and
added, "This is exactly how we act with the Holy One,
blessed be He. He gives to us more and more, without
limits and without considering whether we are worthy
of it, and then at a moment of inspiration, we agree to
give Him back a little of what is His—a little *tzedaka,*
some good deed, one bagel from the tray, one crumb
from what we received from Him."

Hadassah repeated this story and its lesson many
times.[4] ✍

The Rabbis say, "Give Him what is His, for you and what is yours are His." There is a lovely parable of a baby being fed by its mother and putting a little of the food back into its mother's mouth. Although it may only be a little, it is so sweet when we willingly give back to God some of what He gives to us. Hadassah did not become angry, like most people would, at Massouda's disturbed and selfish behavior. Instead, like some other holy people, she saw lessons in everything that happens, and she learned from this unpleasant incident a beautiful lesson that we too can learn.

The Best for Others

Hadassah regularly distributed tremendous amounts of food to countless needy people.

≈&≈ A few times a week, Hadassah went to the Machane Yehuda market with a cart that was specially built for her by a carpenter. She went with her grandchildren at her side and bought produce that the vegetable men offered her cheaply. They kept for her fruits and vegetables that were partially bad and gave them to her for half price, knowing that she distributed them to needy people.

Every once in a while, in the midst of the purchases, her granddaughters would return home with the cart, unload it, take everything in it up the many stairs to her home, and then run back to their grandmother in the market to refill the cart.

At home, Hadassah would go through the produce: the better fruits and vegetables she gave to needy people; the rest she kept for herself and her family.[5]

Hadassah also bought chickens at a very reduced price and distributed them to needy people after she and her granddaughters cleaned and koshered them—a huge job. She then sent her granddaughters to give the innards that are not eaten to the stray cats so that they too would benefit, because, as the psalm says, "His mercies are over all his works." [The Rabbis interpret this psalm verse to mean that God is merciful to animals too.] Afterward, she kept the wings, necks, and feet for her family, along with a few nicer pieces for guests, and then distributed the best pieces to needy people.[6] ➳

A Memorial

➳ One of the sad people who was a regular visitor in Hadassah's home was "Hanna with the Cats"—that was what she was called because of all the cats that roamed freely around her apartment. This Hanna covered her face with so many veils that it was hard to see her eyes, and she used to whisper and talk to herself. She ate the Sabbath meal every Friday night at Hadassah's home.

Yet despite being a lonely and childless woman, she never complained about her situation and was always ready for a pleasant conversation. Hadassah admired her noble restraint, since the woman was sufficiently wise to understand her sad plight, yet she never uttered a word of complaint about it. Toward the end of her life, when this woman became seriously ill, she occasionally said in passing, "When my time comes, no one will remember that I ever lived; no one will be

named after me." Her casual comments made a deep
impression on Hadassah and her husband, Rabbi
Fishel. When a daughter was born to them following
Hanna's death, they named the baby girl after her so
that she would have a remembrance and a memorial
in this world. Although Hadassah had other names, of
family relatives, that she wanted to name her daughter,
she did not forget Hanna; and Hanna is remembered
and mentioned to this day in the thriving family of
Hadassah's daughter.[7] ⁓

Milk and Noodles

⁓ Dinah was also a regular visitor in Hadassah's home.
She had been a pampered only daughter and had never
learned to care for herself. When she married, her mother
ran her home, and when her mother died, her own children did everything. After her children were married and
her husband had passed away, she was left alone with no
one to care for her. She ended up wandering the streets,
collecting rags and junk and filling up her apartment
until there was no room for anything else.

"One rainy winter's day," tells Hadassah's granddaughter, "I visited Grandma and found her falling asleep
on a chair, her head dropping down again and again.
'Grandma,' I said, 'you're tired. Why not go to sleep?'

"'I will,' she said. 'I would have gone to sleep
already, but I haven't finished preparing the fruit and
vegetable packages for the needy people. In a little
while, they'll come to pick them up.'

"'I'll take care of it, Grandma. You go to sleep.'

"She agreed and, after telling me a number of things to do, went to sleep.

"Outside it was raining with thunder and lightning, and the sounds of the storm could be heard inside. I was totally engrossed in preparing the packages when I heard a knock on the door. I opened it and found Dinah standing there; she had come to converse with Grandma. I told her that Grandma was sleeping, and she asked if she could come in to warm up. 'Of course,' I said. 'Please come in.' She sat down on a chair and watched what I was doing.

"'You know,' she said, 'when my mother was still alive, she used to make for me, on stormy days like this, a glass of hot milk and noodles. I would feel as if the warmth was going through all my limbs. But those days are gone now,' she concluded with a sigh.

"No sooner had she finished speaking than I saw Grandma Hadassah going from her bedroom into the kitchen. I thought she wanted to get something. But no, she was taking out the heating plate, lighting it (a difficult task), and putting on it a pot with milk and noodles! In a little while, Dinah was having milk and noodles, to her pleasure and delight."

The minute Hadassah had heard Dinah's "request," her tiredness disappeared; she got up and prepared for this lonely woman this favorite treat.[8] ✥

In a famous teaching, the Rabbis say to do God's will as if it is one's own will. In a less famous but related teaching, for the pious and holy, the Rabbis say to do other people's will as if it is one's own will. Just as God acts to please every living creature, so do holy people like Hadassah Linder act to please every living being on earth. That is their deepest pleasure—to please God and everyone they meet.

Matters of Food

⚜ There was always food to eat in Hadassah's home. Whoever entered hungry left satisfied and was even given food to take with him. Hadassah was particularly scrupulous about *bal taƨh'chit,* the Torah teaching not to destroy or waste anything; she never allowed anyone to throw away food. It is amazing to contemplate that a woman who handled such huge quantities of food could be so careful never to allow any food or drink to be treated with disrespect. After all, she thought, are not these gifts from God that enliven living beings, and mustn't we thank God for them and make blessings over them? How is it possible to throw them away?

"I was once standing by the garbage," said one of Hadassah's granddaughters, describing a childhood experience, "with a half-eaten apple in my hand, about to throw it away. I had had enough to eat, but Grandma noticed what I was about to do. She also knew that if she forbade me to put it in the garbage, I'd just hide it from her the next time I wanted to do the same thing, and I wouldn't understand the seriousness of what was at stake. 'Come, dear,' she called to me. 'Come to me, and I'll tell you about the long journey this apple has made!'

"She then began to tell me in living color about how the apple grew under the hot rays of the sun and was exposed to the pouring rain. She described its long trip until it finally arrived at our home and said, 'Now that this apple has had the good luck to reach the hand of a religious Jewish child who makes blessings over food with devotion, do you want to embarrass it and cast it away?'

"Grandma's words became imprinted in my mind and heart, and to this very day, it's hard for me to throw away fruit because of what Grandma said."

Hadassah was pained at heart to see disrespect and waste of food at celebrations, and she spoke about it again and again.

Her daughter explains, "If some of Mama's *cholent* stew remained after Shabbat, she would telephone me and ask me to send the children over to eat it. How can one throw away food? But what can one do when they don't want to eat it? 'Send them to me,' she would say. My children went to Grandma's home and finished the hot food. 'How come here you didn't want any but there you ate?' I asked them.

"'Grandma gave us each an ice-cream pop,' they said, 'if we'd finish the food.'"

If in any case some pieces of bread were left over at her house, Hadassah made them into crumbs, softened them with water, and put them out in the courtyard for the birds.[9] ᨑ᭝

ᨑ᭝ "I don't like this food," one of the children said.

"You don't have to like it," Hadassah replied; "you just have to eat it! Think how little time we actually feel the taste of the food—for just a few moments or less.

The distance from the mouth to the throat is so short, yet everyone makes such a fuss over whether they 'like' this food or 'don't like' that food. We eat food so that we are able to accomplish our spiritual goals; it should make no difference to us what the food's taste is."

Hadassah bought almost one hundred pounds of fruit every week, koshered dozens of chickens, and cooked scores of hot dishes to distribute to needy people, but she herself made do with very little. She had totally subdued her lust for food. She believed that eating is needed to sustain the body and provide strength for holy tasks, such as studying Torah. But taste? Attractiveness? A nice portion? Personally, these things meant nothing to her, but she was careful to provide them for others. She always chose the worst for herself—a burnt cookie, an overripe or crushed piece of fruit, leftovers from days before that no one else would eat. This way she saved food from being thrown away in disrespect and also subdued her desire for food. It is hard to fathom how someone who knew so well that other people needed more and more of everything— staples and extras too—needed nothing for herself.

When Hadassah asked for something to eat, the children knew to bring her what was suitable for her— namely, food that others would not eat. If someone else might enjoy it, Hadassah would not eat it.

"I sat next to her at a *bris* for a great-grandson," said her granddaughter. "Grandma almost didn't eat anything of what was offered. Chicken she certainly didn't eat. I asked her why she didn't take any.

"Grandma answered, 'The nice pieces of chicken belong to those hosting the *bris*. And whatever is left over they should take home for the new mother and spare themselves a few days of having to cook for her. Why do I need any of it? Don't I have food at home?'

"She also said that it was proper to leave some nice food for guests who had not yet arrived. But she kept on encouraging everybody near her to eat more and more. As long as she thought someone else might derive enjoyment from the food, she would not touch it."

Her son said, "I offered her a bag of cookies; but she, as was her way, began to search for a burnt cookie or for crumbs. I asked her why she did this—was it for religious reasons, because she wanted to afflict herself or break her desire for food?

"She answered, 'What do you mean? The only reason is that as long as someone else can enjoy the cookies, why should I eat them? I can enjoy a burnt cookie; to me it makes no difference at all; let someone else enjoy the whole cookies.' That was her explanation."[10] ⋘

Hadassah attained a high spiritual level of equanimity, when a person is so God-conscious that he does not care whether he eats good food or bad food because everything from God's hand is good.

The Joy of Giving

⋘ Hadassah so much enjoyed giving that she had to give. Her pleasure in giving was most evident when she was ill and suffered pains that made it difficult for her to function.

Once, when she was suffering unbearably, a delivery man entered the house, sent by one of the vegetable men, carrying cartons full of fruits and vegetables that Hadassah had ordered. In her later years, she was no longer able to go shopping in the market herself and had an arrangement whereby she ordered from the vegetable men, who had come to know her well over the years and supplied her with the needed produce at low prices.

The moment that the delivery man put the sacks and crates on the kitchen floor, Hadassah's face began to shine, and she completely forgot all her pain and suffering; she forgot the difficult day and began with renewed vigor—seemingly beyond her powers—to prepare the packages for all the needy people, whom she knew from memory. The best medicine for her pain was giving and distributing to others.

"What will my paradise be?" she asked, and answered, "When I'll be able to distribute food and drink as much as every poor person wants and I won't have to worry that I'll run out of some item or that there won't be enough for everyone."

One of her grandchildren once visited her home and left stocked with heavy baskets of goods. "Grandma, bless me," he asked.

His grandmother blessed him: "May God give you joy, like the joy I have when I give to someone else."

Members of her family say, "We must admit that we never merited to have the kind of joy that our grandmother had, because she experienced a supernal joy in giving, giving, giving."[11] ⇜

Blessings and Curses

⇜ One day the phone rang and on the other end of the line was a man who had become embroiled in a dispute with someone else. Knowing that one of the members of Hadassah's household had influence with his opponent, yet refused, despite many pleas, to become a party to the argument, he decided to harass Rabbi Fishel and Rebbetzin Hadassah. He imagined that this way he would be able to resolve the dispute. He began to swear and curse, and Hadassah held the phone without ever thinking of breaking off the conversation and hanging up.

The man continued to curse, and she let him go on and on, while she answered him—for each and every curse—with a similar blessing. So during the course of this whole long conversation, this man merited to receive a flow of blessings, each of them the exact opposite of the curse that had just left his mouth.

Hadassah understood that his curses came from his pain and heartache. Despite the fact that she considered him in the wrong in his dispute, she poured over him blessings and good wishes that God improve his situation and also return him to the correct path.

This man repeated this maneuver a number of times—with the same result—before the dispute was finally resolved.[12] ⇜

Ironing

◅◈► Hadassah found it difficult to understand how people spent so much time occupying their heads with unimportant concerns about clothing.

She was once present when some women were describing in great detail the ironing they did at home. One expressed pride that she ironed shirts with great care, spending a lot of time until they looked like new. Another said that she ironed just the front and the back parts; another admitted in a lowered voice that she never ironed at all.

Hadassah wanted to tell them that it was a pity to waste valuable time and to give exaggerated importance to trivial matters, especially since a discussion of this kind might put pressure on someone who had no time to devote to such things. Further, spending time on unimportant things would certainly be at the expense of more important matters concerning one's family and children.

Not wanting to offend anyone, Hadassah offered her opinion in the form of some light humor. She said, "Last night, my soul ascended into heaven; and what did I see there? I saw that someone who is fastidious in ironing shirts has the gates of paradise immediately opened before her. Someone who spends less time enters paradise but is treated with less regard. As for someone who doesn't iron at all—*oy!* she never enters paradise at all!"

Her gentle rebuke was received with an understanding smile, and her hint was absorbed in good
humor.[13] ❧

First Aid

❧ Whenever there was a medical problem in the family, Hadassah immediately gave *tzedaka,* for the verse
says, "Charity saves from death." Charity was always
the "first aid."

Her son recalled, "I once came home from *heder*
[religious elementary school] with a high fever and sat
down on a chair, exhausted. Mother put her hand to my
burning brow and said, 'I see that you're not feeling
well. But what can I do? I don't have any money.' It was
understood that the money would be given without
delay for charity, which would be my 'medicine.' Mother
quickly sent one of my brothers to a neighbor to borrow
some money and told him to immediately take it to the
charity collector, Rabbi Moshe Baruch Levine, who collected money for needy people. Of course, right afterward, I received the appropriate medical care, but the
'first aid' that came before anything else was always
charity."[14] ❧

Improvements

❧ During an extensive government project to restore
older Jerusalem neighborhoods, a worker came to
Hadassah in her Knesset neighborhood and offered to
make improvements in her home at a minimal cost.

"I'm fine and comfortable," answered Hadassah. "There's no need for any improvements."

The man tried to convince her that the renovations would make her life easier, but she was unmoved by his arguments.

Finally, the responsible government officials wrote in their report, "This woman has nothing but argues that she has everything."

Hadassah had no desire beyond the minimal physical concerns of living. And she felt no need for "improvements." She did have "everything," but her pleasure and enjoyment came exclusively from her spirituality.[15] ◁◈▷

The Torah Cries Out

It is customary for boys and young men studying in yeshiva and at higher schools to have two vacations between terms. One vacation falls during the whole month of Nisan, when Passover occurs; the other is from *Tisha B'Av* through the holidays in the month of Elul. Yet the ancient Rabbis said that one should study Torah day and night. Therefore, Hadassah believed that there is no such thing as a "vacation" from God's word. Don't the Rabbis say that the Torah itself cries out in pain regarding those who neglect its study?

Yet those who allow for a vacation and recess rely on another rabbinic teaching: that sometimes the neglect of the Torah is what establishes it, meaning in this case that a recess is only for the purpose of renewing strength for the next term and for more study.

◁◈▷ Hadassah was devoted to Torah study in the traditional women's way of facilitating and encouraging men and boys to study. She could not bear to see yeshiva boys relax from their intensive study during the break between terms. During the intersession, she continually spurred yeshiva boys to study constantly as always. When they replied, "It's vacation," she answered, "There will be a long vacation after a hundred and twenty years![16] It is forbidden to neglect Torah study for even a day; the Rabbis tell us God says, 'If you leave Me for a day, I will leave you for two.'"[17] ✑

✑ When Hadassah saw yeshiva boys during the intersession idly standing near the fountain in the neighborhood's central square, she could not restrain herself. "You're neglecting the Torah!" she cried out hoarsely. "The world and the Jewish people need your Torah study!" she added, to soften her call.

All those who were accustomed to hear her cries during the intersession spoke nostalgically of this shouting of hers. They never felt insulted or offended by it. They always felt, they said, that this was the cry of her soul, shouted out with tears in her eyes and from her heartache. It was not Hadassah that stood and made demands; it was the holy Torah itself, in all its glory, that stood and cried out full-throated at its neglect and insult.

The Rabbis say that children's Torah study should not be disturbed even for the sake of building the Temple. "Where is the labor and effort of former times?" Hadassah used to ask. "True, there is an exacting attention to the details of *halacha* today, and people observe many stringencies that are easy to fulfill. But where is the old kind of Jew? Where is the warmth for something spiritual?"[18] ✑

⊰⊱ Hadassah could not bear for men to be unnecessarily interrupted from Torah study. Hadassah's daughter once called her husband away from his Torah study because his signature was needed on a lease for their apartment. He left the study hall, signed, and immediately returned to his studying. But Hadassah was very upset and criticized her daughter; she could hardly forgive her. "He was in the middle of studying!" said Hadassah. "How could you do such a thing? You say this was necessary? His studying is more necessary!"[19] ⊰⊱

How Does One Attain Spiritual Greatness?

⊰⊱ "I once arrived to help Hadassah prepare for a *sheva beracha* party for some newlyweds,"[20] said her niece. "While we were working, I couldn't stop wondering how my aunt had reached such spiritual greatness. My mother, Hadassah's sister, had told me a number of times that Hadassah was by nature a very clean and orderly woman who loved neatness and beauty. 'For her to wash the dishes,' my mother once said jokingly, 'was not a simple task, because they had to sparkle like a mirror; otherwise, she was not satisfied.'

"I can testify that although Hadassah was clean and orderly, such matters were absolutely unimportant to her, compared to her great deeds, and that caring for and beautifying her home were utterly insignificant to her.

"I looked for a good opportunity and asked her, 'Aunt Hadassah, how did you become who you are today? What led you to change yourself?'

"'It's very simple,' she replied, in a rare moment when she was willing to talk about herself. 'I made a calculation, a soul accounting. True, I love nice things and get pleasure from them. But I said to myself, "Hadassah, what's most important?" Once I made my decision about religion, I decided to fulfill it in reality.'"[21] ∽

Hadassah took her determination to do things the right way, to wash the dishes perfectly until they sparkled like a mirror, and turned it to religion—to wash and then polish her soul until it sparkled in reflecting divine light.

∽ Her granddaughter once asked Hadassah a similar question about how she became who she is. "We were preparing for a celebration in honor of the conclusion of a term of study at school. The theme was the Rabbis' teaching about the three pillars of Judaism—'Torah, worship, and kindness.' Of course, we decided to interview Grandma about this subject. I visited her together with a few of my girlfriends, and we asked her the questions we had prepared. Among the questions, I weaved in a personal one about her and asked something that had long piqued my curiosity: 'How did you attain all this? What led to it?'

"Grandma Hadassah replied, 'I once made a soul accounting and thought to myself, "When I reach the World of Truth after a hundred and twenty years, who'll give any thought to this woman named Hadassah? Who'll have pity on her?" I realized that there was no other choice than to begin doing something about it.

So I decided to do deeds of kindness; perhaps in heaven they would then be kind to me, beyond what I actually deserve. I made another soul accounting and thought, "Doesn't God bestow on me every day so many favors and kindnesses? I'm totally surrounded by His kindness, by His unlimited gifts—because He's so good to me! What can I do to return His kindness?" I decided to try, to the best of my ability, to be kind to His creatures.'

"We taped her answers, and on that tape you can hear just then the voice of a little girl from a family that Hadassah often helped, asking, 'Hadassah, can I go to market?' meaning, could she act as if she were at the market and take from Hadassah's home all the fruits, vegetables, and other items that she wanted. Instead of going to the market and buying things, poor people simply went to Hadassah's home and took what they needed. Hadassah, of course, answered cheerily, 'Of course! Of course!' The girl's question and Hadassah's reply illustrated the answer that Hadassah had just given to our question—about how she became the woman she was."[22] ⬥

Learning from the Pious

⬥ In the period preceding the Six-Day War in Israel, Hadassah brought her grandmother, Rebbetzin Rivka, to her home for reasons of safety. And she instructed her children to study their great-grandmother, telling them, "Learn from her ways; engrave them in your hearts." Because Rebbetzin Rivka was a great *tzaddeket.*

When the first air raid siren was heard, the whole Linder family, including Rebbetzin Rivka, took shelter with a neighbor who had a fortified room on the first floor.

When the bombing began, everyone was terrified. Everyone in the fortified room was praying and calling out to God; certainly no one was concerned for cleanliness.

But Rebbetzin Rivka was a very clean and orderly woman. Despite being in a difficult, crowded situation in a room crammed with people, she was troubled by the disorder, although she never said a word about it. So regardless of her advanced age, she began to go around the room picking up papers and trash.

When Hadassah noticed this, she realized what was bothering Grandma Rivka; Hadassah then forgot about her own worries and prayers and put the room in order, in the middle of this war situation—to ease the burden on Grandma Rivka of bending and cleaning, which was beyond her ability and beneath her dignity.

Hadassah was always alert to serve Grandma Rivka, who never asked for anything. Wanting her children to absorb this noble trait, Hadassah often told them, "Look, she needs nothing. In life, you should never ask anything from other people; no one owes you anything—that's the way Great-Grandma Rivka feels. And that is the right way to live. Everything is a gift; no one owes us anything."[23] ⋘⋗

One of the most common reasons for unhappiness in life is that we expect things from people that they do not provide. A pious person believes with total faith that he will receive everything that God wants him to have. Some devout people never ask others for help or favors. When anyone helps them or gives to them in any way, they are pleased and thrilled, because they never expect anything. A woman like Rebbetzin Rivka or Rebbetzin Hadassah is self-reliant, God-reliant, and happy.

The Tzaddeket

During Hadassah's life, her excessive kindness frequently won her not applause but censure. Yet she persevered in her kindness and did good deeds constantly.

~ Toward the end of her life, she once said humbly, "When I was young and had all my powers to do many kind deeds for the sake of heaven, people called me 'different' and 'strange'; many people criticized me. Now that I don't have any energy left and I just sit at home, they call me 'Hadassah the *Tzaddeket*'!"[24] ~

Of course, even when she was elderly, this humble *tzaddeket* never really sat at home idly. She was always doing good deeds and returning God's kindness to her. How? By being kind to His creatures.

Rebbetzin Esther Jungreis

Rebbetzin Esther Jungreis is one of the greatest Jewish personalities of our time. To my mind, she is the *eishet hayil ha-dor,* the Woman of Valor of Our Generation. She has devoted her life to bringing assimilated Jews back to their heritage.

I attended the rebbetzin's annual fundraiser one year when one of the speakers, a woman disciple of the rebbetzin, called her "our Torah mother." Rebbetzin Jungreis gives me an image and idea of what our Jewish Matriarchs were like. I want to recount two personal reminiscences about the rebbetzin.

A Holy Wind

⟨⟩ For many years, I had been reading Rebbetzin Jungreis's weekly column in *The Jewish Press,* and I was always moved by her words.

Then one year, I attended a *Shabbaton*—a festive Sabbath celebration—with her at a Catskills hotel. The rebbetzin spoke during the Shabbat morning services, and her words were so powerful that I began to weep and to shake involuntarily. About half the other people in the audience were also weeping. Her words were so powerful. She spoke with *ruach ha-kodesh,* the holy spirit.

Sometimes people listening to someone like Rebbetzin Jungreis are deeply moved yet fail to understand what they are experiencing. In Hebrew, *ruach* means "spirit" or "wind." Sometimes the "holy wind" blows gently, and sometimes it blows with great force. Hearing Rebbetzin Jungreis's speech, I had felt like a leaf shaking in a strong wind.

Bending Over

⟨⟩ For a number of years, I occasionally went to hear the rebbetzin teach, either in Manhattan or in Brooklyn. I once took my mother, Jeanette Buxbaum, of blessed memory, to see the rebbetzin, who was teaching a Torah class at a synagogue in Brooklyn. I wanted my mother, who was not religiously inclined, to see a *tzaddeket,* a Jewish holy woman. I still occasionally take women friends to see the rebbetzin because I believe it is especially important for women to see a *tzaddeket,* a female model of Jewish holiness.

We were in a small synagogue in Brooklyn that had a *bimah,* a raised stage, in the middle of the room. Half of the narrow synagogue was on one side of the *bimah* and half on the other. The small audience was sitting to one side of the *bimah.* As it turned out, that night was the anniversary of the founding of Rebbetzin Jungreis's Hineni movement (the Hebrew word *hineni* means "I am here," God.)[1] The rebbetzin spoke movingly about how everything she had attained, through Hineni and her many outreach efforts, she had attained because of her holy parents—Rabbi Abraham and Rebbetzin Miriam Jungreis. She spoke very humbly and at length about the greatness of her parents and then called out behind her, "Father, please come to the *bimah* and say a few words to the people."

We had not known that her father was there. He was on the other side of the *bimah,* at the far side of the synagogue, sitting and studying Torah. (The rebbetzin's mother was not present.) The rebbetzin's father got up and walked toward the *bimah.* He was a small man, perhaps five foot one, wearing traditional black garments, with a beautiful white beard, and one could actually see the *Shechinah* glowing on his smiling face. As he approached, I said to my mother, "Ma, I don't think you've ever seen a tzaddik. That's one!" I had taken my mother to see a *tzaddeket,* the rebbetzin; she was also seeing a tzaddik.

As the rebbetzin's father stepped up to the *bimah,* the rebbetzin *bent over double and kissed his hands.* This was so moving to me to see her utter self-nullification before her holy father. *She bent over double* before him.

Rabbi Jungreis spoke briefly in Yiddish, which I do not understand, and my mother translated for me. I remember that he spoke about bringing back to Judaism someone who was very resistant to any religious observance. He had told this man to act as he pleased but pleaded with him to recite just the *Sh'ma* every day. The man agreed, and the ancient holy words brought him back to the Source of his soul. ⪘

Judaism develops a person's reverence for his parents. My own relation to both my parents deepened greatly after my return to Judaism in my mid-twenties. I took my mother to see the rebbetzin because of the profound connection I felt for my mother. The Torah teaches that we must honor our parents—because a person is so much his parents that if he despises them, he essentially despises himself. Everyone who is traditionally religious occasionally meets religious people who have exceptional reverence for their parents. But what if your parents are actually both tzaddikim, as Rebbetzin Jungreis's parents were? Then the reverence becomes unlimited, immeasurable; the rebbetzin bent over double in humility. This incident provided me with a memorable and graphic image of the rebbetzin's greatness and humility. The Rabbis say of holy people that their humility matches their greatness. That is true of the rebbetzin.

Do Not Stand Idly By

Rebbetzin Esther Jungreis writes:

◈ I was born at a difficult period. The winds of war were blowing over Europe, and although the Germans had not yet invaded our city of Szeged, the second largest city in Hungary, persecution of Jews had become an everyday happening.

My father [Abraham] was the rabbi of our community.... Deportations to the concentration camps had not yet begun, but the Hungarian authorities drafted all Jewish young men for slave labor, and since many of the transports passed through our city, our home became a temporary sanctuary for the homeless. The young men who came to our home had to wear yellow armbands.... [Their being conscripted for labor battalions was very often a death sentence.] Szeged was their stopover, and my parents were determined that our home become their home, if only for a brief moment.... The [gentile] superintendent of our building had to be paid off regularly so that he would not report their presence to the police....

There was only one way for these boys to escape the transports and that was to contract some contagious disease that would endanger the health of the non-Jewish combatants. We discovered that the injection of raw milk brought on a mysterious fever, and that a paste made from soybean powder smeared on the eyelids would simulate trachoma, but how to get these concoctions to the Jewish conscripts remained a formidable problem.

As the rabbi of the community, my father had visiting rights to the detention camps, but he was always thoroughly searched and therefore could not carry anything on his person. It was my mother [Miriam] who finally thought of a solution. She sewed pockets into the lining of my coat and secreted the precious potions there, together with some nourishing food and messages from home. Thus, at the age of six, I learned my first lesson in human responsibility: "You shall not stand idly by while the life of your brothers is in jeopardy" (Leviticus 19:16). To me, this was not a remote theoretical concept. Rather, it was a reality which challenged me every moment of the day. Along with this knowledge, I learned the meaning of Jewish pride, for despite the overwhelming risks and constant danger which this responsibility entailed, I also knew that I belonged to a people that demanded such commitment.[2]

Esther Jungreis learned at the age of six self-sacrifice for her fellow Jews. She has followed this path throughout her career as a Jewish leader. It is awesome to think of the bravery of her parents, who not only risked their own lives to save others but risked the lives of their children as well.

Comparing Faces

The rebbetzin and her family were eventually sent to the concentration camps. She writes:

It was faith that enabled me as a child to survive the horrors of Hitler's Holocaust. I recall standing for hours in the mud of Bergen-Belsen waiting for roll call. When the Nazis finally arrived in their immaculate uniforms and shiny boots, cracking their whips and snapping orders, they appeared almost godlike. [Such are the "gods" of the heathens!] Yet strangely enough, I, a little girl dressed in rags, with shaven head and covered with sores, would not have traded places with them for anything. I had only to contrast my father's saintly face with the naked brutality in their eyes to know that it was preferable to die a thousand deaths than to be the daughter of these savages. Although I could not fathom the meaning of the sheer terror that surrounded me, I knew beyond all doubt that God could not be a part of it and that, ultimately, we who believed in Him would overcome.[3] ⁓

Tears for Her People

The rebbetzin's allegiance to God and to the Jewish people and her holy spirit led her eventually to call out as a prophetess to Jews to return to their faith. She writes:

⁓ Often, as I spoke of our people [in speeches to other Jews], I would break down. There may have been those who were embarrassed by my tears, by my open manifestation of emotion, but I have never attempted to disguise my feelings. Live recordings of my speeches have caught these tears, and there have been those who suggested that, in production, I should cut them. But those tears are not my own. They belong to my people and they shall remain.[4]

The rebbetzin's tears are the tears of the *Shechinah*, shed for the suffering of the Jewish people and for the alienation of many Jews from their divine Root. Jeremiah lamented, "My eyes are spent with weeping, my soul is in tumult, my heart is poured out in grief, because of the destruction of the daughter of my people."[5] Elsewhere, Jeremiah tells of "Rachel weeping for her children; she refuses to be comforted for her children, because they are not."[6]

All Children Cry

Rebbetzin Esther Jungreis writes that her parents involved their children in their own religious lives and activities, and that is the way she in turn raised her children. She writes about her life with her husband:

≈ Many people carrying heavy burdens in their hearts came to our home, and we taught our children not only to feel empathy for them but to pray for them, to care for them, and yes, even to cry for them.

I remember one Sabbath eve, when lighting candles, telling my youngest son, Oshie, who at that time was three years old, to pray for the mother of one of his little friends who was very ill. His eyes welled up with tears. A house guest, who was spending the Sabbath with us, wondered out loud at the wisdom of burdening a young child with such a responsibility. "The poor little thing was crying," she protested.

"All children cry," I said, "but some cry for candy and 'give me more,' while others learn to cry because they feel the pain of those in need." ≈

The rebbetzin continues by writing that all of her children have followed in their family's path of helping others, both materially and spiritually.

≈◈≈ "If they feel responsible for their brethren today,
I believe that it is in large measure due to those early
years, when they learned to pray for someone's sick
mom, and even shed a tear."[7] ≈◈≈

Everybody Must Give

One year, just before the High Holidays, Rebbetzin Jungreis was in the
Hasidic neighborhood of Boro Park in Brooklyn to buy some holiday
items. She was sitting in her car, waiting for her assistant, Barbara
Janov, to come out of a store when she saw something:

≈◈≈ Standing a few yards from our car was an elderly
woman, dressed in an ill-fitting black coat, her head covered by a turban. She clutched an open pocketbook in her
hand, and as people walked by, she called out, "*Tzeduka,
tzeduka*"[8] (Charity, charity), and almost without exception, passersby dropped some money in her handbag.

Tzedaka is one of the pillars of Jewish life. . . .
No request for help should be ignored, and most impor-
tantly, the gift must be offered warmly, graciously, and
with a smile. Before the High Holidays, special efforts
are made to intensify one's contributions, so I wasn't
surprised to see even little children respond to the
woman's call. I was about to open the car window to
beckon to her when a teaching of our Sages flashed
through my mind: "The poor are put to shame when they
are forced to go begging. Don't add to their ordeal. Bring
your gift to them." So I walked over to her, wished her a
blessed New Year, and placed some money in her bag.

As I continued to watch as people gave her *tzedaka,* it occurred to me how very grateful to God we must be for having endowed us with a way of life that *demands* that we give.

Suddenly, I noticed a change in her facial expression. With a resolute look, which seemed to say, "OK, that's enough for now. I need a break," she leaned against the wall of a building, took some crackers out of her pocket, and began munching on them. Then something strange happened. Another beggar walked down the street calling, "*Tzeduka, tzeduka.*" Not realizing that she was a competitor, he approached the woman, holding out his hand. What is she going to do now, I wondered.

My little woman opened her pocketbook, took out a coin, and dropped it into the man's hand. I felt like giving her a hug. Good lady! I thought to myself. That coin, coming from her, was perhaps more significant than a major contribution from a wealthy man. Although she herself was a beggar, she totally understood the essence of *tzedaka:* Every person, no matter what his or her station in life, must give.[9] ⊱

According to Jewish law, even a beggar is obligated to give something, however small. And this charity, despite its amount, does more for the giver than for the recipient, because it elevates a person to the status of being in the image of the Giver of all life and of all goodness.

Giving When Things Are Tough

Throughout the ages, every Jewish home contained *tzedaka pushkas,* charity boxes. Children were trained at an early age to always drop

coins into the *pushkas* to teach them their obligation to give to and
to share with others. Rebbetzin Jungreis writes:

≈≫ The impact that *pushkas* had on Jewish life
reached far beyond the confines of *tzedaka.* The extent
to which this was so became apparent to me when I met
Robert, who had just emerged from a nasty, painful
divorce. His wife had left him for her tennis instructor,
but amazingly, there was a calmness and even a gentleness about Robert. I didn't detect any of the cynicism or
bitterness that usually accompany such an experience.

"How did you manage to maintain your positive
outlook?" I asked curiously.

He pondered my question for a moment, then said,
"I guess it's something I learned from my mom."

"Tell me about it. I would like to know."

"My parents were poor people," he began. "My
father was a laborer, and with six children, there wasn't
much to go around. But my mother had at least a dozen
tzedaka pushkas lined up on her windowsill. Every
Friday, before she lit the Sabbath candles, she would
put money into each of the *pushkas* [people often have
a number of *pushkas* dedicated to different specific
charities and causes].

"I remember on one occasion, it must have been a
year after my bar mitzvah, Dad had a particularly bad
week. As I watched my mother drop her coins into the
pushkas, I wondered out loud whether it was necessary
to put money into all of them.

"My mother picked up on my muttering and chided me. 'Borchel'—she always called me by my Jewish name—'you never have to be afraid of giving *tzedaka*, for, whatever you give away, God will give you back a thousandfold. And when things get tough, that's when you really have to double your efforts. If you do that, you will see that God's blessing will always be with you.'

"So Mom kept filling up her *pushkas* throughout bad times as well as good ones, and somehow we always managed. My mom's teaching stayed with me. No matter what happens, no matter where life takes you, you must continue to give. So I guess that throughout my painful experiences, the image of Mom dropping those coins in the boxes even when we ourselves were deprived kept me going. I told myself that if Mom, with all her problems, was able to give, then I too must continue to give, no matter what.

"I was always active in charities, but when my wife left me and my world fell apart, I became even more involved. And that, Rebbetzin, saved my life. I guess that is what prevented me from becoming bitter and depressed."

At one time or another, we all experience personal crises. At such times we have the option of indulging in self-pity and succumbing to depression or of remembering that we have a mission—to make *tikkun olam*—to perfect the world by giving. If we can live by that commitment and remember to help others when we ourselves are in need of help, we will be able to weather the storm and discover that the teaching of King

Solomon, "Charity saves from death," is true in more ways than one.[10] ⬥

The Source of Strength

Rebbetzin Jungreis's mother, Miriam, lived into her nineties and was, as the Rabbis say, a "woman of deeds." Among her good deeds was collecting, laundering, and sorting used clothing for needy Russian-Jewish immigrants to America. The Rebbetzin writes (before her mother's passing):

⬥ A couple of years ago, Mama had to undergo surgery. Her recovery was agonizingly painful, and so during that period, I tried to protect her . . . and didn't bring bags of clothing to her house. But Mama became depressed. "What's the point of living if I can't help people?" she wailed. . . .

Seeing that I had no option, I started to gather the *shmattas* [rags] again. Mama could hardly move. Every step was painful. But she would sit with her bags of clothing, sorting them and deciding which articles would be most appropriate for her needy Russian families.

"Mama," I protested one day, "this is too much for you. You don't have the *koyach* [strength] for it anymore."

"*Koyach!*" she retorted, "*Koyach* you get from giving. When a mother nurses her child, the more the baby takes from her, the more milk God gives her. God gives *koyach* when *you* give."[11] ⬥

Isaiah says, "Those who hope in the Lord will renew their strength [*koyach*]"—those who trust in God and use all their strength to help others, without worrying whether they will have enough, will receive added energy from the Source of all strength.

The Rebbetzin Teaches Children

Rebbetzin Jungreis teaches that to forgive is to emulate God; to harbor resentment is to be a prisoner of your own hatred. She writes that in the secular world, making the first move toward reconciliation is considered an act of weakness. "In the Torah world, however, just the opposite holds true. He who is able to humble himself, suppress his ego, and forgo his honor is the true hero." The rebbetzin tells a story that shows how she helped children, who had learned these Torah values, to have the courage to fulfill them. She writes:

∞ It was one of those scorching hot summer days, but the joy of the bar mitzvah celebration made us oblivious of the heat. My son Yisroel and his wife, Rivke, had organized a beautiful day, and their attention to the smallest details was evident in the seamless way it progressed. Most meaningful of all was the Torah dissertation that Yaakov [the bar mitzvah boy, the rebbetzin's grandson] delivered with ease and eloquence. . . .

The celebration was coming to a conclusion. People were saying their good-byes, and I looked around for my littlest grandchildren. "Where are they?" I asked Rivke.

"Oh, they became restless and went out to play."

Earlier, upon arriving at the synagogue, I noticed that there were many Hasidic boys playing outside. I have always found something very endearing and charming about these children playing their games and having their arguments in Yiddish. I loved watching them engaging in conversation and challenging them with Torah questions, so I was debating whether, despite the heat, I should join my grandchildren and see how they interacted with their newfound friends, when my five-year-old grandson, Yosef, Yaakov's younger brother, came running to me and settled the matter.

"*Bubba* [Grandma], come quickly!" he called out. "Some boys are making fun of Akiva." Akiva is my daughter Slovi's five-year-old, and the two little cousins are great friends.

"What?" I exclaimed in an intentionally dramatic voice. "That's terrible! How can yeshiva boys do such an awful thing—and on *Shabbos* to boot! Come, let's go investigate."

With a satisfied smile, little Yosef took my hand, confident that I would take care of the matter. Yosef led me outside, and sure enough, we found Akiva standing by himself and looking downcast.

"Did someone make fun of you?" I asked.

Akiva just kept staring at the sidewalk and wouldn't answer.

"Yes," Yosef interjected. "I'll show you where those boys are."

And there, just a few steps away, standing where I had seen them earlier, was a group of six to eight little boys. They were the most adorable children you could wish to see. Dressed in their *Shabbos* best, with their long side curls and big black yarmulkes, they looked like a picture.

"Could it be that, God forbid, someone here made fun of Akiva?" I asked in Yiddish.

There was silence as they all stared at me in wonderment.

"If you didn't do it, tell me," I continued, "but if you did, you must apologize. You all know what a terrible thing it is to hurt someone. You must have learned in *heder* that no one is ever allowed to shame someone. It's the biggest sin to do that!"

Still, there was only silence.

"Who will be the first," I asked, "to show the *derech* [correct way] and ask Akiva's forgiveness?"

Not waiting for an answer, I turned away and walked toward Akiva, who was still standing by himself. Without exception, the boys followed me, and each of them approached Akiva and said, "I'm sorry."

I laughed with joy and marveled once again at the power of Torah education. Had I approached any other group of children with the same request, the chances are that they would have responded disrespectfully, but these little boys, because of their Torah background, without exception came to ask forgiveness. As I watched them, in my mind I heard the song that we sang in synagogue in honor of the Torah during the services: "It is a tree of life for those who hold on to it.... Its ways are ways of pleasantness and all its paths are peace."[12] ✑

With Female Prisoners in Israel

The rebbetzin writes the following about one incident of her worldwide outreach work.

⁙ In Israel we visited the female compound of Ramle prison in the heat of a scorching summer day. Accompanying me were my daughter Slovi and Barbara [Janov, the rebbetzin's aide], who was carrying heavy recording equipment to tape the meeting for radio. Not being able to park within the prison compound, we were obliged to walk quite a distance, and as we trudged along, I heard Barbara mutter under her breath, "I don't know how I ever got involved with you. You could have spoken at a normal place, like Jerusalem or Tel Aviv. Why did you have to decide to come to a prison in this God-forsaken place to speak to a few inmates?"

Though it was true that, fortunately, there weren't too many prisoners, our Torah does not consider numbers to be a criterion in determining the value of people. Each and every soul is a world unto itself, and "if you save just one, you save a world." I didn't bother getting into all that, for I was lost in my own thoughts, trying to figure out what I would say to the inmates. As much as I racked my brains, I couldn't come up with anything that would be instructive yet not condescending, meaningful yet not judgmental.

As we finally reached the prison gates, I still did not have the foggiest notion what my message would be. Barbara rang the bell. As the large gate slowly rolled up, she started forward, not seeing the long iron bar at the bottom of the gate, tripped, and fell flat on her face. The prisoners, who were assembled to await our arrival, stood aghast as the guards rushed forward to help.

Barbara got up, brushed the dust off her clothes, and tried to cleanse her scrapes.

Suddenly, it occurred to me that I had my speech. I proceeded to introduce Barbara to the inmates and explained that in all the years that we had worked together, I had never seen her take a flop like that. "But perhaps," I said, "it was meant to be that this should happen here in full view of all of you, so that you might see that it is possible for anyone to fall—but if you do, you have to stand up, cleanse yourself, learn from the experience, and start over again. That's my message," I concluded. "Now I'll take questions."

Of all my programs in Israel that summer, it was perhaps that little speech in the dust of Ramle that was my most moving experience. We stayed there the entire afternoon. The women had numerous questions. They wanted to start classes, study, and find their way back to God.

There was one girl, however, Irit, who did not get involved in the discussion. I noticed her right away. She had a beautiful face, with smouldering, angry eyes, and she sat there smoking one cigarette after the other.

"This is all talk," she called out. "No one will give us a second chance. You're all wasting your time listening to her."

"What you say may be true in the secular world, but not in God's world," I responded. "In the Torah world, things are different," and with that, I proceeded to tell her the story of Rabbi Yochanan and Reish Lakish.

Rabbi Yochanan was one of the most handsome men in all of [ancient] Israel. It is said that women would gaze at his beauty in the hope of having beautiful children. Well, one day, Rabbi Yochanan was accosted by a gang of bandits.

"'What a pity to waste such a handsome face on a Torah sage,' the leader of the bandits, Reish Lakish, said.

"'And what a pity to waste such strength and such a fine mind on robbery,' Rabbi Yochanan answered. Then he added, 'If you think that I am handsome, you should see my sister. If you were a Torah scholar, you might have the opportunity to marry a girl like that.'

"Reish Lakish took Rabbi Yochanan up on his challenge and started to study. He became one of the most celebrated sages of his generation, and he married Rabbi Yochanan's beautiful sister. Throughout his life, he and Rabbi Yochanan, who had become his best friend, studied Torah together.

"So you can see, Irit, that not only did the Torah world offer Reish Lakish a second chance, but it accepted him as a Torah sage as well. And more, Reish Lakish was able to convert all the negative experiences from his past life into positive teachings from which everyone could benefit. So if you turn to God, the miracle can occur for you as well. 'Make for Me an opening as small as the eye of a needle and I will pull you through,' God says.

"Try it, Irit. You'll see. It will work."

"Yeah, and everything will be forgotten and just fine and dandy," Irit scoffed.

"Yes, that's exactly right," I said, deciding to ignore her sarcasm. "'Even if your sins be as red as scarlet, I, the Lord your God, will make them white as snow' is His promise if you follow the formula."

"And what's the formula?" another girl interjected.

"It's a threefold process," I said, "repentance, prayer, and charity. Repentance entails your taking a good, long, and honest look at yourself, admitting where you went wrong, feeling remorse, and resolving never to repeat that act again, and in general committing to God's commandments—observing the Sabbath and living a life of integrity.

"Prayer is something you should do on a daily basis, ideally three times a day—morning, afternoon, and night. Prayer will nourish your soul even as food sustains your body.

"And the third step, *tzedaka*—whatever little you have, you must share, and if you do so, God will give you more. But I must remind you," I added, "of something that I say in all my classes. *Tzedaka* doesn't mean only monetary gifts but giving of yourselves, showing kindness and consideration to others. Perhaps when you leave here, you will do voluntary work with troubled girls and thus convert all this negativity into something positive. The idea is to learn from every life experience, and sometimes you can learn more from failures than from successes."

"Well, I sure had many failures," Irit volunteered.

"Don't be dismayed by them. King Solomon taught that 'Seven times a righteous man falls, and seven

times he stands up,' meaning that a righteous man is
not necessarily someone who is born righteous but
rather someone who *becomes* righteous by standing up
despite the fact that he has fallen.

"But why seven?" someone asked.

"Seven," I answered, "because seven represents
the days of the week—this world, a world in which we are
bound to fall but in which we are nevertheless capable of
standing up. God judges us not so much by the mistakes
that we make but by how we deal with those mistakes, by
our willingness to redress wrongs and make amends."

We went on talking for a while. When we finally
got up to leave, Irit approached Slovi. "We don't want
to impose upon your mother," she said, "but could you
please take this note to Jerusalem and place it in a
crevice in the Western Wall on our behalf?"

On the note was written: "Almighty God, forgive
us," and the names of all the girls were signed on it.[13] ◁◈▷

The female inmates were certainly affected by the holy rebbetzin's
teachings, but I am sure they were moved even more by the great
power of her personality and speech, for she speaks with the holy
spirit. May there be more women like her in Israel.

Two Jewish Girls in Denmark

Two blessings—for wine and then for bread—are traditionally recited
at the Sabbath table. On the table, two loaves of braided bread (*challah*) are customarily covered with a cloth while the *kiddush,* the blessing over the wine, is recited. The Rabbis say we cover the bread so
that it will not be embarrassed by our preferring the wine. Probably

the original reason for covering the bread was so as not to have one's eye fall on it before blessing the wine, because a person would then be obligated to make the blessing over the bread first, out of proper order—following the principle that one does not pass over a *mitzvah* that presents itself—or the person might notice the bread and be distracted while making the blessing over the wine. But the Rabbis, as often, drew a beautiful moral lesson from this Jewish custom of covering the bread: never embarrass another human being.

⊰⊱ Some years ago, I (Yitzhak Buxbaum) taught at the Conference on Judaism in rural New England, which was held at a college campus in Vermont. The Jews in rural New England often live isolated in areas with few other Jews nearby. Years ago, they began an annual summer conference, gathering for a week to study and pray together and to give each other encouragement and support. At this conference, I went to a storytelling session led by an acquaintance of mine named David Fried, who is a tree farmer in New Hampshire (an unusual occupation for a Jew!). David is a quiet, handsome man—a farmer with a big heart. When we spoke about our rebbe, Rabbi Shlomo Carlebach, and I told him some things about Shlomo, tears came to his eyes.

David is a Jewish storyteller, and at this conference, he organized and facilitated a storytelling session where about twenty of us sat in a circle and each told a personal story.

This is the story told by one of the people there, a woman in her forties named Emily Fischer.

Emily grew up in Denmark. She has Scandinavian-Jewish looks, if you can imagine such a thing. She is very beautiful. She had a beautiful voice and a graceful manner as she told the story; she was formerly an actress. She was then living in a small seacoast town in Maine; I am told that she has since moved away.

When she was a girl of about twelve in Denmark, her closest friend was fourteen, only two years older, but this friend taught her everything she knew. Sometimes with adolescents, one friend may be only a little older than the other but seems to know so much more. Emily's friend was wise beyond her years, and Emily adored her. Emily thought that her friend knew that she would die young because she lived life so fully. She did die young, in her thirties, and Emily told this story in her honor.

Emily's friend was Orthodox, and Emily, who is not, would sometimes go to her friend's house for Shabbat. They would light Shabbat candles. Then they would talk as they watched them burn down. The candles would go out, and it was night. Emily said her friend taught her "how to accept the darkness."

Whenever they would get together, they would light two candles having nothing to do with Shabbat but as a symbol of their friendship.

There was a musician, a fiddler, who would come around and play in the courtyards of the buildings, a beggar who played for money. He usually played sad songs. One day when Emily was visiting her friend, this fiddler came. Emily's friend told her that when a beggar plays music for money, you must always give. People would sit inside their homes and hear the music out-

side in the courtyard and would toss some coins out the
window. Although they were just girls and did not have
much money, her friend told her that they had to give
something. She also said that they must wrap the few
coins in paper so that the poor person would not be
humiliated by having to scrounge to pick them up. She
told Emily the Jewish teaching of how terrible it is to
shame another person. Emily worshiped her friend and
took this lesson about not humiliating another human
being into her heart.

She carefully wrapped up her coins in a piece of
paper, as her friend had showed her, and threw the little
package out the window. But her paper broke, and the
coins scattered! Her friend had just explained to her
how terrible it was to embarrass another person, and
look what happened! She was *so* ashamed!

(As Emily told this tale, she was reliving the moment. She closed her eyes and brought both her hands to
her temples in a gesture of shame—she was *so* ashamed!
At the same time, David, the storyteller, was sitting near
her with tears streaming from his closed eyes as he
listened to her story. It was so moving to see them both,
although neither one saw the other.)

Emily's friend told her, "We mustn't look!"—they
must not watch the man as he picked up the coins scattered on the ground so as not to humiliate him. Emily
said that her friend taught her an important Jewish
lesson that day, about not shaming or humiliating
another person.

She ended by saying that *she recalls this story
every time she covers the challahs in front of the wine.*
Often when people tell a tale in honor of someone, they forget to mention the other person's name,
thinking that the listeners would not be interested.
I asked Emily the name of her friend. She said it was
Bonita Polarsky—a Jewish girl who grew up in Denmark
and died young but left this beautiful story behind
for us.[1] ◈

Sometimes when I tell this story I say, "How refined this girl was!
Would we know that when a beggar plays music for charity, you have
to give? Maybe; I would not have known. One might think, 'I don't
like the music.' But this girl knew and she knew to tell her friend."
Would we know that when you give *tzedaka,* you should fold it in a
piece of paper so as not to embarrass the poor person by making
him scrounge for the scattered coins? I would not have known that.
She knew, and she knew to tell her friend.

Someone might say she was trained and had a good Jewish
religious education. Yes, it is true. But could her parents have trained
her in what to do when the paper broke—not to look and embarrass
the man? She knew that by herself. How pure, how refined!

What a great lesson in kindness and sensitivity we can learn
from this wonderful young woman. May we give to the poor with an
open hand and an open heart and spare them embarrassment, in
the merit of Bonita Polarsky—may her memory be for a blessing!—
and in the merit of this story, which she left us.

This story is a classic tale. It shows that there can be tales today that are inspiring and elevated, just like the tales of former times.
But we must notice them and cherish them and collect them—even
tales about friends and family and people we know—just as Emily
told this tale about the dear friend of her youth, Bonita Polarsky.

Allison and the Fruit Seller

A story may or may not be about a great *tzaddeket* but about any one of us at a special moment when we open ourselves to our soul, to God, and rise to holiness.

✍ A young woman named Allison Protas, who is returning to Judaism, attended a synagogue class on Jewish mysticism that I taught in Brooklyn. In one of our class discussions about Hasidic stories, Allison told of an incident that had happened to her earlier that day.

Allison, who is in the advertising business, takes the subway to work, and she sees the way most of the people on the train close themselves off from the outside world and withdraw into a little self-imposed cocoon. She does not want to live that way and resolved to try to be open and friendly whenever possible, as part of her spiritual practice. Every day on the way to the subway, she passes a fruit stand, and although she never bought any fruit, she always made it a point to say hello to the fruit seller.

While she was walking to the subway earlier that day, she was mulling over her spiritual life and became discouraged, thinking that she had accomplished little. As she approached the fruit stand, she realized that that night she would actually need some fruit and decided to buy something.

She selected a nectarine and then took out her wallet to pay, but the seller said, "Oh, no! I'm not going to take money from you. Every day you say hello to me, and I feel so good, it makes my day. Please take this fruit as a gift."

Allison was so moved by the man's gesture but also by the divine providence: that the moment when she had felt discouraged about her spiritual life—and thinking she was not making any progress at all—God had given her a clear sign: "Don't be discouraged, Allison! You are accomplishing something for yourself and for others!"

She told us that she realized from this incident that it takes very little to lift someone's else's spirits—a simple greeting can be so important.

About a week later, Allison sent me the following e-mail message: "Yitzhak, you're not going to believe this. I'm kind of freaking out, but I was going to buy another piece of fruit this morning, for the second time ever, and then I decided naaah, but as I walked by and said my usual smiley good morning to my new fruit-seller friend, he had a nectarine already in a bag for me and passed it off like a relay baton. I actually began to cry because it touched me so deeply and it was just a monumental little moment!"

Allison was probably disturbed by the thought of being offered another gift or perhaps embarrassing the fruit seller and putting him on the spot. But it seems she needed another providential lesson when she was about to close herself off again: "Keep yourself open, keep yourself open! Don't worry so much about being embarrassed or embarrassing others!" Because these moments of giving and taking, of being openhearted and open to the world are the very meaning of life. ✎

God Bless You!

A tale similar to Allison's was told in the same Brooklyn synagogue class by Carole Forman.

⋙ One day, when Carole was in Manhattan, she went over to a kiosk to buy a newspaper, and the man who took her money—someone from South Asia, perhaps a Pakistani—said, "May God bless you"—meaningfully, not just by rote.

Carole, who was a bit down and depressed that day, replied in a low voice, "I hope so."

The man insisted, "No, no, no! God *does* bless you!"

This ringing affirmation of faith brought tears to Carole's eyes.

Sometimes our skeptical mind causes us to forget that God is always blessing us. The newspaper seller, it seems, makes it a religious habit to always bless people when he takes their money, and after Carole's hesitation, he was reminding her of the profound truth—that God is always blessing us; we merely have to be open to receive the blessing. The wind of divine grace is always blowing; we just have to unfurl our sails.

Raise the Torah Banner High

⋙ At the Talmud Torah, the famous Musar school in Kelm, Lithuania, founded by the Elder of Kelm, Rabbi Simha Zissel Ziv, both men and women were encouraged to study *musar*—ethics and perfection of character. The Elder's daughter, Rebbetzin Nechama Liba, was a respected teacher of *musar*. Her father called her "a wonder" for having so successfully accomplished the *musar* task of changing her nature. Noted male *musar* teachers such as Rabbi Yerucham Levovitz, Rabbi Elya Lopian, and Rabbi Moshe Rosenstein visited her regularly once a week to hear her insights on how to live one's life with faith and trust in God.

Her husband was Rabbi Tzvi Hirsch Braude, who later became headmaster of the Talmud Torah of Kelm. Both he and his wife were very devoted to the yeshiva—which was rich in spirit but poor in funds. Rebbetzin Nechama Liba therefore managed a store for boots and galoshes, which she and her husband owned and from which they earned a living. When she was not busy with customers, she sat in the store and studied works of *musar*. The store naturally drew many customers, for in addition to being a respected teacher in the Musar movement, Nechama Liba was the daughter of the Elder of Kelm and the wife of Rabbi Tzvi Hirsch Braude. Her nephew, Reb Nachum Velvel Dessler, helped her with the customers. Periodically, she would ask Reb Nachum Velvel how much they had earned that week. As soon as she reached a predetermined sum, she would immediately close the store, telling her nephew, "The other store owners also have to earn a living." She had faith and trust in the One who provides sustenance to all life, and she did not want to prosper at the expense of others.

During World War II, the revered Nechama Liba was already old in years, and the following story concerning the last day of her life was told by a student of the Talmud Torah of Kelm who survived the Holocaust.

When the Germans invaded Lithuania, they asked
the Lithuanians to assist them in rounding up the Jews.
The majority of Lithuanians responded with enthusiasm, and they volunteered to help with the slaughter
of the local Jewish population. Kelm was no exception.
When the Lithuanians came to the place where most of
the Jews—including the students of the Talmud Torah—
had been gathered, they had already savagely murdered
a number of Jews in Kelm. The Jews were ordered to
march to the town square. From the looks on the faces
of the Lithuanians that morning, their victims had few
doubts as to what lay in store for them. But as they
marched at gunpoint, the men of the Talmud Torah sang
and danced as if it were *Simhat Torah*—the Festival of
Rejoicing with the Torah. Although they knew that their
physical lives would soon end, they also knew that the
life-affirming teachings of the Torah would endure. They
were therefore enraptured in the songs they had sung
so often—"*Vetaher libeinu l'avdecha b'emet*" ["Purify our
hearts to serve You in truth!"] and "*Ashreinu ma tov
chelkeinu*" ["How fortunate are we, how good is our lot
(to be Jews)!"].

Held high on a chair was Rebbetzin Nechama Liba,
whom they carried just as if she were a *sefer Torah,* a
precious Torah scroll.[1] ⪥

When we learn to raise up Jewish holy women who are living Torahs,
like banners to inspire us and lift our hearts, we will be on the way
to the days of redemption and the coming of the Messiah. May it be
God's will.

Notes

Page xxi   Introduction

  1. Isaiah 60:21.

  2. *Yalkut Hadash,* Malachim, 63, 93.

Page 3   Sabbath Candle-Lighting Prayers

  1. This traditional spiritual practice helps a person remember Shabbat every day and adds great power to the holiness of his Shabbat experience.

  2. *Avraham Eved HaShem,* p. 295.

Page 4   Tears Before Candle Lighting

  1. Shimon Vanovo, *Tiferet Nashim,* p. 63.

Page 6   In the Merit of the Sabbath Candles

  1. This tale is a composite of two versions, one heard at the Carlebach Shul, on Shabbat, May 28, 1999, from Channa Schaeffer, who said she heard it from Rabbi Shlomo Carlebach. I've mixed in another oral rendering from Rosalie Eisen and retold the story in my own words. The other tellers told the tale without the heroine's name, which I found in *Sippurim V'Hiddushei Torah MaiHaHozeh MiLublin: Nifla'ot HaRebbe,* p. 60, no. 154.

  I removed the following paragraph from this tale, after the rich man continued his trip: "Shortly thereafter, when the Seer of Lublin was praying the Sabbath Welcoming Service, he ascended, as always, into heaven, and they complained to him, 'You are always blessing people and we have to fulfill your wishes. Is your wife too getting into the act now?' The rebbe

said, 'Let the light shine for him for just half an hour.'" I've removed this because its only point is to indicate that a woman
should not give blessings and that the Seer has to authorize his
wife's blessing.

Page 8   A Prayer over the Challahs

1. Martin Buber (ed.), *Tales of the Hasidim,* vol. 1: *The Early Masters*
(New York: Schocken Books, 1947), p. 213, quoting *Sifro Shel
Yaakov Tzvi.*

Page 8   The Taste of the Garden of Eden

1. *Kodesh Hillulim,* p. 139, quoting *Ohalei Tzaddikim* 17. There is another version of this, about Rebbe Elimelech of Lizensk, in Kalman
Serkez (ed.), *The Holy Beggars' Banquet* (Northvale, N.J.: Aronson, 1998), p. 256. Neither provides the name of Rabbi David's
wife, so I have named her Miriam Shulamis.

Here is another variant of this story, from *Mivasair Tov: Z'chut
Nashim Tzidkaniyot,* p. 94:

Why the Kugel *Tasted So Good*

One Shabbat, the Rebbe of Chantshin tasted his wife's
kugel [noodle pudding], and it was unbelievably delicious,
like the taste of the Garden of Eden. He asked her, "Why is
the kugel so delicious this *Shabbos*? Did you add something
special?"

"No," she said. "I didn't add anything. I made it like every
Shabbos."

After further questioning by her husband, the rebbe, she
said, "Every *erev Shabbos*, while making the *kugel,* I pray
that it should taste good. I did the same this *erev Shabbos*
too, but I did cry a lot about it. And one teardrop fell into the
kugel."

Then the rebbe knew why the *kugel* that Shabbat tasted
so delicious.

Page 11   Healing Food

1. *Reb* is an honorific title, meaning something like "Mister," used with a person's first name.

2. *Mai Ber Yeshayahu,* pp. 43–44. I heard this tale retold on September 3, 1994, by Rabbi Shlomo Carlebach, who said he found it in a book (probably the same as my source).

3. For example, a Hasidic story in *Emet V'Yatziv,* vol. 3, p. 116, no. 45, tells about a woman possessed by a *dybbuk* (the spirit of a deceased person) brought to Rebbe Eleazar of Koznitz. The rebbe tried to exorcize the demon but was unsuccessful. Though the demon yelled it was in pain from being "beaten," it refused to exit. The rebbe then told the family to take the woman home. On the way, she fainted and became well, after which the rebbe said that she was healed because she had eaten cookies baked by his sister, the *tzaddeket* Reizel. The editor, however, claims that the rebbe said this is because he was trying to hide his own holiness. That is not impossible, but it reflects the editor's view, not the rebbe's, and misses the point that women's holiness can also heal.

4. Psalm 45:14.

Page 13   Watching at the Market

1. Retold in my own words from the story in Y. Malka, *B'zchut Nashim Tzidkaniyot,* vol. 2, p. 128.

Page 14   Two Pious Peddlers

1. Malka, *B'zchut Nashim Tzidkaniyot,* vol. 2, p. 131.

Page 17   Are You Not Our Father?

1. *Sefer HaToldot: Rabbi Yisrael Baal Shem Tov,* vol. 1, p. 75; *Kol Sippurei Baal Shem Tov,* vol. 1, p. 251, no. 6, from *Likkutei Dibburim.*

2. *Netivot Shalom,* p. 258.

3. *Ma'aseh HaShem HaShalem,* p. 121, no. 17; p. 138, no. 16.

4. *Tiferet Beit David,* p. 105.

5. Rabbi Eliezer Papo, *Pele Yo'aitz, ot Tof: Tisha B'Av,* p. 303.

Page 19   Riveleh the *Tzaddeket*

1. *Shivhei HaBaal Shem Tov,* p. 145, nos. 70, 71; Dan Ben-Amos and Jerome R. Mintz (eds.), *In Praise of the Baal Shem Tov* (Northvale, N.J.: Aronson, 1994), p. 120, nos. 95, 96; *Likkutim Yekarim,* p. 1, no. 1.

Page 22   Holy Spirit

1. Malka, *B'zchut Nashim Tzidkaniyot,* p. 51. At the end of the original text, the rebbe praises his wife but also denigrates women: "Rebbe Yitzhak Meir answered with surprise, 'Where does a woman get *ruach ha-kodesh* like this? I tell you, when Reb Yaakov died, I heard in the Heavenly Court exactly what she said now.'" I have altered this.

Page 24   Deeds Great and Small

1. Rabbi Elijah, the Torah genius (*gaon*) from Vilna, was one of the greatest Jewish scholars of all time.

2. *Glimpses of Greatness,* p. 193; *Orhot Hasidecha,* p. 350. A version of the tale about the Vilna Gaon's wife can be found in *Shimusha Shel Torah,* p. 19; I found her name in yet another source. For the daughter, I created the name Batsheva.

Page 26   How I Envy You!

1. *Ner Yisrael,* vol. 5, p. 255, no. 62.

2. *Shabbat* 88b quoting Judges 5:31.

Page 29   A Fence to Wisdom

1. Leah Esther Zusmam, *Sarah Shneirer: Sippur Hayeha Shel M'yasedet Bais Yaakov* (Jerusalem: Hochmah, n.d.), p. 103.

Page 30   A Saving Prayer

1. *Orot MiMir,* p. 46. The allusion in the final sentence is to the heavenly scales that decide between life and death, especially in critical moments.

Page 32   Insulting Her Husband

1. Great rabbinic authors are sometimes called by the name of their most famous book, as here; *Noda BeYehuda* was the title of Rabbi Yehezkel Landau's book.

2. *Tiferet Nashim,* p. 8, quoting *Sh'al Avicha VaYagedcha.* The name of the Noda BeYehuda's wife was obtained from another source.

Page 36   Rebbetzin "Devorah Cohen"

1. The *Haggadah,* a traditional text that contains the story of the Exodus from Egypt, is recited at the Passover *seder.*

2. Sara Levinsky Rigler, "Holywoman," from the Aish HaTorah Web site, Mar. 19, 2000.

3. Courtesy of Sara Levinsky Rigler.

4. Sara Levinsky Rigler, "It's So Hard," from the Aish HaTorah Web site, Sept. 10, 2000.

Page 46   If It's Difficult, It Must Be Good

1. This is a euphemism for "after my death."

2. According to the Talmud, a *mitzvah* may be beneath a great person's dignity—for example, the *mitzvah* to help unload another person's donkey or, as here, to stand on the street to ask people for charity money.

3. These prayers accompany the ceremonial casting of one's sins into a body of water.

4. Traditionally, it is a great merit to give *tzedaka,* and a person who solicits *tzedaka* from others "offers merit" to those whom he asks.

5. Avraham, *Hie Tit'hallal,* p. 145, quoting *Tenuat HaMusar.*

Page 49   Using Every Device

1. *Kovetz Sippurim* (1955–1956), p. 4, no. 4.

Page 50   The *Shofar*

1. Avraham, *Hie Tit'hallal,* p. 97.

Page 52   An Angel for the Poor

1. The Musar movement is a pietistic movement begun in the nineteenth century that focuses on ethics and the perfection of character.

2. As noted earlier, it is customary in traditional Jewish religious culture for beggars and charity collectors to solicit at any public gathering.

3. *Tenuat HaMusar,* vol. 2, p. 26.

Page 53   A Generous Wife

1. Adapted from Barbara Rush, *The Book of Jewish Women's Tales* (Northvale, N.J.: Aronson, 1994), p. 68.

Page 55   A Blessing

1. *Butzina Kadisha,* p. 1, no. 3, quoting *Menorat Zahav.*

Page 56   Yenta the Prophetess

1. Moyshe Fainkind, "Yente di Neviete" (Yente the Prophetess), in *Froyen-Rebeim un Barimte Perzenlekhkeytn in Poyln* (Women Rebbes and Famous Personalities in Poland) (Warsaw, 1937), pp. 22–23. Translated by Justin Lewis and edited by Yitzhak Buxbaum. Another version, in *Kovetz Eliyahu,* p. 98, no. 305, reads as follows:

> Rebbe Yehiel Michal of Zlotchov had a daughter named Yenta. Once, her father saw her pause in the middle of her housework and say the *Kedusha*—because she heard the angels in heaven saying *Kedusha.*

Page 58   Loud *Davvening*

1. Adapted from Miriam Samsonowitz, *Grandma: Mrs. Devorah Sternbuch* (Bnai Brak, Israel, 1994), pp. 63, 67, 68.

Page 59   All Prayer

1. *Hayim Sh'Yesh Bahem,* p. 392.

Page 61   Edel, Daughter of the Baal Shem Tov

1. The Rabbis say that because the Jews are such a fiery people, God had to give them a fiery law to tame them. Note that the name Edel would be pronounced the same as the acronym for this verse.

2. *Shivhei HaBaal Shem Tov HaShalem,* p. 164, no. 86; Ben-Amos and Mintz, *In Praise of the Baal Shem Tov,* p. 137, no. 114.

3. *Heichal HaBaal Shem Tov,* p. 282.

4. *Or HaShabbat,* p. 110.

5. *Me'ir Einei Yisrael,* p. 141.

Page 63   Trust in God!

1. *Tiferet Nashim,* p. 177, quoting *Tzofia Halichot.*

2. Ecclesiastes 4:9–10.

Page 67   Elijah's Cup

1. Adapted from Ellen Frankel, *The Classic Tales: 4,000 Years of Jewish Lore* (Northvale, N.J.: Aronson, 1993), p. 605, quoting *Sippurei Eliyahu HaNavi;* other English versions can be found in Serkez, *The Holy Beggars' Banquet,* p. 161 (told by Rabbi Shlomo Carlebach) and in Annette Labovitz, *Time for My Soul* (Northvale, N.J.: Aronson, 1987), p. 350.

2. 1 Samuel 1:8.

Page 70   The Screaming Baby

1. The *Tochacha* is in the Torah portion *Ki Tavo* (Deuteronomy 28:15–69).

2. *Hedvat HaHayim*, vol. 2: *Emunah U'Vitahon*, p. 33.

Page 72   Have Faith!

1. *Kerem Beit Yisrael*, p. 175.

Page 75   The *Bris*

1. The original version reads: "During this whole year, we decided not to kiss our baby, because whenever we were about to kiss him, we asked ourselves, 'How can we kiss an uncircumcised baby?'" My rebbe and teacher, Rabbi Shlomo Carlebach, told me that sometimes he would "change a story without changing it" because he knew it could not have happened as written. I have changed this motif to a vow to strengthen the parents' resolve because I felt that the parents could not have said this as recorded. You decide.

2. *Tiferet Nashim*, p. 253. The rebbe's name, not found in the text, was supplied to me by Rabbi Tzvi Mandel of Brooklyn from *Seder HaHasidut* by Alfasi.

Page 76   A Special Gift

1. *Connections/Hakrev Ushma*, 1987. Rabbi Shlomo Carlebach told this story, which he heard from his brother Rabbi Eli Hayyim, a Bobover Hasid, who told it to Shlomo on the same Hanukkah that he heard it from the Bobover Rebbe.

Page 77   A Covenant in the Flesh

1. I have retold this tale in my own words. It is a composite of Avraham, *Hie Tit'hallal*, p. 86; *Tiferet Nashim*, p. 61, quoting *Netzah Yisrael*; and Yaffa Eliach, *Hasidic Tales of the Holocaust* (New York: Oxford University Press, 1982), p. 175. The first book says the rebbe's name was Abraham Shapiro; the last-mentioned

book is more trustworthy in this matter and says it was Rebbe Yisrael Spira.

Page 80   The Clotheslines

1. The Rabbis teach that sometimes we deserve stern punishment for our sins, but God first sends us a lesser punishment and gives us a reprieve if we accept it penitently. So when a minor mishap occurs, pious people say, "May it be an atonement for me!"—that is, an atonement for one's sins.

2. Adapted from *Tiferet Nashim,* p. 14, quoting *Shalom Bayit;* Avraham, *Hie Tit'hallel,* p. 57, quoting *K'Tzait HaShemesh BiGevurato.* I have removed and changed the following original ending of this story:

> She said that earlier that night, her child had suddenly developed a high fever, which she took as a punishment from heaven for her nastiness that afternoon.
>
> The *tzaddeket,* the spiritual heroine of this tale, was of the belief that she merited, because of this deed, to give birth to a son, who became one of the great Torah scholars of the holy city of Jerusalem. How happy she felt when she managed to get past that single fateful moment in which she could have broken out in a raging fury and hysterical crying—but she preferred the Torah way of restraining herself from the wickedness of disputes! In the end, she never regretted that she had acted correctly. The son she gave birth to that year is one of the great *poskim* [Jewish legal deciders] of our generation, Rabbi Shalom Elyashiv.

We can learn something about storytelling from this tale. The purpose of stories is to teach. If a tale has an element that is unacceptable and disturbing to some of the readers and will prevent them from absorbing the main point, there is no reason to tell the story unless one changes or explains that element. Most people who will read this book will not be able to accept that God punished the one woman's son with a high fever because of her behavior, nor that the good woman was rewarded that year by giving birth to an exceptional son. The main point of the tale in my view is to control one's anger and be patient. As a storyteller I have decided that it is necessary to adapt this tale as I have done. Moreover, I am not obligated by the woman's understanding of the spiritual connections implied by the events. I can tell the story to teach what it means to me; although, if possible, I feel responsible, as a *maggid*, a religious storyteller, as in this note, to inform the reader or listener of the change.

Page 83   The Guest

1. Malka, *B'Zchut Nashim Tzidkaniyot*, p. 110; a version of this tale can also be found in Serkez, *The Holy Beggars' Banquet*, p. 167. Neither work identifies the rebbetzin by name, so I have named her Hanna Hayya.

Page 85   The Sound of Her Blessings

1. *B'Ma'alot Kedoshim V'Tehorim*, vol. 3, p. 47. The rebbetzin's name was supplied to me by Rabbi Kasten of Brooklyn, the aide to the Rachmastrivker Rebbe.

Page 88   The Water Barrel

1. Raichel Horowitz, *The Bostoner Rebbetzin Remembers* (Brooklyn: Mesorah, 1996), p. 17.

Page 89   Even Her Taking Was Giving

1. Adapted from Avraham, *Hie Tit'hallal*, p. 161.

Page 90   A Reward for Kindness

1. This was often the custom of young men who aspired to spiritual heights, but some idlers also did the same.

2. According to the halachic rule of *yihud*, "being alone," a male may not be alone in a room with a female other than a family member—both to protect her from abuse and to protect him from temptation.

3. *Nifla'ot HaSaba Kadisha*, p. 36.

Page 95   One Flesh

1. *Derech HaMelech,* p. 401; permitted interest (*heter iska*) means allowing the lender to take interest by regarding him as the borrower's partner.

2. Nehemiah Polen, *The Holy Fire* (Northvale, N.J.: Aronson, 1994), p. 6; the final verse quoted is Genesis 2:24.

Page 97   At His Wife's Death

1. *Shivhei HaBaal Shem Tov HaShalem,* p. 200, no. 115.

Page 98   How to Accept Suffering

1. *Kerem Beit Yisrael,* p. 229. The original story says that the rebbe blessed the woman with a son. Since this seems to imply a reward of having a son who is of more worth than a daughter, I could not bear to leave this element in the tale.

Page 102   Great Love

1. Rabbi Yisrael Meir of Radin was called the Hafetz Hayim after the title of his most famous book, which means "He Who Desires Life."

2. Avraham, *Hie Tit'hallal,* p. 48, quoting *HaHafetz Hayim: Hayav U'Fa'alo.* The story here says that the tale the rabbi told is in the book *Toldot Adam,* chap. 16.

Page 103   *Tzedaka* as a Cure

1. *Kedushat HaYehudi,* p. 240, no. 244.

Page 104   A Fifth

1. In 2 Samuel 12, the prophet Nathan tells King David a parable about a rich man with a large flock who made a meal of the single lamb of a poor man.

2. *Reb Shlomele,* p. 169, in the words of Rabbi Yitzchok Eisenstadt, slightly adapted. There is another version of this tale, again as told by Rabbi Eisenstadt, in Yitta Halberstam Mandelbaum (ed.),

Holy Brother: Inspiring Stories and Enchanted Tales About Rabbi Shlomo Carlebach (Northvale, N.J.: Aronson, 1999), p. 116. For another story about Pessia Carlebach and her lack of attachment to possessions, see "Pessia Carlebach and the Gentile Maid" later in this book.

Page 107   Standing Up for Herself

1. Exodus 35:26.
2. Esther 1:20.
3. It is traditional to interpret one Torah expression as illuminated by a parallel expression elsewhere.
4. I have combined the version in *Tiferet Nashim,* p. 79, quoting *Imrei Fi,* and the one in *MiGedolei HaHasidut: HaAdmor Rabbi Yeshaya Moskat MiPraga,* p. 15, no. 2. Remarkably, sadly, and typically, the latter book about Rabbi Yeshaya does not contain his wife's name! I have created a name, Havva, to honor her.

Page 109   No Joke Needed

1. Proverbs 31:26.
2. *Sichat Hulin Shel Talmidei Hachamim HeHadash,* in *Otzar Sichat HaHachamim,* the small section about women Torah scholars, "Hochmat Nashim," p. 42, no. 7.

Page 112   The Boldness of Rebbes

1. *Tehillot Baruch,* pp. 66–68; the daughters' names are from pp. 69–74. The fourth daughter's name is not known, so I gave her the name Pessia. Rabbi Shmuel Teich of Brooklyn, the author of *Tehillot Baruch,* is a descendant of Rebbe Baruch of Medzibuz. He told me that there is no family tradition regarding the name of Rebbe Baruch's first wife and that his attempts to find it were unsuccessful. I have given her the name Yitta.

Page 114   Thank God!

1. Tamar Davidovitz, *Eishis Chayil,* trans. Nechama Landesman (New York: Feldheim, 1991), p. 94, with minor editorial changes.

Page 115   Serving a Torah Scholar

1. *Tiferet Nashim,* p. 65, quoting *Derech Yisrael,* p. 212. The name of the holy woman does not appear in the stories; it was supplied to me by Rabbi Menahem Savitz of New Jersey.

Page 116   Her Share in the World to Come

1. I was sent this tale in an e-mail from someone whose name I lost, who heard it from Mimi Feigelson. I have retold it in my own words. I found the name of the Tzanzer's wife in *Rabbeinu HaKodesh MiTzanz,* p. 27.

Page 118   After the Fact

1. Versions of this tale are found in *Sh'al Avicha V'Yagedcha,* vol. 3, p. 204; *Shimusha Shel Torah,* p. 15; and *Gedolei HaDorot,* vol. 2, p. 427. The second of these tells that the couple sold their home to buy an *etrog* (citron), but it has a note that there is another version that they sold their house so that the husband could study Torah. I prefer that version and have changed the text accordingly. The name of the holy woman does not appear in the stories; her name, Hinda, was supplied to me by Rabbi Kalman Redisch, who found it in the *Orchot Hayim* of the Rosh.

Page 119   How to Give Birth

1. *Taanit* 2. This means that not even prophets or tzaddikim can decree about this matter.

2. *Kol Chotzaiv,* pp. 538–539.

Page 120   Facing God

1. Hillel Goldberg, *The Fire Within* (Brooklyn: Mesorah, 1987), p. 181.

2. *Midrash HaGadol* on Exodus 33:20.

Page 120   The Passing of a Woman Who Had the Holy Spirit

1. Avraham, *Hie Tit'hallal,* p. 65 (with some minor adaptations), quoting *Ntzor Lashon; Ntzor Lashon,* end, appended booklet *Lirot Tov,* beginning.

2. Psalms 34:13.

Page 123   My Time Has Come

1. *Be'er Miryam,* pp. 5–6, 10–11.

Page 124   The Dress

1. Delaying payment of a laborer's wages is against Torah law.

2. *Tiferet Nashim,* p. 116, quoting *Lekach Tov.* This tale does not record Rebbe Zusya's wife's name. The author of *Menorat Zahav,* p. 7, says that he does not know the name of Rebbe Zusya's first wife, but the second was named Hendel, so I have used that name, although I do not know which of the two wives the story is about.

Page 126   The Homely Lesson of a Patch

1. Esther Austern, *Silence Is Thy Praise: The Life and Ideals of Rabbanit Batya Karelitz* (Brooklyn: Mesorah, 1990), p. 33.

Page 127   Rebbetzin Malka of Belz

1. All the material about Malka of Belz, aside from material otherwise specifically cited as from a different source, is from "HaRabbanit," *Admorei Belz,* vol. 1, pp. 80–88.

2. *Dover Shalom,* p. 7, no. 5.

3. This sentence is from *Admorei Belz,* vol. 1, p. 87.

4. A related story casts light on this one.

After the death of Rebbe Uri of Strelisk, a rabbi who was one of his great Hasidim traveled for the first time to Rebbe Shalom of Belz. When the rabbi opened the door, he found the Belzer sitting in a chair, and sitting next to him was his rebbetzin. This rabbi immediately shut the door and stepped back because he found such intimacy with a wife strange; he was not accustomed to such behavior with his rebbe, the Strelisker. When the Belzer realized what had happened, he asked his rebbetzin to leave the room and asked his aide to bring the guest in. When this Strelisker Hasid came in, the Belzer asked his aide to bring in two chairs from the adjacent room. After the rebbe asked the guest to sit, the latter asked the rebbe, "For whom is the second chair?"

"For Elijah the Prophet," said the Belzer.

The rabbi said, "I'd like to see him."

The Belzer replied, "It's said that when a worthy guest arrives, Elijah, may he be remembered for good, arrives with him. A person who deserves it sees him."

[The rebbe may have been hinting to his guest about the rebbe's own spiritual level—that he saw Elijah—and that his guest, although "worthy," was unwise to question his behavior or whom he seats next to him. The hint may also be that the guest's vision is not so good: he does not see that the rebbe and rebbetzin are like Adam and Eve in the Garden of Eden.]

Realizing that this rabbi was surprised at his behavior of sitting together with his rebbetzin, the rebbe said, "There are two levels of tzaddikim. The greater one is a tzaddik who has so purifed all his limbs for the sake of God, without any remaining physical feeling, that when he has to do any worldly action, he has to exert himself to inject into himself a little physicality. There is a second, lower level of tzaddik, who has not purified himself to such an extent and who tries with great effort to rise to holiness and purity, so that he not enjoy any activity in a purely bodily way." When the Strelisker Hasid heard these words, he gauged the rebbe's great level in holiness.

> [The rabbi understood that for someone on this level, sitting with and being intimate with his rebbetzin was appropriate, since the rebbe no longer had any sexual desires. We must assume that that was true for the rebbetzin too.]

5. "A candle for my foot and a light for my path is Your Word" (Psalms 119:105).

6. Hasidic tales sometimes show a great disciple or son of a rebbe—a future rebbe—offering wondrous advice and producing miracles before a visitor even reaches the rebbe. The idea is that he is really on the same miraculous level as the rebbe himself. This tale about Malka is a variation on that theme.

7. Another tale follows in *Admorei Belz*:

> Another time the Belzer Rebbe asked his rebbetzin's advice when a rebbe with his aides visited for Shabbat. This rebbe was from *kelipat noga* [he had a "shining shell," meaning that he had an aura of holiness but was in fact unholy]. The rebbetzin said, "Befriend him. If God doesn't push him away, why should you?" [meaning that if God allows him to remain as a rebbe, a leader of Hasidim, why should you expose him?]. That is what the Belzer did. On Shabbat night, that rebbe came to him and the Belzer did not push him away. He asked the man to sit at his Shabbat table, but he did not pay particular attention to him either.

8. Jiri Langer, *Nine Gates to the Chassidic Mysteries* (Northvale, N.J.: Aronson, 1993), pp. 39–40. Langer was an assimilated Czech Jew who became a Belzer Hasid in 1913 and composed a book of Hasidic stories that he had read and heard while in Belz. Other versions of this tale feature the Belzer Rebbe rather than his wife, and the decree is first transferred from the Jews to their cattle and then from their cattle to their poultry.

Page 135   They Are Clapping in Heaven

1. *B'eiro Shel Yitzhak,* p. 51, no. 3. I have expanded the somewhat terse text of the original.

Page 135   Rebbe Edel of Brody

1. This paragraph is based on *Dover Shalom*, p. 15, no. 26, and on Yoram Bilu, "Dybbuk Possession: A Case Study," in Joseph Sandler (ed.), *Projection, Identification, Projective Identification* (International University Press, 1987), p. 171.

2. Dov Sandan, *MiMechoz HaYaldut* (Tel Aviv, 1981), pp. 256–264; originally published in 1938. Thanks to David Assaf, who provided this information.

3. The Torah says that light was created on the first day of creation, but the sun only on the fourth day, so the Rabbis said that the light of the first day was the Hidden Light, the spiritual light of God.

4. Sandan, *MiMechoz HaYaldut*, p. 258.

5. Sandan, *MiMechoz HaYaldut*, p. 260.

6. This alludes to a saying in a Talmud story: "The One who says to the oil [of the Shabbat lamp] that it will burn can say to the vinegar [poured in by mistake] that it too will burn."

7. *Dover Shalom,* p. 15, no. 26.

Page 139   Doubtfully Kosher

1. *Emet V'Yatziv,* vol. 3, p. 159, no. 2; the rebbetzin's name, Shlomtcha, was found in *Marganita DeRabbi Meir,* "Or HaMeir," p. 42.

Page 140   Rebbe Miriam Hayya of Shatz

1. Recall from "Rebbe Edel of Brody" that Rebbe Shalom of Belz is reported to have made a similar comment about his daughter. In different parts of Eastern Europe, rebbes wore different kinds of fur hats, either a *shtreimel* or a *spodek.*

2. Her arrangement followed the arrangement of the different divine emanations in the kabbalistic scheme. All the tales about Miriam Hayya of Shatz are from *Aspaklaria HaMe'ira,* vol. 2, pp. 590–606, with portions of the tale about the coffee taken from *Sippurim Yerushalmi'im,* p. 109.

3. *Nedarim* 29. The reference is to the famous Rabbi Meir of ancient times. Rebbe Miriam Hayya's father was also named Meir—Rabbi Meir of Premishlan.

Page 145   Rebbe Sarah of Chantshin: A High Soul

1. *HaAish Dat MaiOzarov,* p. 88.

Page 147   Sarah Shneirer

1. *Tiferet Nashim,* p. 83, quoting Yehezkel Rothenberg, *Aym B'Yisrael* (Bnai Brak, Israel: Netzach, n.d.).

2. Leah Esther Zusman, *Sarah Shneirer: Sippur Hayeha Shel M'yasedet Bais Yaakov* (Jerusalem: Hochmah, n.d.), p. 114.

3. *Tiferet Nashim,* p. 68, quoting *Moreshet Avot.*

4. *Tiferet Nashim,* p. 68, quoting *Moreshet Avot.*

5. When I returned to Judaism as a young adult, I was astonished at the traditional notion that a person could make "business deals" about spiritual matters and, for example, "sell" his reward or portion in the World to Come! Nothing like that was familiar to me from secular culture. I eventually came to appreciate the idea. Many Hasidic tales tell of a poor man desperately in need of money—for a sick person in his family or a wedding for his daughter—going to a rebbe who is also penniless. The rebbe then offers a rich man a "deal"—to buy the rebbe's portion in the World to Come for the needed large sum, which the rebbe then gives to the poor man. (See "Her Share in the World to Come" earlier in this book.)

6. Zusman, *Sarah Shneirer,* p. 119. The reference to the man working for the "religious community" in the original is *Agudat Yisrael.*

7. Zusman, *Sarah Shneirer,* p. 104. A fuller and slightly different version of the story Sarah Shneirer told is found in *Hemdah Genuzah: Talmidei Besht, Gedolei Yisrael,* p. 101. There we are told that the tzaddik was Rabbi Shlomo Luria, the Maharshal of Lublin, and the vegetable seller and hidden tzaddik was Rabbi Avraham Kashi.

8. Ecclesiastes 9:17.

9. *Tiferet Nashim*, p. 69, quoting *Moreshet Avot*.

10. Ritually washing the hands upon awakening is a halachic obligation.

11. Zusman, *Sarah Shneirer*, p. 183.

12. Psalms 55:15.

13. Zusman, *Sarah Shneirer*, p. 184.

14. Zusman, *Sarah Shneirer*, p. 69. I also paraphrased and used pieces from pp. 64–67 and elsewhere.

Page 161   Why Did the Milk Boil Over?

1. *Rosh Hodesh* is the New Moon and thus the first day of the month. Days on the Jewish calendar begin at sundown, so *erev Rosh Hodesh* is the daylight hours leading up to the appearance of the New Moon that evening.

2. Malka, *B'Zchut Nashim Tzidkaniyot*, p. 172.

Page 163   Sensing Others' Troubles

1. Avraham, *Hie Tit'hallal*, p. 157.

Page 166   Pawn

1. *Tiferet Sh'B'Malchut*, p. 146.

Page 167   Coins That Sparkle

1. In ancient times, mirrors were made not of glass but of metal.

2. The various *sefirot* (divine emanations) in the kabbalistic scheme are not blocked and actually shine.

3. *Kovetz Sippurim* (1958–1959), vol. 2, no. 16.

4. Lubavitch Rabbi Kasriel Kastel of Brooklyn helped me understand this tale.

Page 168   A Disregard for Wealth

1. Psalms 119:72.

2. *Orot Mordechai,* pp. 11–13.

Page 170   A Glass of Water

1. *Beit Yitzhak,* p. 164; the name of the Vorker's mother, Yutta, was taken from *Bain Pshis'cha L'Lublin,* p. 514.

Page 172   In the Merit of His Mother

1. *Avodat Avodah,* p. 264. I was told the name of the rebbe's mother by a Tosher Hasid, Rabbi Shmuel David Gutman of New York.

Page 173   A Mother's Tears

1. *Tiferet Nashim,* p. 29; *HaMe'orot HaGedolim,* p. 272, no. 30. The name of the Hafetz Hayim's mother was obtained from M. M. Yoshor, *The Chafetz Chaim* (Artscroll, 1984), p. 31.

Page 173   Be like My Mother

1. My story is a combination of two versions: the Hebrew version of the tale in the biography of Rebbe Yisrael of Vilednik, *Sh'airit Yisrael,* pp. 13–15 and no. 9, and *Shabbos with Shlomo* (audiotape), *Stories,* side 2, "The Viledniker's Mother."

Page 176   Ungrammatically Correct

1. Yanki Tauber, *Once upon a Chassid* (Brooklyn: Kehot, 1994), p. 161. In 1843, the rebbe successfully defied a czarist attempt to forcibly assimilate Jews in Russia.

Page 177   Which Blessing to Give

1. *Michtavei HaHafetz Hayim HeHadash,* p. 5.

Page 178   The Secret of the Yarmulkes

1. Malka, *B'Zchut Nashim Tzidkaniyot,* p. 133.

Page 180   Pure Thoughts
 1. *B'Yashishim Hochmah,* p. 273, no. 1.

Page 182   Guarding His Studying
 1. Malka, *B'Zchut Nashim Tzidkaniyot,* p. 139.

Page 185   Revelations
 1. *Sippurei HeHag: Pesach,* p. 233. Note that the girl has three grandfathers because her mother remarried.

Page 186   Maxine
 1. Slightly adapted from *Connections/Hakrev Ushma,* 1985, 1(2), 39.

Page 189   Two Cups
 1. *Aliyah* literally means "ascension, going up." To "make *aliyah*" is to "go up" to live in the Land of Israel.
 2. This tale is a composite of *Or HaRashash* [*HaRabbi Shalom Sharabi*], p. 121, and *HaRabbi Shalom Sharabi HaKodesh,* p. 75. There is another version of this tale in *Tiferet Nashim,* p. 82, quoting *Imrei Fi,* and an Eastern European version about a different rabbi appears in *Kovetz Eliyahu,* p. 97, no. 303.

Page 192   Pessia Carlebach and the Gentile Maid
 1. Heard from Rabbi Shlomo Carlebach. Another story about Pessia Carlebach and her lack of attachment to possessions, "A Fifth," appears earlier in this book.

Page 194   He Who Would Live Should Die
 1. Ruchoma Shain, *Shining Lights: Illuminating Stories of Faith and Inspiration* (New York: Feldheim, 1997), p. 209.

Page 198   Golda and Miriam
 1. Based on David Koppelman, *Glimpses of Greatness* (New York: Moznaim, 1994), p. 93, retold in my own words.

Page 200 I Don't Kneel!

1. Adapted slightly from Rush, *Book of Jewish Women's Tales,* p. 180.

Page 201 A Mother's Passion

1. Literally, "a son of the Torah," meaning a Torah scholar.

2. *Ma'aseh Ish,* p. 71, quoting *Zichron Rafael.*

Page 203 Training Her Sons

1. The quotation is Numbers 20:19.

2. *Avodat Avodah,* p. 336; *Tzvi L'Tzaddik,* pp. 6–7; *Yifrach B'Yamav Tzaddik,* p. 8b. The five sons were Rebbe Berish of Ziditchov, Rebbe Moshe of Sambur, Rebbe Alexander Sender of Komarna, Rebbe Lippa of Sambur, Rebbe Tzvi Hirsh of Ziditchov.

Page 205 The Future Redemption

1. Hebrew letters have numerical values, and in Jewish numerology, words whose letters add up to the same value are considered to be related, as is the case with *lekach* [which is Yiddish] and *hatzlacha* [which is Hebrew]; *Imrei Tzaddikim,* p. 7.

2. These words are spoken by Jacob in Genesis 28:17.

3. *Der Yid* (the Yiddish newspaper of the Satmar Hasidim, published in Brooklyn), July 30, 1999, sec. 2, p. 27. See *Beit Shlomo,* p. 14.

4. Genesis 27:27.

5. *Midrash HaGadol.*

6. *Tiferet Sh'B'Malchut,* p. 76.

Page 206 Waiting for Redemption

1. Avraham, *Hie Tit'hallal,* p. 96.

Page 207 In the Cave of Machpelah

1. Adapted from Serkez, *The Holy Beggars' Banquet,* pp. 164–166. This tale was told by Rabbi Shlomo Carlebach, who said that he

heard it in Bobov and that it is a classic tale that appears in many Hasidic books. A version can be found in *B'Zchut Nashim Tzidkaniot,* p. 97. In the English version, the woman is unnamed and said to be the wife of Reb Hersheleh of Kaminka; in the Hebrew version, the woman is anonymous. Charlotte Saunders, a descendant of the heroine of the story, told me in a phone conversation that her name was Fruma Riveleh; she was the wife of Rabbi David of Kaminka and the mother of Reb Hersheleh.

Page 211   *Sukkot* Stories

1. *Chasidishe Masiyos,* beginning of no. 14; translated by Yaakov David Shulman.

2. *Tiferes Tzaddikim,* no. 4 [Yiddish]. Rabbi Yosef's mother's name was obtained from *To'afot HaRim,* p. 64. The original text would ruin the effect of the story for many people, so I have changed it in order to be able to use the tale. The original ends this way:

> The reason for all this was that some distance away stood a church with a cross, whose shadow lay across the *sukkah,* and as a result, Elijah could not enter the *sukkah.* In earlier years, when my father himself was involved in building the *sukkah,* he knew about the shadow, and he built the structure in such a way that the shadow would not fall against it. But this year, my father could not buy the *lulav* and *etrog* before Yom Kippur because he hadn't had the money. And so when he went to buy the *lulav* and *etrog,* he did not have time to help us children build the *sukkah.* We, who did not know about the shadow, paid it no mind. And as a result, Elijah did not come. After my father promised my mother that Elijah would again appear to her, the sky grew cloudy and remained that way for the rest of *Sukkot.* There was no more shadow to lay across the *sukkah,* and so Elijah again came into the *sukkah* and my mother was able to see him.

3. *Be'er Miryam,* "Hadrat Miryam," vol. 2, pp. 188, 220.

Page 215   A Brilliant Female Scholar

1. According to Jewish tradition, there are a total of 613 *mitzvot* (divine commandments).

2. *Haggadah Shel Pesach: Maaseh Rav,* p. 507, quoting *Meged Givot Olam,* no. 15.

Page 218   Hadassah Linder

1. *Nihohei HeHadas,* pp. 115, 136.

2. *Nihohei HeHadas,* pp. 173–174.

3. *Nihohei HeHadas,* p. 259.

4. *Nihohei HeHadas,* pp. 168–169.

5. *Nihohei HeHadas,* pp. 323–325.

6. *Nihohei HeHadas,* p. 327.

7. *Nihohei HeHadas,* pp. 178–181.

8. *Nihohei HeHadas,* pp. 176–178.

9. *Nihohei HeHadas,* pp. 323–325.

10. *Nihohei HeHadas,* pp. 330–331.

11. *Nihohei HeHadas,* pp. 220–221.

12. *Nihohei HeHadas,* p. 346.

13. *Nihohei HeHadas,* pp. 320–321.

14. *Nihohei HeHadas,* p. 256.

15. *Nihohei HeHadas,* p. 309.

16. "After a hundred and twenty years" is a euphemism for "when you're dead."

17. *Nihohei HeHadas,* p. 67.

18. *Nihohei HeHadas,* pp. 67–68.

19. *Nihohei HeHadas,* p. 69.

20. One such party is held every day for seven days after a wedding.

21. *Nihohei HeHadas,* p. 384.

22. *Nihohei HeHadas,* pp. 383–385.

23. *Nihohei HeHadas,* pp. 359–360.

24. *Nihohai HeHadas,* p. 386.

Page 240 Rebbetzin Esther Jungreis

1. The Hebrew word *hineni* ("I am here") was used by various prophets in the Torah when answering God's call. For example, God called "Abraham, Abraham!" and Abraham answered, "*Hineni!*"

2. Rebbetzin Esther Jungreis, *The Jewish Soul on Fire: A Remarkable Woman Shows How Faith Can Change Your Life* (New York: Morrow, 1982), p. 13.

3. Jungreis, *Jewish Soul on Fire,* p. 205.

4. Jungreis, *Jewish Soul on Fire,* p. 35.

5. Jeremiah 2:11.

6. Jeremiah 31:15.

7. Rebbetzin Esther Jungreis, *The Committed Life: Principles for Good Living from Our Timeless Past* (New York: HarperCollins, 1998), p. 13.

8. This is the Yiddish pronunciation of *tzedaka.*

9. Jungreis, *The Committed Life,* p. 49.

10. Jungreis, *The Committed Life,* p. 53.

11. Jungreis, *The Committed Life,* p. 55.

12. Jungreis, *The Committed Life,* p. 115.

13. Jungreis, *The Committed Life,* pp. 118–120.

Page 260 Two Jewish Girls in Denmark

1. I heard this story from Emily Fischer at the Conference on Judaism in rural New England, in Vermont, in the summer of 1995.

Page 267 Raise the Torah Banner High

1. The material about Nechama Liba is from Yosef Ben Shlomo Hakohen, who paraphrased material from *Rav Dessler,* pp. 78–79, 253–256.

Glossary

AGGADA   The legends of the Talmud.

ALIYAH   "Going up" to live in the Land of Israel.

BAAL SHEM TOV   "Master of the Good Name," the title given to Rabbi Yisrael, the founder of Hasidism. See also *Besht.*

BEIS YAAKOV   A network of religious girls' schools founded by Sarah Shneirer.

BEIT MIDRASH   Torah study hall, often adjacent to a synagogue or serving also as a synagogue.

BESHT   The Baal Shem Tov, from the acronym for the title.

BRIS   Circumcision.

BUBBA   Grandma.

CHOLENT   Traditional Sabbath meat and vegetable stew.

CHUMASH   The Five Books of Moses.

DAVVEN   To pray the ordained Jewish prayers.

EREV **SHABBAT**   Eve of the Sabbath; Friday during the day.

ETROG   Citron.

FOUR SPECIES   *Etrog* (citron), *lulav* (palm), *hadasim* (myrtle branches), and *aravot* (willows) ritually waved on *Sukkot.*

GAON   Great Torah scholar; genius.

GEHINNOM   Hell.

HACHAMIM   Sages; title for Sephardic rabbis.

HAGGADAH   Text of the story of the Jews' exodus from Egypt, recited on Passover.

HALACHA   Jewish religious law.

HaShem   God; literally, "the Name" (referring to the unspoken four-letter Name of God, YHVH).

HEDER   Elementary religious school.

KABBALAT SHABBAT   Synagogue service to welcome the Sabbath on Friday night.

KADDISH   Mourner's prayer.

KAVVANAH (PL., *KAVVANOT*)   Kabbalistic formula; intention; devotional focus.

KEDUSHA   Important responsive prayer: *Kadosh, kadosh, kadosh, HaShem Tz'va'ot* ("Holy, holy, holy is the Lord of Hosts; the whole earth is full of His glory!").

KIDDUSH   "Sanctification"; the blessing over the wine.

KOHEN   Jewish priest.

LISHMAH   "For its own sake," with pure motives (hence *Torah lishmah* is Torah study purely for the sake of God).

LOSHON HARA   Slander and other negative speech against others.

LULAV   Palm branch.

MAGGID   Preacher; teller of sacred tales.

MEZUZAH   Parchment scroll with scriptural verses enclosed in a small container, which is attached to the doorpost of a house or a room.

MIDRASH   Ancient collection of rabbinic comments on the Torah, including parables, sayings, and stories.

MIKVEH   Ritual bath.

MINYAN   Prayer quorum of ten male Jews.

MITZVAH (PL., *MITZVOT*)   Divine commandment derived from the Torah.

MOTZA'EI SHABBAT   Saturday night after the Sabbath ends.

MUSAR   Non-Hasidic pietistic movement that focuses on perfection of character and on ethics.

PIDYON (PL., *PIDYONOT*)   "Redemption money"; donation offered to a Hasidic rebbe when making a request, as for a blessing or prayers, by means of a *pitka*.

PITKA (pl., *pitka'ot*)   A petition note given to a Hasidic rebbe with one's name and a request for prayer on one's behalf.

REB   Honorific, equivalent to *Mr.*, used with a man's given name.

REBBE   Hasidic sect leader, also called a *tzaddik;* teacher. A rebbe is always a rabbi, but most rabbis are not rebbes. A rebbe usually has many rabbis among his followers, although most of his followers are ordinary Jews. All those who accept his leadership are called his Hasidim.

REBBETZIN   Wife of a rabbi.

REBBISHE   Pertaining to a Hasidic rebbe.

ROSH YESHIVA   Headmaster of a yeshiva.

SANDAK   The person who holds the child on his lap at a *bris;* godfather.

SEDER   Ritual meal celebrating Passover, during which the *Haggadah* is recited.

SEFER TORAH   Torah scroll.

SHABBAT   Hebrew for Sabbath.

SHABBATON   A special, festive Sabbath.

SHABBOS   Yiddish for Sabbath.

SHALOM ALEICHEM   Greeting: "Peace be upon you."

SHECHINAH   Indwelling Divine Presence; "female" immanent God.

SHEMONEH ESREH   "Eighteen Blessings," the main Jewish prayer.

SHEVA BERACHA (PL., *SHEVA BERACHOT*)   One of the parties given for a newly married couple at the home of a friend or family member each day of the week following the wedding.

SH'MA YISRAEL   The central Jewish credo: "Hear O Israel, the Lord our God, the Lord is one."

SHOFAR   Ram's horn blown on Rosh HaShanah and Yom Kippur.

SHTREIMEL   Fur hat, often worn by a Hasidic rebbe. See also *spodek.*

SIDDUR   Prayer book.

SIMHAT TORAH   Joy of the Torah; holiday when congregants dance with the Torah scrolls.

S'MICHA   Rabbinic or other ordination.

SPODEK   Fur hat, often worn by a Hasidic rebbe. See also *shtreimel.*

SUKKAH   Temporary booth used for eating, living, and sleeping during *Sukkot.*

SUKKOT   Festival of Booths; holiday commemorating the ancient Jews' sojourn in the Sinai Desert, when they lived in temporary dwellings (booths).

TALLIS   Prayer shawl.

TALMUD   The central ancient rabbinic scripture, comprising many volumes of legal and legendary material.

TEFILLIN   Phylacteries.

TEKIAH, SHEVARIM, TEKIA   Blasts on the *shofar.*

TICHEL   Woman's head covering.

TIKKUN HATZOT   Midnight Lamentation Service, mourning the destruction of the ancient Temple.

TORAH   The Five Books of Moses, or the whole Bible.

TU BESHVAT   Kabbalistic holiday, the New Year of the Trees.

TZADDEKET (PL., TZADDIKOT)   Righteous or holy woman.

TZADDIK (PL., TZADDIKIM)   Righteous or holy man; a Hasidic sect leader, a rebbe.

TZEDAKA   Charity.

YAHRZEIT   Yearly anniversary of a person's death.

YESHIVA   Higher religious school; academy.

YETZER HA-RA   Evil inclination.

ZOHAR   The Book of Splendor, the main book of Kabbalah.

The Author

YITZHAK BUXBAUM is an inspired and inspiring storyteller and teacher, one of those reviving the honorable calling of the *maggid* (preacher), who in times past traveled from community to community, awakening the Jews to the beauty of their tradition. The author of the highly acclaimed *Jewish Spiritual Practices*, called "the best book written on Jewish spirituality," Mr. Buxbaum has also written *Storytelling and Spirituality in Judaism*, *The Life and Teachings of Hillel*, and other titles. He teaches at the New School in NYC, where he resides, while lecturing and performing at synagogues, JCCs, and retreats throughout the United States and Canada. Mr. Buxbaum has a Web site at www.jewishspirit.com.

Jewish Tales of Mystic Joy

Yitzhak Buxbaum

$19.95 Hardcover
ISBN: 0-7879-6272-4

Many Jewish tales vividly express the joy, ecstasy, and bliss of holy and ordinary people in exalted moments. This stunning collection contains tales that portray the mystic joy that comes from a passionate love for God and people.

According to the Jewish mystics, the soul's essence is bliss. The soul yearns for joy; it requires joy; but it can only be satisfied with spiritual pleasures that reveal its true nature. The goal is to tap the immense joy that lies within us, to contact our soul's heavenly source of unlimited joy.

Jewish Tales of Mystic Joy reveals the happiness that awaits us if we strive for real spirituality. The stories are about pious rabbis and humble tailors, about dancing, singing, laughing, and crying, but their common denominator is always joyous ecstasy. Drawing us into a world of devotion, the tales allow us to taste the bliss that comes from a life lived from the very center of one's self. Each story comes alive in joy and produces a "holy shiver" that speaks to the soul.

"Yitzhak Buxbaum's *Jewish Tales of Mystic Joy* clearly shows that faith brings joy. His book is filled with Hasidic stories that inspire one to appreciate all that is good in one's life and that guide one on an ascent in the path to joy."
—Joseph Telushkin, Author, *Jewish Literacy* and *The Book of Jewish Values*

"Read these tales of mystic joy out loud and hear them as if Reb Yitzhak Buxbaum is telling them. They are made for the ear that responds to the Sh'ma Yisrael. Let each tale rest on your heart, so that when your heart opens it will drop in and find a place in your memory and awareness."—Rabbi Zalman Schachter-Shalomi

YITZHAK BUXBAUM is a maggid, a traditional Jewish storyteller and teacher, who specializes in mysticism, spirituality, and Hasidic tales. He is the author of nine books including *Jewish Spiritual Practices, Storytelling and Spirituality in Judaism,* and *An Open Heart: The Mystic Path of Loving People.* Yitzhak teaches at The New School University and resides in New York City.

[Price subject to change]